LONDONLAND

LONDONLAND

An Ethnography of Labour in a World City

Simon Bennett

Middlesex
University
PRESS

First published in 2009 by Middlesex University Press

Copyright © Simon Bennett

ISBN 978 1 904750 64 2

A CIP catalogue record for this book is available from The British Library

Cover design by Helen Taylor
Typesetting by Carnegie Publishing Ltd
Printed in the UK by Ashford Colour Press Ltd

Middlesex University Press
The Burroughs
Hendon
London NW4 4BT
Tel: +44 (0)20 8411 4162: +44 (0)20 8411 4161
Fax: +44 (0)20 8411 4167

www.mupress.co.uk

Contents

For Nancy and Raymond. Good people.

Acknowledgements

B EFORE I thank the people who have helped me in my academic career, I'd first like to acknowledge an intellectual tradition: phenomenological ethnography. Because each of us is unique it follows that each of us will have the capacity to interpret the world in different ways. But what if we do more than this? What if our *subjectivity* leads each of us to construct a different world – a personal cosmos composed of different 'facts'? The possibility of there being an infinite number of personal worlds is addressed by John Berger and Jean Mohr in *A Seventh Man*:

> To try to understand the experience of another it is necessary to dismantle the world as seen from one's own place within it, and to re-assemble it as seen from his.... [T]he subjectivity of another does not simply constitute a different interior attitude to the same exterior facts. The constellation of facts of which he is the centre is different.

Phenomenological ethnography raises the possibility that people inhabit *different* worlds. Indeed, that there are as many worlds as there are people. This has implications for communication, both between citizens and between citizens and government. More profoundly, perhaps, it undermines theories of social action. Citizens can no longer be agglomerated or summated. There can be no datum. In a world of multiple realities the only constant is difference. This book's method is informed by phenomenological ethnography. I hope it does it justice.

I have had two careers. The first in computer systems management, the second in academia. I worked as a systems development manager for ten years with some of the most dedicated and amusing people I have ever met (the work was so high-pressure you needed a sense of humour to survive). My second career as an academic has been, well, different. Academia is a curate's egg. It generates insight – consider phenomenological ethnography – but it also generates frustration. Taking everything in the round my best time at university was as a student in the late 1970s. Having failed my A-levels for a second time I was rescued by Sheffield City Polytechnic, specifically by Professor Bob Haigh. It is fair to say that Bob was an inspiration. After working as a coal miner in South Yorkshire he joined the ranks of academe, eventually becoming head of politics at Sheffield City Polytechnic (in the 1970s a fine institution. It is much missed by its alumni). Bob made a big impression on all of us callow youths, not only because of his intelligence and humanity, but also because of his wit. I still smile when I remember how he would enter our seventh-floor seminar room at nine o'clock of a December morn, stride to the windows, open them all as wide as they would go and then proceed to deliver a scintillating fifty-minute lecture in the teeth of a howling gale. His reasoning, of course, was that fresh air was the best cure for undergraduate hangovers. Bob, of course, came prepared. He sported a luxuriously warm woollen overcoat. The rest of us sat there shivering in our fashionable-but-inadequate cotton combat jackets. If I could reprise any period of my life it would be my three years at polytechnic.

My second tranche of academia was also fun – although it was more a means to an end than an end in itself. I did a master's degree (in communication and technology studies) at Brunel University, Middlesex, then a doctorate in the sociology of scientific knowledge, also at Brunel. I'd like to thank my supervisor Professor Alan Irwin for his endless patience and good humour... and for teaching me how to do social science research. While at Brunel I was offered a job at Leicester University's Scarman Centre for the Study of Public Order (SCSPO). While at SCSPO I worked under two directors, Professor John Benyon and Professor Martin Gill, both of whom did me the courtesy of listening to my ideas for course development. Sadly SCSPO, a globally recognised and highly regarded educational 'brand', was eventually erased by our vice-chancellor. I found myself languishing in a criminology department – hardly an appropriate academic home for an MSc in risk, crisis and disaster management. Ideal-type risk management investigations adopt a 'non-blamist' approach, the objective being to learn lessons rather than punish. This is not the case in criminal investigations. Concluding that someone had to make the case for a move I made a nuisance of myself until the university capitulated. On reflection I think I made so much of a nuisance that I irrevocably damaged my career.

My MSc in risk, crisis and disaster management now resides in the Civil Safety and Security Unit (CSSU), an adjunct to the Institute of Lifelong Learning. During my time at CSSU I have worked even more intensively with the aviation industry as a human factors consultant. I work with flight and cabin crew and spend long days and nights on the flight decks of commercial aircraft. I find this work immensely satisfying, chiefly because flight and cabin crew are a close-knit community. They are a band of brothers – mutually supportive, committed, professional. They have always made me feel welcome. They have shown me friendship. Whenever possible they have helped me in my work. For the understanding, camaraderie and sheer good fun I thank them one and all.

Writing meaningful work is not easy. It helps to have a good editor. During the writing of this book I have been fortunate to have Celia Cozens as my editor. Celia has been patient and helpful throughout. She is a big asset to Middlesex University Press. Celia took my book proposal seriously when other publishers would not give it the time of day. Paul Jervis of MU Press provided incisive and constructive comments, for which the book is all the better. It also helps to have a sympathetic academic manager. Jackie Dunne, director of the Institute of Lifelong Learning at the University of Leicester, has supported this writing project. It was Jackie who helped me secure the sabbatical that gave me the space and time to do the fieldwork for *Londonland*.

Finally I'd like to thank playwright Willy Russell for humanising academia. For bringing it, and me, down to earth. *Educating Rita* should be required reading/viewing for every sixth-former. I sign off with the film's most enlightening duel. Rita, the student, calls on Frank, the lecturer. They talk in his study. Frank is dishevelled. He's been drinking.

Frank	Why don't you just go away. I don't think I can bear it any longer.
Rita	Can't bear what, Frank?
Frank	You, my dear. You.
Rita	Yes, well I'll tell you what you can't bear, Mr Self-Pity and Piss-Artist. What you can't bear is that I'm educated now. I've got what you have and you don't like it. I mean good God, I don't need you. I've got a room full of books. I know what wine to buy, what clothes to wear, what plays to see, what papers and books to read, and I can do it without you.
Frank	Is that all you wanted? Have you come all this way for so very, very little?
Rita	Oh yeah. It's little to you, isn't it Frank? Little to you who squanders every opportunity. Who mocks and takes it for granted.
Frank	Found a culture have you Rita? Found a better song to sing? No. You've found a *different* song to sing. And on your lips it is shrill and hollow and tuneless.
Rita	Nobody calls me Rita but you. I dropped that pretentious crap as soon as I saw it for what it was. Rita. Nobody calls me Rita. [Makes for door].
Frank	What is it now, then? Emily or Charlotte or Jane or Virginia? [Door slams. Frank slumps into chair, tired and emotional].

Educating Rita, produced and directed by Lewis Gilbert, screenplay by Willy Russell

Acorn Pictures Ltd. 1983

CHAPTER ONE

Focus, methodology and structure

Focus

> We now recognise that the constraints of geography are shrinking and that the world is becoming a single place.[1]

> For anyone who remembers the dreary Seventies, when rubbish piled in the streets and columnists wrote of Britain going into absolute decline... [London's pre-eminence] is thrilling. But of course it brings challenges, which we have to meet [like] regional divergence, the extent to which London has become almost an island state.[2]

> [T]he reefs and rocks with which [our citizens] have to contend are founded in the structure of our society, while the storms and tides and currents that buffet them emerge from the interplay – as complex as the climate – of economic and political movements operating on a vast and impersonal scale, certainly outside their control, possibly beyond anyone's.[3]

A s Britain's only World City London could justifiably be described as an island state within the fabric of the United Kingdom. Contemporary London with its buoyant economy is a magnet for Britons seeking to better themselves and for the world's dispossessed. London, of course, has always been a melting pot of different cultures and ethnicities, from the admixing of Romans and Britons in Londinium, the original Thames-side settlement, to the influx of settlers from the West Indies in the 1950s and 1960s and of Poles, Estonians and others from the European Union's (EU's) accession states in the new millennium. London is a cosmopolitan place – a global intersection.[4]

London is also a complex place. It is by no means a geographic singularity – a homogenised urban sprawl. Rather it is a collection of discrete villages, suburbs and locales knitted together by ribbon development and 'in-fill' housing and industry. Each has its own character. Brixton, for example, has a large Afro-Caribbean community, while Southall has a large Asian community. Stamford Hill is home to London's Hasidic Jews while Hammersmith has long been a magnet for Poland's migrant workers.[5] Sometimes a neighbourhood's ethnic mix can be read from the shops on its high street. Stoke Newington Road and Stoke Newington High Street, for example, are dominated by Turkish shops (grocers, barbers, travel agencies, etc.) and men's clubs. In terms of architecture, while locales like Preston Road, Rayners Lane and Hillingdon are products of the English penchant for the semi-detached house and tree-lined avenue, inner-city neighbourhoods like Notting Hill and Earls Court are dominated by stuccoed three, four and five-storey Edwardian and Victorian residences. Londonland, then, is a kaleidoscope of ethnicities and architectures, work-styles and lifestyles. It is a heterogeneity.

Today Londonland is a city comfortable in its own skin. It is reasonably peaceful.[6] Migrant groups arrive and assimilate with relative ease. In October 2008 Boris Johnson, mayor of London, wrote: 'We are... open, diverse and welcoming to people from across the globe'.[7] The ebb and flow of Londonland's communities has not always gone smoothly, however. In the eighteenth century, for example: 'The influx of Irish into Spitalfields had led to disturbances in 1736 and during the Gordon (anti-Catholic) riots of 1780, two Irish chapels in Stepney were wrecked'.[8] In August 1958 parts of Notting Hill in north London were scarred by race riots: 'For several days and nights the homes of black tenants in the area were besieged by large crowds of whites, some of them several hundred strong, who smashed windows, shouted racial abuse and threw petrol bombs.... In the next two weeks an escalation of attacks on black people was reported in Harlesden, Hackney, Stepney, Hornsey and Islington'.[9] By the late 1960s attacks on Asians were commonplace: '[A]ttacks on Pakistanis with bottles, boots and knives had become a regular pastime in the East End.... This was the decade when Enoch Powell rose to prominence with his rabble-rousing speeches advocating the end of immigration and a policy of repatriation'.[10] Gradually, however, Londoners have come to accept one another in what one might call a racial and ethnic settlement. Historian Jerry White notes:

> The birth of a multiracial and multicultural society had burst on London almost from nowhere.... The shock waves were at first turbulent, sometimes violent. Surprisingly, things soon settled down. Within twenty years of the first mass arrivals most Londoners accepted that their city had changed forever, and for good. Within another twenty, London was lauded as one of the most tolerant and successful of the world's multicultural societies.... Respect for difference was a hard lesson to learn. It was eventually well learned in London.[11]

While it is true, as White suggests, that things have 'settled down', racially motivated attacks and murders persist. In 1999, for example, a neo-Nazi called David Copeland executed three bomb attacks in London aimed at ethnic minority communities and homosexuals. After his arrest Copeland, who had belonged to both the British National Party (BNP) and National Socialist Movement,[12] told police that as a teenager he had wanted to be reincarnated as an SS officer.[13] Such attacks, although rare, remind us that British society contains within it a *persistent* neo-Nazi residue and that democrats ignore it at their peril.

This book has a simple objective: to describe the working lives of Londoners in a time of rapid social, economic and political change. Thanks to modern communications, burgeoning international trade, greater interdependence between nation states, porous borders and relatively cheap travel we live in an increasingly globalised world. Britain imports fresh food from South America and Asia, coal and gas from eastern Europe, budget television programmes from Australia and the United States and cheap, flexible labour from every corner of the globe. Energised by these imports Britain's economy exports high-value technological and informational artefacts to the world. Current money-spinners include the high-performance wings of the Airbus A380 large-capacity airliner, advanced weaponry, fuel-efficient turbofan engines, financial and business support services and the graphics software used by many Hollywood film studios.[14] Britain's current position as one of the most powerful economies in the world is a remarkable achievement in light of the country's near-bankruptcy at the end of the Second World War (Britain was greatly helped by American aid) and self-inflicted economic and political turmoil of the 1970s (Britain was salvaged by the International Monetary Fund (IMF)). Britain has come a long way since the bankruptcy of Rolls Royce Aero Engines, the 'three day week' and politically motivated strikes (such as those that frequently brought the car industry to the verge of collapse). During the economic turmoil of 2008 when the world banking system teetered on the edge of collapse it was *Britain* that helped fix the problem. As the director of the Peterson Institute for International Economics put it: 'When it came to crisis-response mode, the Europeans, especially the British, did take the lead and the U.S. changed course'.[15] Realising that buying up bad debt was a partial solution at best, Prime Minister Gordon Brown argued for, and secured, a more holistic approach that involved buying equity in and recapitalising the banks. Britain's star was in the ascendancy. In the 1970s Britain was known as the Sick Man of Europe. The country was ideologically bankrupt – an economic basket-case that seemed set on tearing itself apart. In the autumn of 2008 some credited her prime minister with saving the world economy from collapse.[16] With the Americans mired in free-market dogma[17] it was left to free-thinking Gordon Brown (and a select group of other European leaders like French President Nicolas Sarkozy) to come up with a workable salvage plan.[18] Laissez-faire ceded ground to Keynesianism and big government. On 18 October, the *Economist* observed:

> [C]apitalism... is at bay. This week Britain, the birthplace of modern privatisation, nationalised much of its banking industry; meanwhile, amid talk of the end of the Thatcher–Reagan era, the American government has promised to put $250 billion into its banks.... Interventionists are in full cry... all the signs are pointing in the same direction: a larger role for the state, and a smaller and more constrained private sector.[19]

The globalisation dynamic

The structure and modus operandi of the British economy places it at the epicentre of the globalisation phenomenon. Globalisation is a key dynamic of our new millennium world (and is probably *the* key dynamic). Writing in 1995 Malcolm Waters, professor of sociology at the University of Tasmania, defined globalisation as 'A social process in which the constraints of geography on social and cultural arrangements recede and in which people become increasingly aware that they are receding'.[20] While the origins of globalisation can be traced back to the sixteenth century,[21] says Waters, the foundations of modern-day globalisation were laid in the four decades prior to the Great War:

> [T]he [three] key features of this world economy had been 'knitted together' between 1870 and 1914.... The first was the development of transportation and communication networks that physically linked together different parts of the planet, especially by railways, shipping and the telegraph. The second was the rapid growth of trade with the accompanying pattern of dependency, especially between the relatively industrialised countries of Western Europe and the rest. The third was a huge flow of capital mainly in the form of direct investment by European firms in non-industrialised areas.[22]

Like Waters, Steven Schifferes[23] draws our attention to the nineteenth century origins of globalisation. Schifferes sees globalisation as an accelerating and accelerative process:

> Globalisation is not new, but is a product of the industrial revolution. Britain grew rich in the 19th century as the first global economic superpower, because of its superior manufacturing technology and improved global communications such as steamships and railroads. But the pace, scope and scale of globalisation have accelerated dramatically since World War II, and especially in the last 25 years. The rapid spread of information technology (IT) and the Internet is changing the way companies organise production, and increasingly allowing services as well as manufacturing to be globalised. Globalisation is also being driven by the decision by India and China to open their economies to the world, thus doubling the global labour force overnight.

China today is a global economic player. It sucks in raw materials[24] and dispatches usually well-designed and well-made finished goods around the world. This has benefited both China and its more dynamic neighbours. As the Institute of Development Studies's (IDS's) John Humphrey and Hubert Schmitz[25] write in *China: Its Impact on the Developing Asian Economies*:

> China is the engine of a regional production system which has brought enormous benefits in terms of jobs and incomes to those countries that are fully integrated [with it].... China's growth has been phenomenal and the government is justly proud of the economic achievements.

If China has become one of the world's foremost centres of manufacture, India has become a linchpin of the service sector. Schifferes[26] notes:

> Many service sector jobs are now under threat from outsourcing and offshoring.... What China has become to manufacturing, India has become to the new world of business process outsourcing (BPO) – which includes everything from payroll to billing to IT support. India is the world's leading exporter of IT services, with its volume of offshore business doubling every three years.

According to the IDS,[27] although powerful, India and China do not act in a vacuum. Their actions are influenced – indeed constrained – by their relationships with other nations: '[India and China] do not engage with the world in a vacuum. Countries increasingly place demands on them. They are not economic and political juggernauts whose impacts overwhelm the rest of the world'. Today's globalised world is therefore a world of mutualities and interdependencies – a cat's cradle of linkages.

According to Waters, contemporary globalisation advances along seven axes: trade; investment; production; financial exchanges; labour migration; international economic cooperation; and organisational practices. World trade, says Waters, is 'The original and continuing fundamental of economic globalisation'.[28] Schifferes[29] concurs:

> Trade has been the engine of globalisation, with world trade in manufactured goods increasing more than 100 times... in the 50 years since 1955, much faster than the overall growth of the world economy. Since 1960, increased trade has been made easier by international agreements to lower tariff and non-tariff barriers on the export of manufactured goods, especially to rich countries. Those countries which have managed to increase their role in the world trading system by targeting exports to rich countries – such as Japan, Korea and now China – have seen dramatic increases in their standard of living.[30]

One aspect of world trade is the migration of successful business concepts across the globe. By 1995, fast-food giant McDonald's was opening two-thirds of its new outlets outside the USA. With these outlets came McDonald's own brand of management.[31] Another aspect is the international division of labour with manufacturing industry relocating to the world's less developed countries, creating a 'third-world proletariat'.[32] This migration, says Waters, serves to reinforce the economic and political hegemony of the world's advanced economies:

> One of the revelatory discoveries offered by social science in the twentieth century is that colonialism and imperialism produce an international division of labour of the social kind. Core or metropolitan societies do capital-intensive, high value-adding production while peripheral societies do labour-intensive, low value-adding production. This division of labour produces a relationship of domination and mutual dependency which is self-reproducing.[33]

It should be said that the global division of labour is rather more subtle than Waters would have us believe, especially with regard to high technology products where work-share agreements create networks of more or less equal partners. In the case of Boeing's new 787 passenger aircraft, for example, components are sourced from and elements manufactured in all four corners of the globe. For example, while the 787's nose section is manufactured in the USA, it 'includes an installed Messier-Dowty landing gear made from parts manufactured in Canada, France, China and England'.[34] The 787's horizontal stabiliser and centre fuselage section are manufactured in Italy (by Alenia), the engines are manufactured in England (Rolls Royce), the wings are manufactured in Japan (Mitsubishi) and the wing tips in Korea. The various elements are transported to the USA for final assembly in a Boeing 747 'jumbo jet' with a greatly enlarged fuselage.[35] A similar work-share system is used for the new Airbus A380 'super jumbo'.

According to Waters the increasing de-materialisation of production in the world's most advanced economies (Japan, Germany, Britain, etc.) and export of manufacturing industry to low-cost developing countries (like Brazil and China) exacerbates global inequalities in the distribution of income and wealth (although it does benefit those fortunate enough to find employment with multi-national corporations). As Waters notes, it was the industrial revolution that set the world on its current twin-track development route:

> On an income per head basis the rich:poor ratio was about 2:1 in 1800, by 1945 it was 20:1 and by 1975 it was 40:1.... Poverty is accompanied by pathological rates of literacy, life expectancy, infant mortality, nutrition, morbidity and population growth.... [36]

While such deprivations are painful for those directly affected they are fortuitous for countries like Britain whose increasingly post-industrial economy requires large numbers of cheap, mobile and malleable workers. Faced with the choice of suffering deprivation at home or taking their chances abroad many of the world's poor choose to migrate – even though jobs in advanced countries like Britain are often low-skilled, insecure and badly paid. As Waters notes economic migrants are absorbed into an increasingly bifurcated economy: 'One group of workers [constitutes the] dominant professional and technical class, another is an urban underclass producing menial services in a context of uncertain employment'.[37]

Of course London's incomers hail not only from the developing world but also from other parts of the United Kingdom where persistent regional inequalities intensify the capital's magnetic pull. Sometimes factors other than economic inequality come into play. In the 1970s and 1980s, for example, Northern Ireland's low-intensity civil war persuaded many Ulster people to resettle in London. The abatement of civil strife in recent years (thanks to the efforts of the Major and Blair administrations) has seen the process begin to reverse. People are also attracted by London's greater tolerance of difference, whether in regard to lifestyle, race or ethnicity. London's 'pull' has long found expression in popular culture, as in the seminal 1960s film *Alfie* in which a naive Sheffield teenager hitches down the M1 motorway only to fall into the clutches of a self-absorbed, neo-misogynist cockney played by Michael Caine.[38] London's role as a melting-pot city is long-standing:

> Londoners came from everywhere. At any one time around a third of people living in the County had been born outside it, mainly in the provinces of England and the nations of Britain. In outer London this rose to more than half. Londoners were 'an alloy of the people of Britain', it was said in 1941. They would become an ever more complex amalgam of elements before the century was much older.[39]

Methodology

This book copies the methodology of two volumes of popular history produced by the Workers' Educational Association (WEA) in conjunction with London's Centerprise Trust in the 1970s. The books *Working Lives. Volume One 1905–45* and *Working Lives. Volume Two 1945–77* consisted of extended interviews with a selection of residents of the London Borough of Hackney.[40] Those interviewed included an embroiderer, demolition worker and lighterman[41] (Volume One) and a barber, hairdresser and taxi driver (Volume Two). One of the researchers described the methodology thus:

> The two volumes were compiled mainly from taped interviews conducted by members of the group [the Centerprise Publishing Project] but these were only a starting point, because we were concerned with the written, not the spoken, word. The original interviews were transcribed in full, including 'Ums', 'Ahs', slips, contradictions, discontinuities and repetitions, but this was only a first stage. After transcribing, the authors expanded and edited their original tapes to produce coherent written accounts.... [42]

The methodology used to assemble the two WEA/Centerprise Trust volumes was an amalgam of popular history and ethnography. This study employs a broadly similar methodology.[43] Gilbert[44] offers this definition of ethnography:

> [T]he techniques are likely to include interviews (usually more like a conversation than a standardised interview...), the analysis of documents, direct observation of events, and some effort to 'think' oneself into the perspective of the members, the introspective, empathetic process Weber called 'verstehen'.

The methodology at the heart of this book is that of qualitative research. Unlike the quantitative data generated by, say, Whitehall's Office for National Statistics, the data generated here consists primarily of interviews with workers. It is subjective and intimate. Denzin and Lincoln[45] offer this definition of qualitative research:

Qualitative research is a situated activity that locates the observer in the world. It consists of a set of interpretive... practices that... turn the world into a series of representations, including field notes, interviews, conversations, photographs, recordings.... At this level qualitative research involves an interpretative... approach to the world. This means that qualitative researchers study things in their natural settings, attempting to make sense of... phenomena [work, for example] in terms of the meanings people bring to them. Qualitative research involves the... collection of a variety of empirical materials – case study; personal experience; introspection; life story; interview... – that describe... moments... in individuals' lives.... [Q]ualitative researchers deploy a wide range of... interpretive practices, hoping always to get a better understanding of the subject matter at hand.... [E]ach practice makes the world visible in a different way.

Interviews with workers were tape-recorded then transcribed verbatim. A semi-structured interview format was used allowing the interviewee to develop a more textured account of her/his work experience where appropriate. The interview questions are reproduced as an appendix. To protect interviewees' identities false names are used. Interviews were conducted either at the interviewee's home or at her/his place of work. For example, the interview with the off-licensee was conducted in the back room of his shop which doubled as a kitchen and office. (During the interview one of his customers came in to make tea and toast.) The interview with the black cab driver was conducted in the back of his taxi. The interview with the bus driver was conducted in the canteen of his bus garage. In some cases time pressures meant it was not possible to administer the entire questionnaire – as with the black cab driver. Because the cabbie was on duty it was decided to miss out the 'Social' questions altogether (see Appendix).

The verstehen aspect of ethnographic research is addressed in two ways. First, through the author's own experience of living and working in London for some sixteen years (in the 1980s and 1990s) and of keeping a flat there to the present day. Clearly this encounter with the Metropolis gives the author a basic understanding of what it is like to live and work in London. Secondly, in a literal way through the reproduction in the text of some of the author's own experiences (under the rubric 'Verstehen').

There is a strong popular history tradition in British writing, from the documentary accounts of the lives of ordinary people produced by the Mass Observation project before, during and after the Second World War to George Orwell's *Down and out in Paris and London*. From the Greater Manchester Low Paid Unit's (GMLPU) *Workers' Voices: Accounts of Working Life in Britain in the Nineties* to *Pit-Talk*, a University of Leicester study of miners' work-place argot. From Tom Pickard's 1980s study of Sunderland shipyard workers *We Make Ships* to *A Sociology of Commercial Flight Crew*, my own study of aviators' life experiences. In-depth studies of British society can also be found in the broadsheets (see below) and in specialist journals like the *Economist*.

In 1986 Tom Pickard spent six months interviewing workers at the doomed Austin & Pickersgill shipyard on the River Wear. Wearsiders had been building ships for 600 years. That ended in 1989. During his time at the shipyard Pickard amassed 70 hours of interviews. The interviews were reproduced in *We Make Ships* in the form of interviewer–interviewee exchanges. Sometimes Pickard talked to two workers simultaneously. For example:

Pickard:	The Tories went mad when some of the bishops started [drawing attention to unemployment].
Chris [ship-yard worker]:	That's right....
Eddy [ship-yard worker]:	What you touched on about people being on the dole: luckily, meself [*sic*], I've only been on the dole twice. My lad – he's on the dole. It's crap. He wants a job.
Chris:	But what's more obscene: that, or somebody saying 'fuck' on the telly?[46]

The interviews were usually conducted *in situ*: 'Many of the interviews and conversations took place either at the men's places of work, or in their cabins during the morning and lunch breaks'.[47] Pickard was careful to protect interviewees' identities: 'Because there is a very real danger of workers in this book being blacklisted for their thoughts... and because jobs in the North-East of England are so difficult to find, I have decided to identify none of the workers.... I find the necessity for anonymity... alarming'.[48] Besides interview data the book also contained Pickard's own impressions of shipyard work. For example:

> Mack then took me on to the half-completed ship.... He pointed out the hole in the deck which the welders have to climb through to get beneath the engine bed.... The ship has two skins... and the welders have to crawl between them along narrow seams, wearing bulky protective clothing and dragging their masks and tools. They also pull an extractor pipe after them. Their journey is through steel hatches and over steel ribs which stick up every few feet and scrape the spine. Once inside they work in cramped conditions, usually alone, lying on their sides in a steel box sometimes no higher than eighteen inches high, breathing fumes all the while. Almost every welder I spoke to dreaded working in the 'lube oil' and they all, without exception, recalled at least one occasion when they had 'thrown a wobbler' [experienced fear and/or claustrophobia] in the double bottoms.[49]

Pickard's admixing of interview data with his own impressionistic accounts (informed by his extended stay at the yard as writer-in-residence) and startling black-and-white photographs produces a book that is illuminating, engrossing and *genuine*. In social scientific terms Pickard's book is a classic ethnographic study. His time at the yard as writer-in-residence constitutes the cultural immersion dimension of ethnography, while his interviews and conversations reveal workers' lived experience of ship building. The book's voice is fundamentally that of the shipyard worker.

The GMLPU publication *Workers' Voices: Accounts of Working Life in Britain in the Nineties* consists of interviews with twelve workers. One interviewee, Margaret, who sometimes held down several part-time jobs to make ends meet, described how it felt to have to scratch around for work in an increasingly affluent society:

> You watch the television and it's all this fabulous lifestyle and how good it is and how we should all have the latest technology and everything and they seem to forget that most of the world are actually finding it difficult to pay the rent and eat.... When I was doing all these little part-time jobs it was like being on a string. I used to get home from work and I would sit down because cleaning is quite strenuous and people want it done nicely, so it meant humping and lifting of furniture. I would get in from work and I would sit down. Peter would quickly cook some tea. I would have an hour and a half indoors and then I would have to go out again. I would get in about half past nine at night and I would go to bed and I would get up again in the morning and that would go on. Even at the weekends I had to start at eight in the morning and I finished at three in the afternoon. I had half an hour dinner break.... It's fine people saying, 'Oh well, set up these nice little packages of part-time jobs'. They want to try doing it. I used to get in at night and I would be like zombie woman. I didn't know where I was. I was always on edge. I was always geared to go. I could never relax because I knew if I relaxed I would lose it and then I wouldn't be able to get up. It's easy for people to think it's part-time jobs, but you have to get yourself into a mental attitude which says 'I'm going'. You've got to do the job well so you have to gear yourself up.[50]

In *A Sociology of Commercial Flight Crew* pilots talk about their work and home life, their hopes and fears, their highs and lows. They talk about relationships, affairs and broken marriages. They talk about lonely stays in bed-sits and the exhilaration of flying. Here are some of their observations:

> We must recognise that low-cost, high-intensity flying with very short turnarounds is much more fatigue-producing than conventional aviation work patterns.

> Life 'on the road' is tough. Over half a year is spent sleeping in hotel beds. When something goes wrong at home (sick spouse/children, financial worries, etc.) it always seems to happen when you are away. This is a great career, and I enjoy it immensely, but I had no idea about how the lifestyle would affect my personal life. Chasing jobs around the south-west [this respondent flew for US airline SkyWest] I was often in a new city, no friends for good times or bad, and with a schedule that prevented planting roots. You asked about failed marriages. I have never been married but I was engaged once and my career choice definitely played a part in us not getting married. It actually ended up being a good thing. However it does illustrate how difficult it is maintaining a healthy relationship when you are away

from home 3–4 nights each week. Your partner must understand not only your job and the nature of it, but also be secure with the relationship as a whole. If I had known from the beginning how difficult the road ahead was going to be it would have given me pause. I probably would have made the same choice, but at least I would have been warned. Working at an airline as a pilot is, at its best, the most enjoyable, and frankly the 'coolest' job I can imagine. At its worst it is lonely, tiring, stressful and sometimes, when the chips are down and Mother Nature is seemingly angry just at you, frightening.

My departure from Cathay Pacific was prompted by the death of my first wife (from whom I was separated) and need to take care of my children at a critical time in their lives. While at Cathay I had travelled back to Europe for a weekend visit with them every month, which was extremely tiring on top of my regular long-haul flying (of which I had nine years).

Once I have driven 1,200 miles a month (minimum), flown 85 hours (average) plus the rest of the duty-time, kept up with all the company paperwork and checks, done two lots of housework and the shopping, put in enough hours of Open University study (to be able to get a real job), kept up to date with Eastenders [the BBC soap opera], oh and slept.... where on earth do I have time for a relationship?[51]

The Leicester University–Vaughan College publication *Pit-Talk* records the argot of midlands' mining communities – the English of the working class. In November 2006 the *Guardian* newspaper's *Weekend* supplement carried a series of photographs of small traders taken by David Bailey. The photographs were accompanied by traders' observations about their chosen profession. Baker Karl observed: 'Our bread is better than the supermarkets', but people can't be bothered to go to two places to do their shopping'. Rag-and-bone man[52] Alf explained: 'I was 13 when I started. There were 30 or 40 rag-and-bone men round my way then; now it's just me'. Farrier Pippa said: 'In the past there would have been a forge in every village and your customers would have come to you. Now I go to them. I've got a portable gas forge in the van'. Labourer Arthur said: 'I came here from Poland.... Before that, I was studying, and then I was working in McDonald's. I came for the money.... It doesn't exactly make me a rich man, but I can afford to buy more things here than I could back home'. Bespoke shoemaker Louise noted: 'In London in 1900 there were 200 bespoke shoe-making companies. Now there are six or seven.... A pair of handmade shoes will cost you £1,200 to £1,300'. Fishmonger Spirit explained: 'I got my shop from the council in 1993 and spent over £40,000 redeveloping it from derelict. In 2000 the council told me they wanted to sell the property.... But in the end they took the building to auction.... The new landlord tripled the rent. I got into arrears... one night, at 3 a.m., I heard a banging. There was a policeman and two bailiffs outside.... I have fought the eviction order in court and won'. Carpenter Alison said: 'You have to throw your shoulders back and be very confident.... I've got a successful business now, but it has been a struggle as a woman carpenter.... There've been times when jobs have gone to men, even though I've provided insurance and a 12-month guarantee. Somehow people think a man will do a better job'.[53] It is evident from these and other works of popular history that valuable insights can be gained by giving ordinary people – the foot soldiers of the economy – the opportunity to talk about themselves and their work. Unmediated accounts are by definition more accurate than interpretative accounts where the author's voice may overwhelm that of the subject.

The importance of listening – of creating a space for ordinary folk to express themselves – was perhaps best understood by the founders of Mass Observation. In 1937 three idealistic Englishmen established the Mass Observation project to illuminate how ordinary people lived:

> Mass-Observation [was] set up in 1937 by Tom Harrison, a self-styled anthropologist and adventurer, Charles Madge, a poet and journalist, and Humphrey Jennings, a documentary film-maker working at that time with the GPO Film Unit. Their aim was to create an 'anthropology of ourselves' – a comprehensive survey of ordinary people's feelings and activities using a very wide variety of techniques to gather information. Most of their early work centred around the observation of people's behaviour but they were also interested in how people wrote about their own lives – hence the diaries.[54]

It was the diary element of Mass Observation that provided the most intimate and probably the most accurate impression of Britons' day-to-day lives. In 1939 Mass Observation set out to record Britons' experiences during the Second World War: 'Mass-Observation invited members of the public to record their day-to-day lives in the form of a diary. These diaries... would be used as a basis for the study of civilian life during wartime Britain'.[55]

Clearly no methodology is flawless. While the reproduction of interview responses verbatim gives *Londonland: An Ethnography of Labour in a World City* a degree of integrity, the fact that it was the author who decided which occupations to feature means the book is still a construct – a product of the author's own agenda of concerns. Consequently, although only a sub-text, the author's voice can still be heard.

Structure

The book's structure is straightforward. The scene-setting first chapter is followed by a detailed examination of British society with a special focus on work and the distribution of income and wealth. Given that Britain has had a nominally left-wing government for the last ten years it is interesting to reflect on the degree to which the Blair–Brown administrations have promoted social justice and equality of opportunity (staple ideological commitments of the Labour Party). Britain may be one of the most powerful economies in the world but is it a just society, a true meritocracy, a new Jerusalem or just a clone of the USA with its neo-con, winner-takes-all, wait-for-the-trickle-down zeitgeist?[56]

The second chapter also examines the social, economic and political life of Britain's capital through the work of established commentators like Steven Humphries and John Taylor, Jane Cox and Jerry White. A series of reports on poverty and deprivation published by the *London Evening Standard* in the mid-1990s features strongly, as does research conducted by the Department of Geography at Queen Mary College, University of London in 2005. Sociologist Zygmunt Bauman's insightful analysis of globalisation is used to pull the chapter's myriad observations together. Workers' interview-derived testimonies are reproduced in the third chapter. The interview responses are reproduced verbatim (although 'Ums' and 'Ahs' are edited out). The questionnaire itself is reproduced as an appendix. All the interviews were conducted during the summer of 2007.[57]

Using the secondary data presented in Chapter Two and primary data presented in Chapter Three the final chapter identifies the major themes and trends of the London employment market. It describes the highs and lows, pluses and minuses of working in London. It is hoped that the personal accounts contained in this book will add to our understanding of London labour and that politicians, employers and trades unions will assimilate the messages.

Endnotes

1   Hamilton cited in Waters (1995)
2   McRae (2007)
3   Harrison (1983) pp. 12–13
4   In her book *London's East End Life and Traditions* historian Jane Cox describes London as a 'transit camp'.
5   Hammersmith is home to London's Polish Centre.
6   It is important not to allow oneself to be overwhelmed by media crime reports. In 2008, for example, knife crime found itself in the media spotlight. Considered in the context of London's vast population, however, knife crime poses a very minor risk to public safety. Media-induced moral panics are socially dysfunctional. They cause unnecessary worry and induce governments to introduce ill-thought-out measures (as happened some years ago with the Dangerous Dogs Act).
7   Johnson (2008)
8   Cox (1994) p. 143
9   Humphries and Taylor (1986) p. 122
10   Humphries and Taylor (1986) p. 130
11   White (2001) pp. 405–6
12   Copeland joined the BNP in 1997 and the National Socialist Movement in 1998.
13   Hopkins and Hall (2000)
14   'Services... can... increasingly be exported by electronic transmission which is especially the case for financial services. Aesthetic commodities can be exported more

directly, especially insofar as broadcasting technology becomes more widely available'
notes Waters (1995, p. 75).

15   Bergsten cited in Schwartz (2008)

16   *Economist* (2008a)

17   Most contemporary US politicians have a deep-seated mistrust of Keynesianism and big
government.

18   Schwartz (2008)

19   *Economist* (2008b)

20   Waters (1995) p. 3

21   During the sixteenth century nation states began to construct a network of
international relations.

22   Waters (1995) pp. 65–6

23   Schifferes (2007)

24   Sometimes to the detriment of the globe's ecology (Humphrey and Schmitz, 2007).

25   Humphrey and Schmitz (2007) p. 31

26   Schifferes (2007)

27   Institute of Development Studies (2008)

28   Waters (1995) p. 66

29   Schifferes (2007)

30   While China may be richer today than she was during the Cultural Revolution it is
important to remember that many Chinese still live in poverty. China has an army
of rural poor. Poverty is one of the main drivers of Chinese economic migration (see
Chapter Two).

31   McDonald's working practices are Taylorist: there is a 'one best way' to perform each
food preparation task. Staff are indoctrinated in this one best way. Work becomes
automatised.

32   Waters (1995) p. 66

33   Waters (1995) p. 70

34   Mecham (2007) p. 48

35   De-centred design and production does not always go according to plan, however. In
2007–8 Boeing's 787 project suffered several setbacks when sub-contractors failed
to perform as expected. The 'hollowing-out' of major corporations is far from a fully
matured process. There is much still to learn (see, for example, Anselmo, 2008).

36   Waters (1995) p. 71

37   Waters (1995) p. 75

38   *Alfie* is fundamentally a film about the iniquities of back-street abortion in the years
before Britain provided this service on the NHS.

39   White (2001) p. 91

40   Understandably, perhaps, the two volumes did not sell in large numbers. They can,
however, be found in university libraries (the University of Leicester's library, for
example, holds both volumes). Local authority libraries can source them from the
British Library.

41   Lightermen navigated barges (lighters) on the Thames.

42   Gray cited in Centerprise Trust (1976) p. 7

43 In point of fact this study is somewhat more elaborate. The original WEA/Centerprise Trust volumes consisted almost entirely of interviewees' accounts. There were no conclusions drawn. Each volume ended (abruptly) with the final interview. A two-page introduction provided the framing. In contrast this study offers a comprehensive 'scene-setting' chapter ('Britain and its capital') and a summation ('Eternal city'). It must be said, however, that the original volumes' lack of embellishment is a strength rather than a weakness. There is much to be said for leanness. The author's voice can too easily overwhelm the data.

44 Gilbert (1993) p. 157

45 Denzin and Lincoln (2003) p. 4

46 Cited in Pickard (1989) p. 67

47 Pickard (1989) p. 2

48 Pickard (1989) p. 1

49 Pickard (1989) pp. 34–5

50 Cited in Greater Manchester Low Pay Unit (1995) p. 8

51 These statements, made by different pilots, are all taken from *A Sociology of Commercial Flight Crew* (Bennett, 2006).

52 A rag-and-bone man buys householders' discarded items door-to-door for repair and re-sale.

53 Cited in Atkinson (2006)

54 The Mass-Observation Archive and the Centre for Continuing Education (1991) p. 1

55 The Mass-Observation Archive and the Centre for Continuing Education (1991) p. 1

56 It remains to be seen to what degree President Obama will modify this agenda. America's enduring zeitgeist is that of free-market economics.

57 Because of the need to 'frame' the interviews with contemporary data, Chapter Two focuses on Britain's economy as it stood in 2006–7. Clearly this data pre-dates the economic slowdown of 2007–8.

Britain and its capital

Work and reward

You see in the old days you felt differently. There are no poor people if you're all poor people. It's only when you see the rich that you realise 'God, I'm poor'.... [1]

THESE are the best of times... and the worst of times. For the young, educated and enthusiastic, Londonland[2] is a honeypot of career opportunity and entertainment. For the rest, Londonland is a grinder that abrades, reduces and, eventually, exhausts. London is a *hard* city. It is a city of razor-sharp contrasts in which wealth and opportunity rub shoulders with poverty and entrapment. In Londonland the economically successful reify their wealth in profitable real estate, expensive automobiles, cosmetic surgery and luxuriant fashion while the rest – Poles, Slovaks, Czechs, Brazilians, Chinese, Filipinos, Nigerians, Ghanaians and others – generally struggle to earn a decent wage. Many – but by no means all – eventually return home to their families and friends, sometimes wealthier, always wiser.[3] London is simultaneously a city of expensive baubles and cheap trinkets, of privilege and exploitation, of comfort and cold, of security and fear, of permanence and transience. Londonland is a paradox of economic and social geography.

In 2006 bonus payments to City workers hit a record high. The *Guardian*'s David Teather noted: 'City bonuses this year are expected to reach a staggering £8.8bn.... The Centre for Economics and Business Research estimates that 4,200 City workers will receive bonuses of more than £1m'. It was not only the high flyers who benefited: 'Almost everyone... gets some kind of bonus. A secretary might receive between 6–10% of his or her salary. People in back-office functions... might get 40% to 60%. The big money, though, is "front of house" – the traders'.[4] Previous windfalls had boosted consumption of such items as vintage Christian Dior fur coats, Rolex watches (at £10,000 each), Italian sports cars, cosmetic surgery (for women and men) and bumper nights out (where tens of thousands of pounds might be spent). One investment banker chose to celebrate her birthday in style: 'There was the time I flew all my friends to New York for my 30th birthday. I did do some silly stuff and that was quite fun'.[5]

Verstehen

In June 2007 I had some business in the City, or rather with a group of educators whose offices just happened to be in the City. After my meeting I cycled to Liverpool Street. Feeling in need of a caffeine injection I stopped at a coffee bar on Brushfield Street opposite a rather swanky arcade of shops that stood on the site of Old Spitalfields Market. In true postmodern style the developers had retained the market frontage, appending the stylish air-conditioned retail units to the ancient (but buffed-up) brickwork. The pavements in front were unusually broad, spotless and spirit-level even, creating a cat-walk for the City's most successful young ladies, whom I watched parading up and down in their new outfits and shiny shoes *desperate* to be noticed. Brushfield Street, it seemed to me, was the reification of Blair's Cool Britannia project (which Brown seems determined to continue, albeit in a lower key): a mix of old and new design, of tradition and innovation, of old and new money, style and vulgarity, understatement and vanity. On exiting the locale I noticed a small sign attached to one of Brushfield Street's carefully styled and freshly painted lamp posts (elegant enough to be called designer lamp posts). It warned that cycles chained to lamp posts would be removed. Clearly nothing could be allowed to impede the progress of the street's well-heeled clientele – even environmentally friendly and health-bestowing bicycles.

The 2006 bonuses were predicted to have a significant impact on property and land prices. According to the Halifax building society, London property prices rose by 8.5 per cent between 2005 and 2006.[6] Teather observed: '[Bonus recipients] favour Chelsea, Kensington, Notting Hill and Mayfair – in the first half of this year [2006], Savills reckons that prices in sought-after parts of London rose by 22.5%... Outside London, City workers are buying homes in the Cotswolds, Hampshire and Sussex. The number of homes being sold for more than £2m grew by 79% over the past year, according to the Land Registry'.[7] In April 2007 average house prices in Britain stood at £236,490, up nearly £31,000 since April 2006.[8] According to estate agent Rightmove annual house price inflation reached 15 per cent in April 2007.[9]

Verstehen

> In 1978 I left my working class roots in South Wales to start a degree course
> at Sheffield City Polytechnic. After graduating I landed a job in London. It was
> 1982 and Thatcherism was beginning to bite. Britain's industrial base was in
> decline. There were closures and lay offs. The miners were branded The Enemy
> Within by the prime minister. The service sector, on the other hand, was in the
> ascendancy. I worked in the service sector. Life was good. I got a promotion.
> I found myself flush with cash. One of my workmates bought a drop-head
> Jaguar XJ6 sports car. On summer evenings we would motor up and down the
> King's Road in Chelsea, showing off. We hopped from pub to wine bar to pub
> to restaurant in pursuit of our Sloane Ranger quarry. We spent as much as we
> could, as quickly as we could... and without any guilt. Money, it would appear,
> insulates and intoxicates. It colours your world view. Crucially it gives you
> options (life chances). I learned to sail. I learned to fly gliders. I bought a big,
> showy car. I would like to say that I felt guilty about the vanity and indulgence.
> But I didn't. The opportunity was presented to me (ironically by a political
> party whose values I had always disliked) and I took it. I wonder what that says
> about human nature? And what does it say about me?

Opinion was divided on how the British public would react to such large City
payouts. The Trades Union Congress (TUC) observed: 'People clearly need to be
rewarded for doing a good job, but the huge amounts being paid out in City bonuses
continue to beggar belief. Many working people helping to deliver vital services
can only dream of earning what a small number of City high-flyers receive each
year in their annual bonus'.[10] One Labour MP claimed that 'excessive, ridiculous
bonuses' were creating 'a sick society'.[11] Even the right-wing *Daily Mail* voiced
concerns: 'It wouldn't be so bad if, like the Victorian rich, the beneficiaries spent
their windfalls on philanthropy. As it is, most prefer to splash out on... cars, houses
and yachts, presenting a revolting spectacle of greed and self-indulgence... [S]uch
disproportionate wealth is feeding the politics of envy, ever bubbling below the
surface in Britain'.[12]

So much for institutional perceptions. But what of the woman and man in the
street? The following opinions were reproduced in the *Guardian*:

> There is a huge amount of evidence that great disparity of wealth is profoundly
> damaging to the social fabric and to individual health and well-being (M. Jones,
> Cornwall).

> I work hard in the public sector for my £26,000 salary but I am starting to feel
> resentful of [City] people getting these sums (Anonymous).

You will find that a salary of £26,000 leaves you among the 13.69% richest people in the UK, and the 2.25% richest people in the world (S. Cleland, Aberdeen).

[City people] work incredibly long hours, sometimes seven days a week, in extremely stressful environments. Would you really give up your cosy pension, job security and 36-hour week for that? London is one of the world's top financial centres, so instead of resenting our high flyers we should congratulate them and stop moaning! (K. Boother, Twickenham).[13]

Stewart Lansley, author of *Rich Britain, The Rise and Rise of the New Super-Wealthy*, claimed that consensus politics and civic selfishness had rendered City bonuses a non-issue:

There has been a dramatic shift in the political and cultural climate in the past 25 years. These kinds of rewards simply wouldn't have been acceptable in the 50s, 60s or early 70s. The Americans called it the 'shame gene' that used to act as a kind of limit to the extent to which people could exercise their natural greed. But that's gone now. The gap will keep getting wider between the super-rich and the rest. The egalitarian era was a blip.[14]

According to Lansley, 'The people who envy the super-rich are the rich.... The middle classes and poorer people are much more rooted'.

While some in government were critical, others, like the economic secretary to the Treasury, were sanguine: 'If the City is doing well, we are all doing well'.[15] The economic secretary may have a point. While the City's most successful people are well-rewarded, bonuses tend to be ploughed back into the economy. As one former foreign exchange dealer observed, City folk are not natural savers: 'Your expenditure expands to fill the income available and that is true even when you go up the ladder'.[16] *Country Life*'s editor noted: 'Lots of houses that had fallen into disrepair... or had been turned into hotels are being bought and turned back into homes'.[17]

It is therefore possible to frame City bonuses – and the resulting extravagance – as a social good. Could it be that we are witnessing an accommodation between Thatcherism[18] and Keynesianism in a new economic settlement – one in which personal spending supersedes state investment as the key driver of economic development?[19]

At the same time that over 4,000 City workers were receiving million pound plus bonuses, Londonland's other workforce – its waiters, cleaners, nannies, bus drivers, shop assistants, nurses, ambulance drivers, traffic wardens, care workers, clerical workers, etc. – were endeavouring to balance income and expenditure in an unforgiving Metropolitan economy. In 2003 Citizens Advice London published its response to the mayor of London's anti-poverty strategy. *Tackling poverty in London* gave numerous examples of poor pay and conditions. For example 'a young man aged 23 who was employed in a shop and paid £2 per hour, less than half the national minimum wage... the client was concerned about losing his job and decided not to pursue the matter'; 'a young woman who works in a restaurant and whose tips are paid into her salary. She is paid the national minimum wage but because her tips are included in this they effectively subsidise her wages... [consequently] her wages never go above the minimum wage'; 'a young woman aged 18 who worked for a hairdresser. She worked twelve hour shifts with no lunch break and was paid £1.30 an hour. When she was off sick she received no statutory sick pay'.[20] It is revealing to contrast this last example with one of the testimonies from Centerprise's *Working Lives. Volume Two 1945–77*, that of Hackney barber Lew Lessen. Before the Second World War Lessen found himself working in a barber shop in West Kensington:

> The hours we worked there were of gigantic proportions.... 12 hours a day, less about 30 minutes for lunch.... We worked 13 hours on Saturdays.... If you were out of the shop by a quarter to ten on a Saturday night, it wasn't bad going. More often it was 10 p.m. This meant that, with lunch times deducted, we worked 68 hours a week.... We were always afraid of losing our jobs and many did.[21]

In one barbers, Lessen found himself sacked for taking time off sick:

> I woke up one Friday morning and knew that I had 'flu. As I was too conscientious at my job I went on working Friday and Saturday anyway. By the time I finished on Saturday night I was the worse for wear and went straight to bed and stayed there until Wednesday morning. Meanwhile my father had phoned the boss.... I rested all day Wednesday and decided to go back into work on Thursday morning.... When I got there I found my job already filled.[22]

In her book *Wigan Pier Revisited. Poverty and Politics in the 80s* Beatrix Campbell investigated working life in the 1970s and 1980s. For some workers conditions were not that different to those of the 1930s. Workers complained of exploitation and alienation:

> Among many skilled workers there is real pleasure in the skill of manufacturing things and in their skill being valued. There is also pleasure in workmates. Yet there is usually a feeling of powerlessness to influence the work process, and this seals the experience of alienation.[23]

One interviewee described her experience of working in a small factory in Sunderland in the 1970s:

> We had no breaks at all. You'd eat as you worked.... It killed you. There were no cleaners in there, we had to clean it ourselves, and if you didn't keep up with the work you were sacked. Actually you were threatened with the sack all the time. They liked young people because the wages were low, it was slave labour.[24]

The oppressive character of manual labour vested time spent away from the broom or bench with special significance:

[Tea] breaks were sacred because the work was a clamour of concentrated, brain-bending production. Twenty minutes off the bench or the track [assembly line] meant so much more than they seemed. It was time off the job and away from the job.[25]

Tea breaks represented much more than an opportunity for refreshment. Tea breaks allowed workers to re-assert their individuality and independence: '[T]ea breaks and washing-up time... challenged the idea that, once through the gate, your time is only the company's time'.[26] Tea breaks were social punctuations.[27]

The fate of British manufacturing industry in the years since Campbell published *Wigan Pier Revisited* gives the following observation a special significance:

A fitter I met in the Midlands served his time on 'machines made of reconditioned scrap – they used to give me electric shocks'.[28]

The abuses highlighted by Beatrix Campbell in 1984 continued into the new millennium. Some employers remained locked in a battle with labour. In *Tackling poverty in London*, Citizens Advice London drew attention to employer malfeasance. The 2003 document talked about 'employees struggling to achieve their rights to the minimum wage' and recommended 'that further action is needed to increase... employers' awareness of their statutory duties'. Citizens Advice London noted that it was left to the most vulnerable – employees with grievances – to secure employer compliance with rules and regulations:

In the main it is individuals who enforce employment law by taking cases to Employment Tribunals.... [W]here people fear to complain this will not work as a compliance strategy.... We would ask the Mayor [to join with us] in calling for the establishment of... a dedicated employment rights enforcement body empowered to investigate... complaints [and] carry out random spot checks.... Without this the poverty and hardship caused by employers who fail to comply with their obligations will remain a feature of London life for those in low paid work.[29]

As to the dubious practices of some employers, *Tackling poverty in London* described the case of 'an employer that had deducted without proper written authority, nearly £2,000 from an employee's salary when he left his job. They claimed that this was for a training course.... Our client maintained that there had been no... agreement that the fees should be repaid... an Employment Tribunal... found in our client's favour'.[30]

The various cases cited by Citizens Advice London confirm a politically inconvenient truth – that without adequate publicity, education, policing and enforcement, legislation cannot be fully effective. It is one thing to pass into law measures like the European Union's Working Time Directive, the Working Tax Credit scheme and National Minimum Wage. It is quite another to ensure employers' compliance. Employees' lived reality of work can be very different to that intended by politicians. Despite the best efforts of amplification stations like trades unions, welfare associations and advice centres,[31] employee protection initiatives inevitably lose some of their momentum. Factors implicated in attenuation include low profitability, size (small firms can be overwhelmed by complex legislation) and, of course, employer greed.

If life was tough for Londonland's new millennium low-paid, then it was even harder for the capital's unemployed, marginally employed and retired. Interviewed in 2005 by Julian Knight of the BBC[32] a London supermarket worker explained how, after turning to loan sharks, he had become trapped in a spiral of poverty:

> I wanted a few little luxuries [like] the odd take away meal.... I felt that having a job meant I deserved a few nice things.... I didn't have acceptable identification and the bank wasn't interested in me.... [When I lost my job] I wasn't able to make my repayments. I started to get aggressive letters from lenders.... I told the lenders I had a problem and they referred me to another credit firm which said it would take on my debt but at an even higher interest rate.... I sold everything I had bought but the pawnbrokers gave me only a fraction of what I owed. There seem few options for poorer people with money troubles apart from the pawnbrokers and loan sharks.

In the same interview a mother of two from south-east London explained how her judgement had been clouded by the Christmas frenzy:

> It is a difficult time of year and he offered me a £300 loan.... They came into your home... no awkward questions were asked.... I knew it was expensive – £25 a week over 20 weeks – but what do you do when your washing machine is broken and you have a young family? It seems to me that [the] burden of poverty falls heaviest on those with children.... [33]

Poverty amongst Britain's pensioners can have potentially lethal outcomes, as Nicholas Davies's[34] 2005 portrait of a London pensioner illustrated:

> Mr Purvis is 68. He lives in a small, dark flat, near Kings Cross.... It is damp, and a thin skin of mould lies on some of his furniture.... He has a rule that he never spends more than £5 a week on gas. In winter, the flat is often cold, so he may spend most of the day in bed.... He has the same rule for electricity – just the £5 a week. From time to time, he does have to sit in the dark.... Another £5 for the phone – he'd get rid of it, but he has a bad heart...

That such conditions and ways of living persist should be a matter of concern to everyone. That they persist in one of the most powerful economies in the world (governed for ten years by a nominally left-of-centre government) is puzzling.

Ten years before Mr Davies's interview with Mr Purvis, London's most prominent daily newspaper, the *London Evening Standard*, ran a series of articles on poverty and disadvantage in the capital. The *Evening Standard*'s investigation revealed sharp economic and social disjunctures. In the first article the *Standard*'s editor, Stewart Steven, described a burial ceremony:

They had just buried the baby. There was a minister of the Church who said a few words.... Noticeably there was no mother present.... You can get a lot of babies in a pit 20 feet long, three feet wide. Where is this sad place? Somewhere in some awful recess of the Third World? ... The exact place: the East London Cemetery, Grange Road, Plaistow. Four miles down the road is the City – the greatest financial centre in the world. Five miles away and there is the glitz and glamour of the West End, the trendy restaurants, the smart clubs and the elegant shops. Not so far away is that temple to modern capitalism, Canary Wharf. A few miles maybe, but a few million also.[35]

The story of Canary Wharf and its Docklands environs tells us much about late/post-industrial Britain. The terminal decline of London's docks and failure of GLC-led efforts at regeneration[36] prompted the Thatcher government to establish the London Docklands Development Corporation (LDDC), a state-funded body that set out to fill the economic void with sunrise industries like currency dealerships, publishing houses, advertising agencies, software houses, specialist high value-adding manufacturers and the like, all supported by a modern, integrated and cost-effective transport infrastructure.[37] While the LDDC was largely successful in its mission to build a new economic base, many of the jobs went to accomplished economic migrants from distant locales. One interviewee claimed that even the initial construction jobs went to outsiders:

When they were building Canary Wharf they brought in people from all over the country. But you promised us jobs, we said. They produced lists to show that the workmen lived locally. Of course they did. They were all in digs, going home to the north or wherever at the weekends.[38]

An ex-warehouseman described a two-tier labour market with semi- or unskilled locals left to fight over menial jobs:

The regeneration was supposed to bring jobs. What really happened was they closed down what little industry there was to make way for the offices and blocks of luxury flats and the companies that moved in brought their own workers.... The only jobs for us were as car park attendants and security guards.[39]

Asked to summarise the overall impact of the LDDC's regeneration programme on Docklands' indigenous population a local doctor, Maurice Rosen, commented:

In the 24 years I have been a GP here, I have seen very little that has been to the advantage of local people. They are treated like outcasts, third-class citizens.[40]

One of the *Standard*'s investigating journalists, Keith Dovkants, summarised his experiences in this way:

Much of the steadiness has gone from people's lives. Their children cannot find homes, they move away and family roots – so precious here – have been torn up. The loss of the docks aches, even now, like a bereavement.

Another of the *Standard*'s journalists observed:

> It is not just a matter of material poverty [in Tower Hamlets 70 per cent of secondary school pupils received free school meals, more than three times the national average]. There is a spiritual poverty, a lack of self-regard and care manifested through the exceptionally high incidence of cigarette smoking and obesity, both recognised contributors to heart disease.[41]

In her Annual Report as director of public health for the East London and the City Health Authority, Dr Bobbie Jacobson commented: 'If there were one magic bullet that could transform health in the East End it would be to reduce the extreme poverty experienced by most East Londoners. The new census points to an unequivocal picture of worsening levels of poverty in East London... high levels of ill health are one of its many consequences'.[42] In 1994–5 the mortality rate for one-to-four-year-olds in west London's Riverside health authority stood at 23.3 per 100,000. In Tower Hamlets [an east London borough] it stood at 50.2.[43]

The Jarman Index, developed by Professor Brian Jarman of St Mary's Hospital, Paddington, measures multiple deprivation in local authority areas. Factors considered in Jarman's scheme include the local unemployment rate, number of unskilled workers, number of single parents and number of overcrowded properties. Using data from the 1991 census the Jarman Index revealed the three most impoverished inner London boroughs to be Southwark (ranked 11th most deprived), Hackney (ranked 12th) and Tower Hamlets (13th).[44] According to *Standard* journalist David Taylor, 'Jarman captured, in unassailable scientific terms, the appalling reality of life in East London in the closing years of the millennium. What he was unable to convey was the sheer human suffering'.[45]

As far as London's blue collar workers were concerned the evisceration of the capital's docks (and collapse of numerous associated industries like warehousing and distribution) proved a financial and psychological body-blow. In its *Regeneration Statement* of March 1998[46] the LDDC noted 'the severe economic, physical and social damage caused to East London by the closure of London's docks'. The speed and scale of the disinvestment (or, less euphemistically, abandonment) was remarkable: between 1978 and 1981, 10,000 jobs disappeared; between 1971 and 1981 the area's population fell by 20 per cent; by 1981 '60% of the area was derelict, vacant or under-used'.[47] Free market economics can be brutal. It was clear to at least one Conservative politician that something had to be done. Speaking in 1981 Michael Heseltine described the problem in these terms: '[T]he area displays more acutely and extensively than any area in England the physical decline of the urban city and the need for regeneration'.[48] [49] The Thatcher government's solution was to set up a Development Corporation. The LDDC set out '[T]o create the circumstances... in which private investment would fund the economic regeneration of London Docklands, while at the same time... improve the social infrastructure and public amenities from their low base'.[50]

As mentioned above, local residents (and their representatives) were less than welcoming – a fact recognised by the LDDC itself in its 1998 *Regeneration Statement*: '[R]elationships with the three Boroughs got off to a rocky start and there were many tensions and disagreements throughout the 1980s'.[51] The LDDC's strategy was simple – it pump-primed the Docklands economy in the hope of attracting significant private investment. The Conservative government's New Keynesianism[52] worked: by 1998 (the year of the Corporation's abolition) the LDDC's £1.86 billion infrastructure investment had attracted £7.2 billion-worth of private investment (in offices, hotels, shopping malls, restaurants, factories, etc.).[53] Docklands' working population was predicted to be 175,000 by 2014.[54] A 1997 survey of Docklands employees showed that while 56 per cent held white-collar jobs (in the financial services sector, real estate, local government, etc.), 43 per cent had blue-collar jobs. Surprisingly, perhaps, 19 per cent of Docklands employees worked in manufacturing (plus 9 per cent in transport and communication and 8 per cent in wholesale, retail and repair).[55] By 1997 there were more manufacturing jobs in Docklands than in 1981.

Further help arrived in the form of improvements to public transportation (the Docklands Light Railway (DLR) with its numerous stations and London Underground's Jubilee Line Extension, for example) that enabled Docklands residents to fill vacancies across London. As for the Docklands environment itself, many of the LDDC's policies had green outcomes. The Corporation's determination to redevelop brownfield sites, for example, obviated the need for virgin land. The development of an integrated transport network encouraged workers to leave their cars at home. The new network 'delivered a modal split on the Isle of Dogs Central Business District... of 27% private to 73% public transport at peak hour travel'.[56] Other policies with green outcomes included cycle routes, riverside and dock-side walks (in 1981 only 3.7 miles of waterfront were accessible: by 1998 thirty-one miles were accessible), new parks and open spaces, wildlife sanctuaries and 'more energy-efficient approaches to electricity supply including combined heat and power stations supplying developments through local networks'.[57]

It is clear that different groups constructed the LDDC's regeneration programme in different ways. Captains of business and industry usually cast the Corporation in a positive light – as evidenced by this analysis from the chairman of the East London Partnership (and group services director of Grand Metropolitan), David Tagg:

> Many big companies have moved to east London because of cheap rents and Canary Wharf. But contrary to popular belief, most of these companies are investing in the area because they believe in its future.... These companies bring new people and new expertise to east London. They are also prepared to use their collective muscle to lobby for the area. Business played a major part in fighting for the extension to the Jubilee and East London Tube lines.[58]

Not unsurprisingly Michael Pickard, chairman of the LDDC, was equally upbeat:

> There are now more than 2,500 companies in the area – up from 1,000 in 1981.... And they exist not in isolation, as the myopics persist in believing, but as part of a real and flourishing community. Why else would so many new shops, supermarkets and restaurants be opening in Docklands?... Who has benefited from all this? Contrary to some views, the take-off of Docklands serves more than the newcomers who work there. The longer it continues to attract private investment and government support, the wider will the benefits spread.[59]

Those with direct experience of the dock closure programme, those who experienced the social and economic dislocation at first hand, were less sanguine, however. (Unsurprising, perhaps, given that the closures destroyed a venerable way of life.) As noted by Dovkants, the indigenous residents of Docklands were a proud and independent people with a strong sense of place:

> [T]he recent history of the Isle of Dogs suggests an aboriginal people engaged in a constant battle for concessions to their sense of belonging, their desire to live where they have always lived, in their own way.[60]

In 1957 sociologists Michael Young and Peter Willmott published their seminal study of life in London's East End *Family and Kinship in East London*. Focusing on Bethnal Green they revealed a world of close family ties and mutual obligation. Every family member understood what was expected of her/him.[61] Bethnal Green was a society of mores and tacit codes – an intimate and sometimes claustrophobic society:

> [I]n one street containing 59 households, 38 had relatives in other households; in one block of buildings containing 52 households, 28 had relatives in it; in another block, with 176 households, 64 had relatives.... Over half the married women saw their mothers within the previous twenty-four hours and 80 per cent of them within the previous week.[62]

It is reasonable to assume that a similar society had developed in Docklands and that its communities were as close-knit as those of Bethnal Green in the 1950s.

Trends in the distribution of income and wealth

In 1985 Britain's Heir Apparent, Prince Charles, expressed his desire that Britain should not become a 'divided realm'. The 1980s, claim Hudson and Williams, set in train two significant dynamics: a sustained economic recovery following the successive slumps and partial recoveries of the 1970s and early 1980s,[63] and the re-emergence of a distinct underclass[64] in British society:

If there is such a being as the average UK citizen, then in 1989 he or she was probably better off than they had ever been – leastways in material terms.... Nearly two-thirds of households own their homes and 73 per cent have central heating. There is also widespread ownership of consumer goods with, for example, 74 per cent owning freezers. Not only have such items become almost universal possessions but the consumer boom has encompassed an ever increasing range of household goods.... While the national economy was certainly experiencing a boom of sorts, it was equally evident that the benefits were not being spread equally within the UK. It is as easy to draw a portrait of a divided and impoverished UK as it is of a prosperous nation. Indeed, this was the objective of the Divided Britain declaration issued by the Child Poverty Action Group in 1986. It stated that 'Britain is divided into different worlds by extremes of wealth, income and prospects. In north and south there is a widening gap between rich and poor... sick and healthy, employed and unemployed'.[65]

The economic expansion of the 1980s continued into the 1990s, as Majorism emulated Thatcherism. The Major government's fiscal prudence saw a widening of the gap between rich and poor:

The 1980s and 1990s were a time of conspicuous wealth and economic growth.... By most measures the gap between rich and poor grew as unemployment topped 3m and taxes on the wealthiest people were cut. At the same time [the government] reformed the Welfare State and kept benefits to a minimum. The aim was to cut costs and to encourage people into work.... However, moves such as ending the link between the state pension and average earnings led to an increase in pensioner poverty. And analysts identified the rise of a poor underclass in UK society.[66]

The United Nations Development Programme's (UNDP's) 1996 Human Development Report noted: 'The United Kingdom, unfortunately, has an exceptionally high degree of inequality'.[67] Lean and Ball commented: 'The report shows that the poorest 40 per cent of Britons share a lower proportion of the national wealth – 14.6 per cent – than in any other Western country. This is only marginally better than in Russia, the only industrialised nation, east or west, to have a worse record. Measurements of the gap between rich and poor tell a similar story. The richest fifth of Britons enjoy, on average, incomes ten times as high as the poorest fifth'.[68]

While of concern, it is important to place these figures in a broader context. In July 1996 the *New Internationalist* investigated global long-term trends in the distribution of income, wealth and opportunity. It noted a widening of the gap between the world's richest and poorest citizens in three key areas: income, trade and commercial bank lending:

Widening gaps between rich and poor[69]		
Percentage of global economic activity, selected categories		
Income	**1960/70**	**1989**
Richest 20%	70.2	82.7
Poorest 20%	2.3	1.4
Ratio of richest to poorest	30 to 1	59 to 1
Trade		
Richest 20%	80.8	81.2
Poorest 20%	1.3	1.0
Ratio of richest to poorest	62 to 1	86 to 1
Commercial bank lending		
Richest 20%	72.3	94.6
Poorest 20%	0.3	0.2
Ratio of richest to poorest	326 to 1	485 to 1

What these figures demonstrate is the increasing economic polarisation of the world community up to the end of the 1980s. Wealth (and the opportunities afforded by wealth, like travel and education) became concentrated in fewer and fewer hands. Of the US experience the *New Internationalist* wrote:

> Between 1983 and 1989 the richest 0.5% of US households increased their share of total private wealth from 24% to 29%.... Then, between 1989 and 1995, the valuation of the Dow Jones Industrial Average of shares doubled, and with it the value of the 80% of all US financial assets that are held by the top 10% of American households, hugely increasing the value of their assets.[70]

The stock market-fuelled enrichment of America's elite in the 1980s demonstrates a key economic dynamic: that wealth creates wealth, and that those without it will struggle to lift themselves up. Only the wealthy can exploit stock market booms and banks' lending facilities to the full: 'The richest 20% of the world's people now have a virtual monopoly of access to commercial bank lending – an astonishing 485 times more than the poorest 20%, who in effect have no access at all. The main reason for this is that the richest 20% own assets which they can use as "collateral" for loans, whereas the poorest 20% own virtually nothing'.[71] (The very poor are often not able to open a bank account. The banks – which, as businesses, are out to make as much money as possible – don't see them as money-spinners.)

In 2000 the *Economist* printed an article about America's poor. 'Poverty in America: Out of sight, out of mind' described the users of Chicago's Wacker Drive and Lower Wacker Drive:

A stroll down Wacker Drive... offers an instant snapshot of America's surging economy. Young professionals stride along, barking orders into mobile phones. Shoppers stream towards the smart shops.... But there is a less glamorous side to Wacker Drive, literally below the surface. Lower Wacker is the subterranean service road that runs directly beneath.... It is... a favourite refuge for the city's homeless, many of whom sleep in cardboard encampments between the cement props.... As Wacker Drive, so America.[72]

What is perhaps most disturbing about this scene is that people can live such completely divergent existences under the same flag. Advanced capitalist societies may (perhaps unwittingly) have entered an era of social parallelism. In his 1983 book *Unemployment* Jeremy Seabrook talked about the impact of modern capitalism – of the bifurcation of the UK's labour force into core workers and peripheral workers, labour shake-out, casualisation, extended periods of inactivity between (often unsatisfactory) jobs and long-term unemployment – on social relations. His observations were prescient:

[T]he price paid by working people for the 'successes' of capitalism has been in terms of the breakdown of the old neighbourhoods, the destruction of human associations, the loss of solidarity, indifference between people, violence, loneliness, mental illness, alcoholism, drug-dependency, a sense of loss of function and purpose.[73]

In 2004 the Institute of Fiscal Studies (IFS) noted of the British economy: '[T]he level of inequality inherited after the big inequality rise of the 1980s has not been much reversed and remains at a 40-year high'.[74] The *Guardian's* economics editor commented: 'The richest 1% of individuals... took 3% of national income in 1979 but 8% by 2000, representing a return to the position of the 1950s'.[75] While New Labour's real-terms benefits increases had helped the poor,[76] and while Britain's poor were still much better off in *absolute* terms than the poor of most Third World countries, Britain remained a deeply divided society.[77]

The 2005 edition of *Social Trends* noted: 'Throughout the period 1984 to 2003, more than three quarters of adults in Great Britain considered that the gap between those with high incomes and those with low incomes was too large'.[78] While such an opinion could, of course, be attributed to the politics of envy, it is clear that the earnings differential in Britain is a significant feature of economic life:

In April 2004, directors and chief executives of major organisations, with median earnings of £1,791 per week, topped the earnings league for full-time employees in Great Britain. Senior officials in national government, medical practitioners and aircraft pilots and flight engineers also had median weekly earnings exceeding £1,000. The lowest paid of all adult full-time employees were leisure and theme park attendants and floral arrangers and florists, with median earnings below £200 per week, only just over a tenth of the earnings of the highest paid occupational group.[79]

On 21 October 2008, in the midst of the banking crisis, the Organisation for Economic Cooperation and Development (OECD) published a report on income distribution. The OECD, said the *Economist*, concluded that 'Britons get neither equal outcomes nor equal chances. Income is distributed more unequally than in most OECD countries... and more unequally than in any rich one except America and Italy. Nor is equality of opportunity much in evidence: a son's income depends more strongly on his father's in Britain than in any other country for which the OECD has data. Across the developed world the gap between rich and poor has grown for two decades now. *That has been particularly true in Britain's open economy* [my emphasis]'.[80] Even in times of economic turmoil it would seem that rich Britons get richer.

Other 'lineaments of division' (to borrow Hudson and Williams's term) include regional variations in wealth and prospects. In 1997 the *Financial Times* noted:

> People living in the north east or Scotland... are twice as likely to be living in a household without a car as those living in the south east, while in Merseyside they are twice as likely to be out of a job as in the rest of the north west. Some disparities are growing, too.[81]

Verstehen

In 2006 I went for an interview at Liverpool University. As the interview was scheduled for mid-day I spent the morning walking around the city. It was only my second visit to Liverpool and I wanted to get a feel for the place. Three things stood out. Firstly the pawn shops. Secondly the pre-opening queues outside the pawn shops. Thirdly the way many people looked and dressed: they looked and dressed poor. They wore hard faces and cheap clothes. Even the children had hard faces. The meanest streets were in Toxteth, a neighbourhood with not a single redeeming feature. During the 1980s and 1990s Liverpool's economic and social fabric had been ripped apart. True the Blair government and European Union had started to reverse the city's decline. But it takes years to restore confidence and rebuild lives. In fact, it takes generations. Society, trust, respect, pride, confidence, tolerance, patience and other positives cannot be bought off the shelf. They develop organically, at their own pace. Nature abhors a vacuum. Take away hope and despair moves in. Take away jobs and crime moves in. Take away dreams and drugs move in. Take away obligation (like having to be at work at a particular time) and anarchy sets in. Until my morning stroll around Liverpool I had forgotten that pawn shops still existed. But they do. And they're used.

In its 2004 report *Poverty: The Facts*, the Child Poverty Action Group's (CPAG's) Dr Paul Dornan observed:

> Poverty spreads across the length and breadth of the United Kingdom. The fact that of all industrial nations we are ranked as second to Mexico in terms of regional inequality is shocking.[82]

According to David Teather: 'The City bonus... is underscoring the north–south divide in Britain'.[83]

Stratification

In his 1995 book *The State We're In* Will Hutton argued that post-Thatcher Britain was made up of three basic social strata. Holding up the economic edifice were the *disadvantaged*. Many of the disadvantaged were unemployed. At the apogee were the *privileged* – full-time and self-employed core workers and long-term part-time employees. Stuck in the middle were Britain's *marginalised and insecure workers* – short-term part-time employees and casual workers.[84] In his review of Hutton's book sociologist Terry Ward noted: 'People in this category are in poorly protected jobs that carry few benefits... 80% [of part-time workers] are women and 2 million of these work under 16 hours per week'. As to the ratio of the *disadvantaged* to the *marginalised* to the *privileged* Hutton proposed a 30-30-40 split. Ward observed of these ratios: 'Presumably, the segments might change in size, depending on economic and other trends: in time, 30-30-40 might become 20-40-40, for example, or even 30-20-50'. In the mid-1990s conventional labour market theory proposed only a two-way split between 'secure, well-paid, "core" workers in the primary sector and... insecure, part-time and poorly paid workers in the secondary sector or periphery'.[85] Ward also took issue with the size of Hutton's top stratum, which encompassed investment bankers (who in the mid-1990s could earn £100,000 per annum) and teachers (who started out on under £12,000 per annum).

In *The State We're In* Hutton complained that British society had become venal and trivial:

> The sense that the aim of financial and corporate life is personal enrichment at any price is accentuated by the extravagant remuneration packages for senior executives.... Great personal wealth has not translated into wealth for the community.... The media are the mirror for the economic and social disintegration of the country. The focus of the newspapers, notably the tabloids, has narrowed to a right-wing populism that pays scant attention to accuracy, the brew leavened by sexual tittilation and obsessional royal family watching. The power to form opinion has been accompanied by a more careless attitude to the way such power is exercised.... Britain in the 1990s has lost its sense of direction and its people are at odds with themselves. It needs to revitalise its economy [and] rewrite the contract between the members of its society.... [86]

While Hutton may have been right about Britain's greed culture and the petty obsessions of its media,[87] he was conspicuously wrong about the direction of the British economy. Ten years on from *The State We're In* Britain had (depending on which analysis you chose to believe) the fourth or fifth largest economy in the world – albeit an economy different in kind to that which existed in 1995. In new millennium Britain the knowledge industries were becoming the touchstone of British success. The British economy had been reconfigured to perform a value-adding role: workers were educated and trained to *add value* to building-block products made in cheaper countries (in 1996 the *New Internationalist* observed: 'The countries of the south now account for 80 per cent of the world's "working class", its industrial workforce. In the North more people now work in service industries than in factories').[88] Britain's value-adding core workers were supported by an army of semi- and unskilled workers on exploitative long- or short-term contracts – the peripheral people.[89] For sociologist Zygmunt Bauman a precondition of the modern industrial system is *forgetfulness*:

> The pressure today is to *dismantle* the habits of permanent, round-the-clock, steady and regular work; what else may the slogan of 'flexible labour' mean? The strategy commended is to make the labourers *forget*, not to *learn*, whatever the work ethic in the halcyon days of modern industry was meant to teach them. Labour can conceivably become truly 'flexible' only if present and prospective employees lose their trained habits of day-in-day-out work, daily shifts, a permanent workplace and steady workmates' company; only if they do not become habituated to any job, and most certainly only if they abstain from (or are prevented from) developing vocational attitudes to any job currently performed.... [90]

If Bauman's vision of the new millennium workforce is correct where does that leave the current obsession with keeping as many young people in education for as long as possible?[91] What use is extended (and increasingly costly) education to a casualised and robotised workforce? Rather than raising expectations should we not be lowering them?

As mentioned above an increasing proportion of Britain's peripherals come from the EU's accession states. They come to Britain looking for a better life. What many find is poor accommodation, tabloid hostility, ignorant stereotypes, expensive metropolitan transport and menial work:

> It's bright and early on a pleasant spring morning, and a group of men in their early 40s is waiting at the side of the road. Every half an hour a minivan with an English-speaking driver stops and some of the men disappear into the vehicle. They negotiate a price and drive off. This is a ritual that repeats five times a week. It takes place not on the border of New Mexico, but in Hammersmith, London. The men are not illegal immigrants, they are Polish workers who came to England after the EU expansion in May 2004.... [T]hey prefer the black market, often waiting hours for an appropriate van.... They stay in rented houses, often sharing bedrooms with a dozen other eastern European workers.... [92]

According to the director-general of the British Chambers of Commerce 'Poles have been taking the jobs because they have a far better attitude to work than local people, and they have much better skills'.[93] Journalist Heather Stewart says that Polish migrants have boosted productivity and helped keep interest rates down:

> For firms employing them, these hundreds of thousands of staff have been a bonus, and for the broader economy there have been considerable benefits. Thousands of young, mobile workers, often ready to work for relatively low wages, have created a more flexible pool of labour and helped to keep inflation, and thus interest rates, down. Peter Spencer, of the Ernst and Young Item Club, estimates that rates are a full percentage-point lower than they would have been otherwise. Based on this boost to the labour supply, Gordon Brown [in 2007 Labour's chancellor of the exchequer] increased his estimate of the economy's long-run trend rate of growth from 2.5 to 2.75 per cent, banking on a continued influx of productive workers.[94]

Despite the economic benefits bestowed by migrant workers, concerns have been expressed that indigenous workers have been excluded from employment opportunities. According to right-wing lobby group Migrationwatch, while indigenous workers are reluctant to come off benefits to take low-paid jobs, workers from eastern Europe have few concerns: 'It has been suspected for some time that benefit levels are a real disincentive to take work that is on offer and our research spells out why this may be so. An important factor is that wages are now so close to benefits that there is very little financial incentive for unskilled British workers to find a job. By contrast, Poles have very strong financial motivation. On the minimum wage in Britain they are earning four to five times what they would earn at home'.[95] [96] According to the National Bank of Poland by 2007–8 Polish migrants in the UK were sending home about £9 million each day.[97]

While the EU supplies many of Britain's migrant workers, other countries like China also play a part. Chinese workers fill many of the lowest-skilled vacancies – sometimes with tragic consequences. On 5 February 2004, twenty-three Chinese cockle-pickers drowned in Morecambe Bay on the north-west coast of England. The cockle-pickers, all from Fujian province in southern China, were directed by a gangmaster. Many had never seen the sea before. Their English was poor. But they were desperate for work.[98] As they ventured onto the treacherous sands of Morecambe Bay on the evening of 5 February they met other gangs headed for shore. Unaware of the forecast high tides and poor weather the Chinese workers pressed on. When the tide turned all but one of the cockle-pickers drowned (the survivor had to be rescued by a lifeboat). Some had their clothes ripped from them by the force of the water. As Helen Carter, Hsiao-Hung Pai and Riazat Butt of the *Guardian* noted, Morecambe's Member of Parliament had warned of the dangers in 2003:

There had been warnings of potential disaster before the 23 cocklers drowned. The MP for Morecambe and Lunesdale, Geraldine Smith, wrote to the Home Office in June 2003 expressing concern about the safety of Chinese cocklers. She pointed out: 'They are being transported 20 to a boat in waters renowned for their currents and quicksands, where experienced fishermen would not consider carrying more than six'. She added that they were unable to speak English, were controlled by a gangmaster and were being paid one-fifth of the rate for their work. At the time, Fiona Mactaggart, the Home Office minister, said the immigration service had too few resources to deal with the problem. An investigation was ruled out, as it would 'serve little useful purpose'.[99]

In 2004 the *Guardian* used an undercover reporter to investigate the living conditions of Britain's Chinese migrant workers. The reporter, Hsiao-Hung Pai, observed:

> [T]heir lives are ruled by gangmasters who house them in appalling conditions, steal their identity and put them to work in dangerous, low-paid jobs that no one else will do.... they come to find work and a better life, instead they find misery.[100]

Hsiao-Hung Pai found accommodation with a group living on the outskirts of Thetford in Norfolk. The house had three upstairs bedrooms, each of which accommodated four Chinese. Hsiao-Hung Pai slept in a downstairs room that contained three mattresses and a double bed. Because the three mattresses and bed were in use, Pai slept at the foot of one of the mattresses. The house had a 'tiny' bathroom with no sink (which meant that residents had to brush their teeth over the bath) and a small kitchen which people used in shifts. Amongst the residents was a group of three from Shanghai. In Britain for a year, they had been constantly on the move. They had picked daffodils in Plymouth, worked as cocklers in Morecambe, picked flowers in Birmingham and worked for a communications company in Coventry (doing low-skilled work). All the jobs had been low-paid and insecure. Sometimes gangmasters made unexplained deductions from their wages. Sometimes they were not paid at all. One of the workers, who was forty-five years old, said of cockling: 'It was incredibly hard work, and my health simply couldn't cope'. Of the flower picking in Birmingham he said: 'We worked like hell there for two weeks, but got only £15 each for our work. The gangmaster refused to pay us any more than that. We were just totally powerless. We had to leave'. Asked why Chinese migrant workers put up with such abuse he said: 'We wanted to do something to stop these middlemen.... But instead we fight against each other and some of us act as oppressors themselves, to the extent that we become even more defenceless in this society'.[101] The need to make a living in a risky economic (and legal) environment had the effect of turning one worker against the other. Gangmasters' power of patronage created a situation of divide and rule. Workers feared they would be shunned if they complained. As another of the Shanghai migrants observed: '[W]e always have our immigration status to worry about. How do we speak out if we do not have the same rights as everyone else?'[102] [103]

In April 2007 the BBC broadcast the results of its undercover investigation into the conditions of migrant workers in Britain. A Lithuanian journalist posing as a migrant seeking work in Britain uncovered evidence of substandard accommodation, engineered indebtedness, underpayment, inaccurate record-keeping and the forced movement of labour. BBC journalist Allan Little wrote: 'We have uncovered conditions that – taken together – amount to a form of bonded labour which is creeping back into the low paid and hidden corners of the country's otherwise booming economy.... [T]hose at the bottom of the heap – the unskilled, who do not speak English – are becoming a new kind of workforce. They come expecting a reasonable... wage and in the belief that they will work full time... they find themselves part of a vast... pool of casual day labourers, not knowing each day whether they will be working tomorrow or not, and often bonded to their employer by debt and circumstance'.[104] The undercover journalist spent six days in Hull waiting for work. Then he was told he was being moved to Yorkshire and given twenty minutes to pack. He was taken to a converted farm building near Richmond:

> There were more than 20 migrant workers already living there. There were 12 people in his room alone – men as well as women, including one couple. They shared one shower and two toilets. There was no privacy. [The agency] deducted up to £50 a week from the wages of each employee for rent.[105]

Responding to the BBC's investigation, the director of the UK Human Trafficking Centre, Deputy Chief Constable Grahame Maxwell, said: 'This quite clearly is labour exploitation. Certain elements are there; there's a deception and there's a movement of people with an expectation of being paid a reasonable and appropriate wage. This is a kind of forced or bonded labour. This is modern day slavery'.[106] The deputy general secretary of the Transport and General Workers' Union called for tougher legislation to counter unscrupulous employers' exploitation of vulnerable migrant labour. The chief executive of the Gangmasters' Licensing Authority (GLA) noted that the withholding or docking of wages from debt-ridden workers sounded suspiciously like bonded labour. One of the companies investigated by the BBC insisted that it had not broken the law.

Despite the GLA's efforts, abuses continue. In early 2008 the GLA launched a major crackdown on unscrupulous gangmasters. According to the *Guardian's* Steven Morris 'Officials discovered that labourers employed to pick daffodils and vegetables in Cornwall were being paid below the minimum wage [of £5.52 per hour], living in dirty and cramped conditions, and being forced to pay over the odds to be driven to the fields in dangerous vehicles'.[107] The GLA interviewed eighty Bulgarians, Latvians, Poles and Lithuanians. Few refused to cooperate with the GLA. Possibly they were glad that someone was taking an interest in their well-being. The GLA's chairman said:

> Labour providers who continue to ignore the rights of workers... should be in no doubt that we will catch them through our unannounced raids and other enforcement activities. Where we find abuses we will apply the maximum sanctions. We will not stand for worker exploitation and we will stamp it out.[108]

The problem, of course, is that despite the efforts of the GLA, local authorities and police there seems no end to the abuse. Buoyed by an endless supply of desperate (and vulnerable) migrants unscrupulous gangmasters have every incentive to devise new ways of avoiding detection. One is reminded of General Booth's late-nineteenth-century observation that there exists a 'Greater England' of progress and aspiration and a 'Darker England' of exploitation and despair. Today's Darker England is populated by unemployed or unemployable indigenous workers and migrant labourers. Both groups live in substandard accommodation. Both are afflicted by bad diet and a general lack of amenity. Both have little chance of escaping their dreary lot. Mobility is either horizontal or down.

Regarding Hutton's 30-30-40 model it is clear that the middle 30 per cent (Hutton's *marginalised*) are more than ever before a mix of indigenous workers and economic migrants. Today's work force is – perforce – adventurous, globalised, flexible and mobile. Labour mobility is driven by lack of opportunity at home[109] and facilitated by cheap travel.[110] Borders are more porous. For the desperate of Africa and Asia, criminal gangs offer a last chance. One of the most powerful influences on human behaviour is the unequal distribution of wealth and opportunity both within and between countries. Why else would Chinese workers tolerate the kinds of conditions and treatment described above? Modern China may be developing at a phenomenal pace but there is endemic rural poverty together with unemployment amongst China's urban dwellers. As the *Guardian*'s undercover reporter observed: 'Fierce competition as a result of China's opening-up to world markets and international capital means privatisation, lay-offs and high levels of unemployment'. China's economic migrants, observed Pai, ranged from the rural poor to sophisticated degree-holding urbanites. Thrown together by lack of opportunity they wanted to make a better life for themselves and their families. As a degree-holding resident of the Thetford house explained to the *Guardian*'s reporter:

> We all know that the only thing that drove us to leave our homes is poverty. I have a son studying in the university and I want the best education for him. He's bright and he will find himself a good job after university. I must give him all the support he needs.[111]

This man slept on a mattress in a room with four others, in a house in a country with a nominally left-of-centre government.

Contemporary Britain

What sort of country has Britain become? Is it now (in 2008) after ten years of New Labour a New Jerusalem, a genuine meritocracy, a green and pleasant land? Not according to UNICEF, and not according to social commentators David Robins, Irvine Welsh, Ruaridh Nicoll, Lynsey Hanley, Anne Treneman and Beatrix Campbell. In February 2007 UNICEF reported on children's welfare. *Child Poverty in Perspective* ranked Britain 'bottom of 21 industrialised countries for children's well-being.... Only the US is close to Britain at the bottom of the table, based on 40 separate indicators of children's well-being'. UNICEF wrote:

> Britain is one of the richest countries and should be doing much better than it is. We have known for some time that Britain has comparatively high levels of child poverty and children living in workless families. However the UK performance on this league table is shocking.[112]

The chief executive of the Children's Society responded:

> We simply cannot ignore these shocking findings. Unicef's report is a wake-up call to the fact that, despite being a rich country, the UK is failing children and young people in a number of crucial ways.[113]

A spokesperson for the Department for Education and Skills reminded Britons that in 2007 there were 700,000 fewer children living in relative poverty[114] (compared with 1998–9). 'We recognise that Unicef does vital work in this area. But in many cases the data used is several years old and does not reflect more recent improvements' she claimed.[115] [116] Some of UNICEF's findings hinted at a more general social malaise. For example, while 73.2 per cent of Dutch children found their peers 'kind or helpful' only 43.3 per cent of British children found them so.[117] This finding suggests that British society is more individuated – and possibly more competitive/aggressive – than Dutch society.[118]

The government's sensitivity on the issue of child poverty is understandable: in 1999 Prime Minister Tony Blair pledged to eliminate child poverty in the UK within a generation, 'A bold target and one that no other government in the world has yet managed to achieve' noted the BBC's Tom Cheal.[119] Unfortunately for New Labour, eradicating child poverty has proved a difficult task – especially in London, where high living costs squeeze even the relatively prosperous:

> The stark truth is that London has the highest rate of child poverty in the UK and the most children living in poverty. Despite being the most prosperous region in Europe almost a fifth of the UK's poor children live in London. So the government faces severe challenges in trying to combat child poverty in London: high housing and childcare costs and expensive transport. And London's higher basic living costs means money does not go as far in the capital as elsewhere, making it even harder for many parents to move into employment.[120]

In 2006 in response to the plight of London's children the mayor of London, Ken Livingstone, established an independent commission to investigate child poverty in the capital. In 2006 'Across London, 41% of children live[d] in poverty, compared with a national average of 28%'.[121] Despite Livingstone's left-wing credentials (he was often out of favour with Blair's New Labour) the mayor's initiative received the support of the London Assembly's Conservative Group. The Leader of the Conservative Group, Bob Neill, said: 'It is a disgrace that child poverty is so high in a city as wealthy as London'. The chairman of the Association of London Government (ALG), Sir Robin Wales, 'said they could not allow half a million children to live in poverty while trying to showcase "what is brightest and best" about London in time for the 2012 Olympics'.[122]

So much for UNICEF and the mayor of London. What about social commentators David Robins, Irvine Welsh, Ruaridh Nicoll, Lynsey Hanley, Anne Treneman and Beatrix Campbell? What do *they* think of the 'sceptred isle'? The short answer is 'not very much'. They see Britain as a land of economic fissure in which Hutton's bottom 30 per cent are sidelined on sprawling council estates or shoehorned into decaying inner-city neighbourhoods. Robins comments:

> In the 80s, with the departure of the white working classes, 'inner city' became a euphemism for urban ghetto.... Black and ethnic minority people were being walled in by institutional racism. Throughout the 80s a series of uprisings took place.... It was mainly directed at the police.... But the real pressure came from the demoralising effect of unemployment.[123]

Responding to the case of Michael McGarrity, a 'three-year-old who managed to fend for himself for two weeks after his mother died in the flat they shared in Leith', Irvine Welsh commented:

> Social problems [that is, 'problem' people] have been removed from the city-centre to the peripheries, out of sight and mind of tourists and professionals...

British cities, claimed the author, had become bifurcated: 'Glasgow is Hillhead or Easterhouse, Edinburgh Merchiston or Muirhouse'.[124]

For Ruaridh Nicoll, the McGarrity episode was 'a story about what happens out on the edge, where there is real deprivation. A fundamental breakdown is occurring in places that most of us are unwilling to look'.[125] In her book *Estates: An Intimate History*, Lynsey Hanley, who spent the first eighteen years of her life on Birmingham's Wood Estate (along with 60,000 others), described the psychological impact of life on a 'reservation'. Of tower blocks[126] she said: 'They sap the spirit, suck out hope and ambition, and draw in apathy and nihilism. It's hard to explain why I feel so strongly about housing in this way, other than that I know I had a lucky escape where others did not, and that too many people will not know what I mean by that'. Of council estates in general she said:

Council estates... are a physical reminder that we live in a society that divides people according to how much money they have to spend on shelter. My heart sags every time it senses the approach of those flat, numbing boxes that prickle the edges of every British town.... Play word-association with the term 'council estate'. Estates mean alcoholism, drug addiction, relentless petty stupidity, a kind of stir-craziness induced by chronic poverty and the human mind caged by the rigid bars of class and learned incuriosity.... people fight themselves or each other, rather than the system, simply because it's easier and there's an obvious way to do it.... Council homes were once the gold standard for a bright, uncynical working class.... To get a council house in the immediate post-war period was to have a full stake in society [post-war council houses were spacious and generally well-built, with gardens front and rear]. Council homes were never intended to be holding cages for the poor and disenfranchised, but that's how they ended up.

Of the media's portrayal of council tenants she observed:

In newspapers and on television, every reference to a council estate is prefixed with the word 'tough'.... Any connection between the physical, economic and social isolation of council estates and the sometimes desperate behaviour of their tenants is ignored, or dismissed, or laughed at.... The shorthand for proletarian hell used by those who don't live on them is 'council estate', and this is what they mean.

Of the prospects of the Wood Estate's residents[127] Hanley observed:

In 2001, a man in Solihull proper could expect to live 71.4 years and a woman 77.6.... On the Wood, they could expect only to reach 61.8 and 66.1 respectively. Ward unemployment reached 23.3% in 1992, prompting the EU to list it as one of the most disadvantaged estates in Western Europe....[128]

In early 1999 journalist Anne Treneman visited a council estate in Bradford. She wrote:

Here the rubbish is everywhere, and shocking. It fills gardens and spills on to pavements. In some gardens you cannot see green for the layers of old clothes, food wrappers, boxes, papers, nappies. Ripped bin-bags and bits of rubbish hang from trees as if taking part in some sort of grotesque urban spring. A long-time resident would later tell me that the technical term for all of this was 'shit tip'. 'It's an old English expression', she said, and laughed as I wrote it down. Many of the houses are empty, with boards for windows. There is graffiti, and a general decay that makes those houses where people have attempted a flower bed or two look all the more pathetic.... This place feels threatening and alien. Here someone else is in charge.[129]

Treneman's fin-de-siècle portrait resonates with that drawn by Beatrix Campbell in her 1993 tome *Goliath. Britain's Dangerous Places*. A former resident of Newcastle's Jubilee estate[130] told Campbell how, after supplying the police with information about local criminal activity, she had been bullied off the estate:

I had loved it there. I had fought to get to that estate.... The danger turned me out of my home... why should people have to put up with all that crap? I think back and what I remember is lads running round the estate with black plastic bags. They'd broken into people's houses and the next morning the stuff would be on sale. For all the harassment we had, they'd even come to our door selling other people's stuff. That's how they live. It needs some sort of community gathering-together to sort it out.[131]

It could be argued, of course, that for such people as Welsh, Hanley and Campbell the glass will always be half empty – that however prosperous and contented the majority of Britons become, left-leaning commentators will habitually accentuate the negative (and attenuate the positive).[132] In February 2007, following a spate of shootings in London and general concern about alienated youth with easy access to guns, the Conservative Party leader David Cameron expressed his concern at the direction society appeared to be taking. In a clear break with Thatcherism (which prioritised wealth creation in the expectation that the benefits would trickle-down the social ladder) Cameron called for a realignment of society's values. The Tory leader claimed that a future Conservative administration would prioritise the family over wealth creation.[133] As for Welsh, Hanley and Campbell, so too for Cameron: certain of society's values (consumerism, vanity, superficiality, excess, the politics of envy and social Darwinism) had become a source of risk. As he put it:

We need to recognise that our society is badly broken and we need to make some big changes, starting now. When you look at the people caught up in these events, what you see is a complete absence in many cases of fathers, and a complete presence of family breakdown. That, I think, is what's at the heart of it. Young people have more leisure opportunities than ever before.... What they don't have is a sense of responsibility which is imparted to them at a young age.[134]

One reading of Cameron's analysis is that he was just politicking – he saw an opportunity to make political capital and grabbed it. Another reading is that, like Treneman, Welsh, Hanley and other commentators, he was genuinely worried about the consequences for social cohesion of almost three decades of 'me-ism' and 'now-ism'. The prime minister was defensive. '[T]his tragedy is not a metaphor for the state of British society', he asserted.[135] He then went on to announce a series of special measures to address the issues of marginalised youth and gun crime. The *Guardian* editorialised: 'Violence in the inner cities... cannot be tackled by criminal-justice policy alone: it is a symptom of deeper problems in the communities dwelling there. David Cameron was right to acknowledge that yesterday'.[136]

Just before the shootings and ensuing moral panic, one Labour minister had talked about the potential negative consequences of relative poverty. Peter Hain, secretary of state for Northern Ireland and MP for Neath (a working-class Welsh constituency), told a national newspaper:

There's a real problem of people on average incomes feeling there's a sort of super-rich class right at the top.... What is it? Four thousand City workers receiving more than £1 million each in bonuses. People don't feel that's proportionate.... That sort of thing creates a society where you start getting envy being promoted and a sense of real antagonism and that breeds all sorts of socially undesirable behaviour.... I don't believe that people will only work in the City because they get those sort of bonuses. They don't need to offer them. Why don't they give two-thirds of that £8.8 billion and invest it in charity or invest it in regeneration schemes for unemployed kids who are living a mile away from the opulence that there is in the City?[137] [138]

The obvious riposte to Hain's analysis, of course, is that it ignores the multiplier effect of such a massive injection of cash into the economy (although cash spent chasing properties or on such ostentation as fine art, fast cars, drunken weekends in Prague, season tickets to Chelsea FC or plastic surgery would produce little direct benefit to the 'unemployed kids who are living a mile away from the opulence that there is in the City').

Verstehen

In the 1970s I studied public administration at Sheffield City Polytechnic. Pre-Thatcher Sheffield was an economically and socially vibrant city.[139] Saturday nights were raucous, the city centre overflowing with cash-rich working class women and men looking for a good time. But even then the city had its dark corners, like Hyde Park flats. One weekend a friend came to visit. I thought I'd show him the sights, which included Hyde Park. As we strolled through the concrete maze we came across a neat pyramid of dog faeces. We looked up. There we saw a balcony and a dog. Evidently the dog's owner let it defecate on the balcony, then shovelled or brushed the offending material over the edge... to land in *exactly* the same position every time. Quite a skill, we agreed. (Of course, it is just possible that the dog had learned to hang its rear over the balcony in *exactly* the same place each time it wished to defecate. If this is what was happening the dog could have gone into show business.)

Regarding contemporary discourse about council estates two points should be made. First the warning signs of alienation and dysfunction were noted by sociologists Young and Willmott some *five decades* before Hanley's *Estates: An Intimate History* was published. Consider, for example, these observations taken from *Family and Kinship in East London*:

We have... described some of the effects of migration [from Bethnal Green to an estate built on the outskirts of London by the London County Council (LCC)]. People's relatives are no longer neighbours sharing the intimacies of daily life.

Their new neighbours are strangers... and they are... treated with reserve. In point of services, neighbours do not make up for kin.... They frequently complained of the unfriendliness of [the new LCC estate].[140]

One of Young and Willmott's interviewees noted:

That busy sociable life [in Bethnal Green] is now a memory. Shopping in the mornings amidst the chromium and tiles of the Parade is a lonely business compared with the familiar faces and sights of the old street market. The evenings are quieter too: 'It's the television most nights and the garden in the summer'. Mrs Harper knew no one when she arrived at [the LCC estate], and her efforts to make friends have not been very successful.... It is the loneliness she dislikes most – and the 'quietness' which she thinks will in time 'send people off their heads'.... Mrs Harper has taken a part-time job. 'If I didn't go to work, I'd get melancholic'. Her verdict on [the LCC estate] – 'It's like being in a box to die out here'.[141]

For a few, however, the anonymity of the peripheral estate provided a welcome change from the clamour and close associations of inner-city Bethnal Green. 'In London people had more squabbles. We haven't seen neighbours out here having words' said one interviewee who, according to Young and Willmott, 'actually welcomed seclusion'.[142] The majority, however, were disappointed by the lack of amenity,[143] a symptom of which was the dramatic increase in television ownership (in 1955 while 32 per cent of Bethnal Green households owned a television set, 65 per cent of estate residents owned one). The lack of amenity obliged residents to entertain themselves. The age of the nuclear working-class family had dawned.[144]

The second point is that those in government are well aware that the poor have become ghettoised in decaying sink estates.[145] This is why communities secretary Ruth Kelly commissioned a report into the issue. Written by Professor John Hills of the London School of Economics the report recommended the promotion of different types of housing on large estates. As journalist Matt Weaver explained: 'The document... examines ways of breaking up large sink estates, which it says have become concentrations of poverty.... [I]t suggests that council and housing association homes should be sold off to higher income groups or let out at market rents as they become vacant in order to create more economically mixed areas. Cash raised from the scheme would be used to build replacement affordable homes elsewhere'.[146] Given the poor condition and physical isolation of many of the country's housing estates one wonders what attractions they could possibly hold for middle-class 'settlers' used to more prosperous locales (like Primrose Hill or Fulham) with pleasant parks, cinemas, sports halls, nurseries, welcoming public houses, good shops and transport links? As Jonathan Glancey has pointed out, while local authorities were able to meet the capital costs of housing estates, they often failed to spend enough on their maintenance, resulting in premature decay. Of Britain's sink estates Glancey says: 'Sink estates are places where hearts sink lower than any forgotten south London canal or river... few tears are likely to be shed when these concrete streets in the sky fall to earth'.[147] For Blake Morrison estates mean: 'Poverty, ignorance, drugs, graffiti, junk food, feral children'.[148]

This scene-setting would be incomplete without a description of Britain's privileged – those perched at the apogee of the economic Ziggurat. How do they live? The answer would seem to be 'very well indeed'. In February 2007 the *Independent* published a 'Special Issue on Boom Britannia'. Staffers analysed London's hyperactive economy. London, they argued, had become one of the richest and most dynamic cities in the world. Its beating heart, the City, had eclipsed even New York with £29-billion-worth of company flotations.[149] In almost every domain London was in the ascendancy:

> It has over 15 or 20 years become the most international place on earth.... You can measure this in terms of its cost. It has... the most expensive industrial property, which is around Heathrow.... More people fly in through its five airports [London City Airport; Stansted; Luton; Heathrow; Gatwick] than any other place in the world. More books are published than anywhere else. On most of the City indicators of international business London is number one, ahead of New York. And within the M25 there is the largest non-national professional community on the planet.... London... has become a magnet for global talent as well as for global money.[150]

But there was, argued the newspaper's editorial, a dark underbelly to London's success – the increasing marginalisation of both the bottom and middle 30 per cent of its citizens:

> Without doubt, this is a special time in the history of London. But amid the goldrush, there is concern that much of the money is in the hands of a relative few. Though the City generates one fifth of all corporate-tax revenues in Britain, it does so with fewer than 350,000 employees. And it does so in a city where the gap between rich and poor is growing rapidly. Children born in poor areas have a life expectancy six years shorter than elsewhere. The middle classes feel the impact too, with house prices trebled over the past decade.[151]

Regarding the position of London's middle 30 per cent the following testimony from a twenty-five-year-old, £30,000-per-annum advertising agency account manager who decided to emigrate says much:

> I loved London but was finding it hard to get a foot on the property ladder. I didn't want to be in my early thirties and not own a property. I had a great time in London but unless you have serious money, it is difficult to make ends meet and enjoy it. There is also a lot of competition for work. I felt like I had to take the step [to emigrate]. It was a hard decision. I have a lot of friends in London but it's such an expensive place to buy property. Two of my friends bough a flat in Wimbledon for £300,000. For that you can get a four-bed house with a pool here

[Perth, Australia], two minutes from the sea... my commute is now extremely pleasant: a seat on a modern train which runs on time.

In May 2007 the chief economist at the Royal Institution of Chartered Surveyors (RICS) noted the 'terrible affordability problems amongst first-time buyers'.[152] In April 2007 the average house price in the capital stood at £333,785.

Thatcherism's great promise was that all would benefit from wealth creation through the trickle-down effect. While the early years of the new millennium saw consistently low unemployment and increasing consumption of consumer durables (in 1996–7 16 per cent of households had a mobile telephone: by 2002–3 70 per cent had a mobile) the income gap between rich and poor grew ever wider. As the *Guardian's* John Carvel noted in 2005:

> The majority may have never had it so good, but the trickle-down theory of income growth did not work. After adjusting for inflation, the poorest 10% of households earned £100 a week in 1971, while the richest 10% earned about £320. By 2002–3 the household incomes of the poor were still under £170 a week, while those of the rich had swelled to nearly £670. The inequality gap between the two groups more than doubled to about £500 a week.[153]

While Britons may be generally better off, British society is more economically polarised than ever before (see the October 2008 OECD report, above). The British economy is increasingly configured and driven by the markets (which, as Margaret Thatcher observed, cannot be bucked). Economic polarisation is not a peculiarly British phenomenon, however:

> The gap between rich and poor in America is the widest in 70 years.... In 1979, the top 1% received just 7.5% of national income, compared to 15.5% in 2000. The share of the poorest 40%, in contrast, declined from 19.1% to 14.6%.[154]

In 2005 Anatole Kaletsky of the *Economist* forecast that while the British economy would have its ups and downs there was a good chance it would perform well in the long term.[155] If Kaletsky's forecast is accurate Britain's political class will have a unique opportunity to close the gap between rich and poor, enhance the working lives of this country's ever-growing army of 'peripherals' and save a lost generation of alienated, angry youth. The question is: will they do it? Why challenge the hegemony of the markets when they have delivered sustained growth? Why risk everything for the bottom 30 per cent? The answer may lie in Neal Lawson's state-of-the-nation analysis following the February 2007 moral panic over gun crime:

> The free-market spirit of competition... is the code of our mean streets. It is the spirit that is transferred into our schools.... Miserable rusting estates offer no sanctuary, just a playground of violence for children far beyond the fear of Asbos or prison. When you have nothing to lose, why care?... [T]he social norm we teach is the cult of the winner. There is no solidarity, empathy or humanity for the loser

in [our] harsh meritocracy. For endemic social problems we offer... pitifully weak individualised solutions.[156]

The answer, then, is that the bottom 30 per cent merit attention not only because their actions may threaten the prosperous, but also because the condition of the bottom 30 per cent is a barometer of the values of the top 70 per cent. Dead-end jobs, sink estates, unemployment, underemployment, brutish and brutalising behaviour, philistinism (sometimes induced by the gutter press) and dysfunctional lifestyles are not inevitable. They are not facts of life. These and other dysfunctions are *socially produced*. Consequently they can be un-produced.

Verstehen

One January morning in 2007 I found myself in Bedford at six, waiting for a seven o'clock train. Needing to find a cashpoint, I decided to take a stroll into town. It was cold and dark. As I walked I encountered numerous small groups of pedestrians, all headed for the town centre – specifically Bedford's employment agencies. I eavesdropped on their conversations. Most were eastern Europeans. Most were young. Most looked to me to be too thin to withstand a typical British winter. Having registered for work they stood outside the agencies, smoking, conversing amongst themselves, chatting on mobile telephones. Then they boarded a van or people carrier and were driven off, perhaps to a building site, perhaps to a poultry farm. I thought to myself 'There must be a better way than this'. I got my cash then walked to the station. I bought an expensive coffee and sat in the foyer. I watched. I like watching. Londonland's office-fodder began to arrive. A trickle at first, then a flood. I was struck by how well-heeled they looked. Shiny black shoes. Pristine brief cases bulging with papers, Blackberries and lap-tops. Sumptuous dark winter coats. Colourful scarves (a muted rebellion). Casual but smart – the new millennium dress code. They, too, bought expensive coffees from the attentive young woman at the Italian coffee shop. Pleasantries and jokes were exchanged. It was a Friday. Best day of the week.

Londonland

Like any great human enterprise, London has had its ups and downs, triumphs and tribulations. The Great Fire and Blitz knocked it back, but it rebounded, feeding off the energy of its luminaries, visionaries and residents to become one of the great cities of the world. London may not be as pretty as Paris or Venice or as spectacular as Sydney, Hong Kong, New York or Rio, but it is unmistakably a World City – a magnet for bright young Brits, foreign investment, tourists and the world's globalised workforce. Individually each of these elements is a force to be reckoned with. Together, however, they generate synergies that drive London forward with an enormous, irresistible momentum.[157] If you stand on Westminster Bridge and take London in (as I have done many times) you *know* you are at the heart of something great – something bigger than the sum of its parts and certainly much, much bigger than you.

Bouncing back

London's industrial sector was at its peak in the 1950s when the port city received and processed raw materials from around the world (and especially the Empire).[158] London's value-adding role created enormous wealth and economic opportunity (for Londoners). In 1956 one thousand ships docked in the Port of London each week to be handled by its 30,000 dockers. Tate & Lyle employed nearly 8,000 workers. London was more than just the docks, however. The city produced large volumes of motor cars (Ford), buses and lorries (AEC), electrical goods (Belling and Osram) and aircraft (Vickers and DeHavilland). London hosted around seventy US multinationals, including Kodak, Gillette, Hoover and Firestone.[159] London was one of Britain's major industrial cities, and its workers took great pride in that fact. As one AEC worker recalled:

> It was a wonderful place to work... we had a damn good team spirit; we were cock-a-hoop because we were the world leaders in producing trucks and buses. We had a fine body of craftsmen... and [the vehicles] went all over the old Commonwealth and Empire, and the rest of the world as well.[160]

Of course not every company had such a contented workforce as AEC. At its Dagenham site the Ford Motor Company tried to improve productivity by speeding up its assembly lines. Ford's 'speed-up' harmed industrial relations. As one Ford worker explained:

> They were constantly cracking the whip and trying to get more and more out of us... time study caused lots of disputes and strikes. Sometimes the men would try to cheat the time-and-motion man by taking longer than they needed for the job while he was timing them, but they usually took that into account.[161]

Industrial relations at Dagenham were fraught. In the early 1960s several operations were consolidated into a new plant – the Paint, Trim and Assembly (PTA) plant. As Huw Beynon noted in his book *Working for Ford* the PTA became a strike hot-spot:

> In 1960 the men in that plant took part in strikes that accounted for 100,000 man-hours. In 1961 the figure had jumped to 184,000 and in 1962, 400,000.... Faced by an intransigent shop floor organisation the Ford Motor Company decided to operate the 'firm line' advocated in the 1960 Ministry of Labour talks.[162]

Perceptions and actions are, of course, influenced by context. Working on the line was far from pleasurable:

> Working on the line was filthy, dirty and noisy. Basically, you had to have a bath every night. The metal dust that was flying around would turn all your underclothes rusty. No matter how much you washed the sheets they would go rusty and so would the pillows.[163]

For some, working on the line was also an admission of defeat – an acceptance that you would never be anything more than a very small cog in a very big machine. Teachers' and politicians' talk of possibilities and options, of 'realising the potential of every citizen', was clearly a deception.[164] As one of Beynon's interviewees put it:

> You don't achieve anything here. A robot could do it. The line here is made for morons. It doesn't need any thought. They tell you that. 'We don't pay you for thinking' they say. Everyone comes to realise that they're not doing a worthwhile job. They're just on the line. For the money. Nobody likes to think that they're a failure. It's bad when you *know* that you're just a little cog. You just look at your pay packet – you look at what it does for your wife and kids. That's the only answer.[165]

Verstehen

Many years ago, when I was still a child, I watched a BBC Wales journalist interview a coal miner. Until that moment I had understood the world through various stereotypes. For example: people who did white collar jobs were educated and 'decent'; people who did manual jobs were uneducated, unimaginative, crude and hopeless. By the end of that interview my prejudice had evaporated. The miner, asked about his work and hopes for the future, reflected on his situation. He knew he was trapped. He knew he could have made something of himself had the opportunity arisen. He spoke with great eloquence and dignity about his life, the comradeship he had found at work and his love of books and learning. He chose his words carefully. The more he spoke the more ashamed I felt about my stupid prejudices. That interview – that man's dignity – has stayed with me for forty-odd years. Life is short. Everyone should be given an equal chance. Success should not be a function of how much money your parents have, where you live, how you speak, who you worship or how you look.

Huw Beynon passed this judgement on the car assembly line:

> If you stand on the catwalk at the end of the plant you can look down over the whole assembly floor. Few people do, for to stand there and look at the endless, perpetual tedium of it all is to be threatened by the overwhelming insanity of it.

The sheer audacious madness of a system based upon men... wishing their lives away.[166]

Regarding the Ford Motor Company's work ethic Beynon commented:

Throughout his life [Henry Ford] maintained a single-minded, autocratic hold over his company, entirely convinced of his right to run it as he thought fit. *This conviction outlived him, entrenched in the ideology of Ford executives in the 1950s and 1960s.* Every car plant was a hard place to work in. The philosophy of Henry Ford was to add a special bite to the organisation of work on the shop floor of a Ford plant [my emphasis].[167]

Of the Ford 'speed-up' Beynon wrote:

The speed-up had a particularly violent effect upon the older workers in the plant. At the best of times men in their fifties can't compete as equals on an assembly line with men half their age. Speed-up and the clamp-down on the organisation of work resulted in many of these men asking for their cards.[168]

One worker described how it felt to work on the line in middle-age:

I was told that the only job for me was on the assembly line.... I know what the company was up to in my case. They hoped to kill me off. The line had been so speeded up that even young men couldn't cope. And I was fifty-two at the time.... So I went on the line. It was terrible. I had a job where I was chasing conveyor belts up and down all the time without a moment for a breather. I used to work myself silly. When I got home I was whacked out. To be honest, the work was too much for any one man. The foreman kept having to come and help me out. The only reason he did it was because he also knew that the job needed two men.[169]

Verstehen

For most of my working life I have been fortunate enough to work in offices. Offices are clean. Offices are warm in winter. Offices are relatively quiet. In an office you can make a coffee or pop to the toilet when you want. You can light up when you want (outside the staff entrance, of course). If you work in an office you don't get rained on. Office workers don't have to wear waterproofs, steel-toed shoes, hard hats or ear-defenders. Office workers can show off their Saturday afternoon purchases of clothes and shoes to colleagues in the Monday morning fashion parade. They can celebrate the superficiality and banality of consumer society *at work*. I am not unfamiliar with manual labour, however, thanks to summer jobs and my academic research. For two summers I worked as a store man in the vast kitchens of an oil refinery in South Wales. The food store was located under the canteen. Because of the steam pipes it was warm down there – ideal for cockroaches, flies and other scavengers. The roaches gorged themselves on the spillages. They grew. They bred. They chattered. They scuttled around the store while above, in the canteen, hundreds of men (and in the 1970s, all the oil workers at that refinery were men) tucked into lunch. One of the high points of the day was a mid-morning visit by Stan, one of the foremen. Roy, the store manager, Stan and I would sit at a small table at the back of the store drinking tea and eating cheese and crackers. As the roaches navigated around our feet Stan would tell us about the latest management débâcle. As far as Stan was concerned most managers were 'c*nts'. The *most* inept were 'f*cking c*nts' (these were often graduate trainees). I had never heard those words used so often and with such venom until I met Stan. I learned a lot in that store. I remember Stan and Roy and our cheese-and-cracker mornings with *great* affection. With Stan and Roy what you saw was what you got. There was no affectation, no pretension, no showing-off. One day Roy decided to move the garbage bins in the loading bay so we could hose it down. It was the height of summer, a blistering hot day. I helped move the large, over-full bins. The wall against which the bins had stood was white with maggots. Thousands and thousands of them, pulsating and glistening in the sun. Big black flies buzzed lazily around our heads. We fitted a hose to a hydrant and got to work, flushing them down the drains. Above us the day-shift men were trooping in for lunch. They never saw the below-stairs.

Companies tried to sweeten an increasingly bitter industrial pill with giveaways:

During the 1950s many companies in London compensated for increasingly monotonous work by using some of their profits to improve conditions for their workers. This was the heyday of company paternalism, when every major company felt it was essential to provide canteens, sports grounds, entertainments and paid holidays for workers.[170]

During the 1950s working Londoners became wealthier than they had ever been before. By the end of the decade they were almost twice as well off *in real terms* as they had been before the Second World War. The 1950s economic zeitgeist of cheap mass production and credit-fuelled mass consumption[171] produced real benefits for Londonland's labour force. Unfortunately for Londoners, however, the foundations of this prosperity   cheap raw materials from, and protected markets within, the British Commonwealth – were about to crumble into dust as more and more countries achieved independence.

Verstehen

In the early 1990s I spent a lot of time in west London, specifically Hammersmith and Fulham, conducting research for my PhD. Like most immigrants to London I had always conceived of the city as a centre of government, business and the arts – not industry. To me industry was a northern and Celtic phenomenon. Engineering and manufacture belonged in the midlands, coal mining in Wales, Nottinghamshire and Yorkshire, tin mining in Cornwall, cotton spinning in Lancashire, ship-building on the Clyde and Tyne, etc. After spending some weeks going through the London Borough of Hammersmith and Fulham's archive (housed in *The Ark*, the spectacular bronze-coloured glass edifice visible from Hammersmith fly-over) the scales of prejudice fell from my eyes – London had been, and still was in many respects, an industrial city. My PhD focused on the industrial heritage of Sands End, a hamlet on the north bank of the Thames once noted for its market gardens and basket-weaving. I came across Victorian and Edwardian photographs of Sands End that showed a river frontage crammed with every sort of industry, from wharfage and warehousing to gas production (from coal), engineering and tile-making. The photographs were similar to those I had seen of the Avon, Taff, Tyne and Clyde. By the 1990s, of course, things had changed somewhat. The power station had been demolished and much of the engineering had moved on. But Sands End was still an industrial hamlet. The RMC concrete plant and gasometers remained, supplemented by numerous small industrial units, car-wrecking yards and the waste transfer station. The waste transfer station was surrounded by high nets to prevent dust from wafting over the adjacent Chelsea Harbour residential complex. (Chelsea Harbour was one of the most exclusive developments in London. Michael and Shakira Caine had once owned a penthouse there.) The nets didn't work. Dust (and odour) migrated regardless. To my knowledge the transfer station operates to this day. I still wonder what Chelsea Harbour's well-heeled, globetrotting residents think of it? I wonder what Michael and Shakira thought of it when they lived there?

London was both an industrial city and centre of administration. The 1950s saw the beginning of an office building boom intended to meet the demand for pleasant, efficient and cost-effective office space. A magnet for government departments and corporate headquarters, London needed to build offices fast:

> [T]he aspirations of modern office users were sky-high, for the post-war world had seen an explosion in office employment through company formations and mergers, the expansion of government bureaucracy, and the enlarged economic significance of advertising and marketing over manufacturing. Brand-new headquarters in London were an essential requirement for domestic and foreign firms, for new government departments and for newly nationalised industries. By 1962, 60 per cent of City floorspace would be devoted to offices as against 45 per cent before the war.[172]

Besides offices, London also needed more and better housing. The early post-war period was the era of 'comprehensive development' with large swathes of the capital bulldozed and rebuilt according to some enlightened master-plan (often no more than a cheap imitation of Le Corbusier's 'machines for living' vision). The government's 1956 housing subsidy changes 'which gave councils more money per flat the higher it was from the ground'[173] encouraged councils to build high. The cityscape changed:

> A notable feature of... early post-war council estates was their scale – generally much larger than any inner-London estate of the first half-century.... That fitted the aspirations of the time for 'comprehensive development': the Stepney–Poplar Comprehensive Development Area, adopted by the LCC [London County Council] in 1946, proposed the clearance over thirty years of much of 1,300 acres housing 75,000 people.

While some new building had architectural merit, much did not. Residential towers and low-rise blocks (and accompanying squares, green spaces, elevated walkways and shopping malls) were bleak and functional. Many new office complexes were built to the standard steel frame, concrete floor and curtain wall formula, adding yet more blandness to an increasingly anonymous cityscape.[174] This did not seem to bother business tenants, however, who snapped up even the most radical developments – like London Wall:

> [T]he seminal development in the City which demonstrates that the financial sector had espoused wholeheartedly the virtues of architectural modernism was the development of London Wall... straddled by six anonymous curtain-walled towers and lower slabs which proved irresistible to modern commercial tenants. They sealed the fate of development in the City.... [175]

As London's skyline changed, so did its population. Post-war immigration, facilitated by the 1948 British Nationality Act, transformed London into a multi-ethnic city. Two forces acted synergistically to bring about this transformation. The first was the Attlee government's commitment to make Britain accessible to those who had helped her during the war. Two million Indians had fought for Britain during the war, and ten thousand Afro-Caribbeans had served as RAF ground crew. The 1948 Act satisfied a debt of honour. The second factor was the desperate shortage of labour in London's manufacturing, transportation and construction sectors. While London had seen waves of immigration in previous centuries (for example Jews from eastern Europe, Huguenots from France and many, many people from rural Ireland) the post-war years saw significant population movements. During the mid-1950s, for example, about 3,000 people were arriving from the Caribbean each month. Many immigrants were forced to endure colour prejudice – both covert and overt:

> Their arrival helped to unleash a rising tide of racial colour prejudice in the capital. Assumptions about the racial superiority of the English over their subject peoples were several centuries old and were closely linked to the development of the slave trade and the Empire. Stereotypes about the inferiority of non-whites remained very strong.... The result was that many Londoners who had never met a black man or woman nevertheless had a rather negative image of what they were like.... In the late 50s signs stating 'no coloureds' appeared on boarding-house doors and windows all over the capital. One common excuse was that the white residents would not want to use the same bath as a black person.[176]

Prejudice, of course, was an age-old malaise of the metropolis. As Jane Cox notes in her book *London's East End Life and Traditions*:

> Always the newcomers were hated and reviled, mocked for their strange way of speaking, resented for their successful businesses and suspect because of their eating habits. In the Peasants' Revolt of 1381: '...many Flemmynges loste here heedes... namely they that koude nat say Breede and Chese, but Case and Brode'. Three hundred years later Dr Welton, the Jacobite incumbent at Whitechapel Church... railed against the Huguenot immigrants, thundering from his pulpit: 'This set of rabble are the very offal of the earth...' [177]

Poverty, says Cox, magnified racial and ethnic tensions:

> Maybe Gentile shared bread pudding with Jew, but there was a good deal of racial feeling around and tension between different groups was magnified, as it always is, by poverty. Everyone was fighting for the same crust. The Protestants hated the Catholics and the Catholics hated the Protestants and everybody hated the Jews.... Little had changed since the old days when everybody hated the Flemings, then the Dutch, then the French Huguenots, not to mention the Irish, Scots and Welsh and anyone who spoke 'funny' or ate strange food.[178]

Despite such problems, however, London continued to attract the world's dispossessed. Each new wave of immigration bent some aspect of the capital to its own ends:

> The Great Synagogue in Brick Lane says it all – it changed from being a French chapel into a Wesleyan one; then it became a synagogue and, until recently, was a mosque. German sugar bakers, Welsh dairymen, French weavers, Dutch brewers and printers, Spanish pedlars – intermingled with English farm labourers – came to London to seek their fortune or save themselves from starving. Then there were the Irish and the Jews. All was coming and going.[179]

The rot sets in

London's economy began to unravel in the 1960s. Subsidised for decades by protected markets and lucrative government contracts many companies were unable to cope with the halving of Commonwealth trade that resulted from the decline of Empire. Companies' economic woes were magnified by the capital's high costs, increasingly inadequate infrastructure and shortage of building land. Unable to develop new, more efficient sites many companies migrated to the New Towns (like Crawley and Stevenage) and other parts of the country. This pleased the government which was determined to relocate industry to Britain's less prosperous regions. A spate of takeovers and mergers saw the birth of numerous mega-corporations. To satisfy their need for cheap building land, efficient transport, cheap labour, low rents and low rates companies like the newly formed British Aircraft Corporation and British Leyland Group abandoned London in favour of more suitable locales. The complexion of London's industrial base began to change.

Between 1960 and the dawn of the new millennium the number employed in London's manufacturing sector fell from about 1.4 million to just over a quarter of a million. As Jerry White notes in his acclaimed *London in the Twentieth Century*:

> Closures happened first and worst in east London, in the older industrial areas that had grown up around the river. West London was last to be affected, but it was inexorably ravaged in its turn. London's manufacturing workforce was 1.29 million strong in 1966, already a drop from 1.43 million just five years before. By 1974 it had fallen to 940,000, by 1989 435,000, and by 1997 274,000. In the thirty years from 1966, manufacturing in London lost nearly 80 per cent of its jobs.[180]

Every sector and locale was affected, from north London's furniture industry, to west London's automotive parts industry, to east London's docks, warehouses and distribution centres:

> [T]he north London furniture industry employed 16,390 in 1960 but 1,320 in 1984... the west London vehicle-parts industry virtually evaporated with the

closure from 1979 of Smith's Industries, Firestone Tyres, Champion Spark Plugs, Zenith Carburettors, Lucas, Glacier, British Leyland and others.... The gaps that firms left in the 1960s – just like the bomb sites of twenty years before – stayed empty or ruined because there was just nothing to take their place.[181]

As we have already seen, the most dramatic closures occurred in London's docks. Two forces conspired against Docklands: the dockers' fight for better terms and conditions; and the technology of containerisation. While the end of the casual dock labour system with its degrading scramble for work benefited dockers in the short term, the resulting increased costs encouraged the shipping companies and their associated industries to look for savings. Salvation seemed to lie in containerisation, big ships and deep-water ports like Tilbury in Essex. The exodus began in earnest in the 1970s. By 1981 every one of London's major upstream docks had closed. The economic impact on London's riverside boroughs was significant:

> It was the end of an era for a labour force of around 20,000 people.... For every job lost in the docks, another three were lost in dock-related services and industries.... Unemployment in the dockland boroughs of Tower Hamlets, Newham and Southwark increased from 10,000 in the late 1960s to 80,000 by the early 80s.[182]

Finding themselves cut off from supplies of raw materials and an efficient transport artery (ships no longer ventured upstream) companies with riverside plants either relocated or closed. The combination of government grants and a property boom in luxury riverside apartments and watering holes for the well-to-do meant that some relocators did rather well: '[T]he property boom in the capital meant that companies could "asset-strip" their factory sites, and make an enormous amount of money out of redeveloping them for offices and warehouses'.[183] Despite skyrocketing property prices, however, the capital remained scarred by derelict land:

> At the end of the century great tracts of evacuated industrial space were still marketed as 'opportunities' in east and south-east London, the Lea Valley, Park Royal, the Wandle Valley and elsewhere.[184]

Of course not all was doom and gloom for London manufacturing during the '60s, '70s and '80s. By the end of the 1960s, for example, the Ford plant at Dagenham was employing some 30,000[185] people thanks largely to the success of the Cortina: 'More than 4 million Cortinas were to run off the production-line at Dagenham, many of them for export. The millionth Cortina to be exported was transported by helicopter from Dagenham to Belgium amid much pomp and ceremony'.[186] Such a plant would support thousands of jobs in other industries and professions too – like transport, catering, advertising, accounting, the law, construction, cleaning and maintenance and repair. On the other side of London, Heathrow was expanding at a phenomenal rate, trying to keep pace with the increasing demand for air travel.

Gatwick, Stansted and Luton were also growing. The brand-new London City Airport would create yet more jobs. Air transport created tens of thousands of skilled and unskilled jobs for Londoners and served the transport needs of sunrise industries like tourism, banking, financial services, business consulting, cultural production, distribution, fashion and higher education. London's economic tectonic plates were shifting. As one era ended, so another began. Smokestacks gave way to smoked glass.

Bouncing back again

In the 1980s and 1990s the engine of London's economic recovery was the City. The massive inward investment of the final two decades of the twentieth century had begun in the 1970s when numerous foreign banks established themselves in London. The advent of the electronic dealing room in the 1980s[187] saw City employment soar. In 1966, half way through the Swinging Sixties, employment in London's banking, insurance and financial services sector stood at just 275,000. By 1998 the figure had increased to 790,000 people, almost 25 per cent of the capital's labour force. The City's capacious electronic dealing floors and efficient air-conditioned offices were productive: 'The productivity of the sector meant that it created around 38 per cent of London's GDP at the century's end'.[188]

Well-paid City workers and their families began to re-colonise London, ploughing much needed investment into local economies. And it wasn't just Hampstead, Chelsea and Blackheath – London's established investment hot-spots – that benefited: 'In these years gentrification invaded areas that it had only just reached... in the 1970s. Stoke Newington... became especially desirable around old-villagey Church Street... recovering middle-class ground lost from the 1930s to the early 1950s. Parts of south Shoreditch that had not seen an indigenous middle-class for over a century found abandoned warehouses turned into lofts.... Even Hoxton... began an unlikely new career in the early 1990s in media production and the arts'.[189]

Verstehen

> While doing my PhD in the early 1990s I ran short of money, so I decided to take a part-time job as a clerical assistant in a firm of City architects. The major attraction for me was the location. The firm occupied a floor in a converted warehouse in what had been one of London's most dilapidated inner-city parishes – Shoreditch. Located to the north of the City, Shoreditch was being colonised by high-tech reprographic firms, sellers of upmarket household fixtures and fittings, firms of architects and a supporting cast of sandwich shops, coffee bars and better-than-average Indian restaurants. It wasn't exactly pretty – the streets were pot-holed, the pavements uneven and dirty, the street-furniture faded, battered and bruised, the roads chokingly narrow – but the area had a remarkable vibrancy to it. I actually looked forward to going there. It was an enjoyable place to work. It was lively. It was varied. It was different. The fact that the practice was run by a talented female American architect made it even more appealing. It is easy to sneer at gentrifiers and developers. Indeed there is much to sneer at – the conspicuous consumption, the aloofness, the vanity, the superficiality, the self-obsession. But where else could the huge sums of money needed to turn Shoreditch around have come from? The Major government? Definitely not. The Blair project? I doubt it. The local authority? Paralysed by dogma. No, the money had to come from a dynamic private sector willing to take risks in a run-down inner-city neighbourhood. Imaginative, risk-seeking professionals like my American architect have done much for London.

The 1980s saw contradictory forces acting on London. On the one hand there was the private realm of the City: liberated, energetic and prosperous. On the other the public realm of the inner-city local authority: trapped by outdated dogma; inefficient; impoverished; unimaginative; shabby. In 1983 London's population reached its lowest point of the twentieth century. Unemployment was worse in London than in the rest of the UK (a surprising reversal). Crucially for the bottom third of London's population there were fewer and fewer semi- and unskilled jobs available. As the capital's industrial base shrank it coalesced around a limited range of activities, chiefly financial services and the leisure industry. The consolidation trend continued into the 1990s leaving the capital more and more dependent on the fortunes of its financial sector. No-one knew what would happen if this sector caught a cold. Some were uneasy:

> London seemed to be divided within itself, 'the City' divorced from the city's deindustrialising heartlands and suburbs. More and more it seemed to have just one arrow in its quiver, ending up 'with a highly volatile and unbalanced economy' where a 'collapse in the financial services sector would see London's economy in a very bad way'.[190]

Of course there were pockets of resistance, like Docklands' new manufacturing and distribution sector, carefully nurtured by the LDDC during the 1990s (see above), and the frantic economic activity around Heathrow. Generally, though, it was the City's health that determined London's prosperity. Londoners' fortunes were increasingly tied to the forces of international capital.

New millennium metropolis

In 2005 and 2006 a research team based at Queen Mary, University of London published a series of papers on the lifestyles and prospects of migrant labour in London. In their 2005 paper *Making the City Work: Low Paid Employment in London* Evans, Herbert, Datta, May, McIlwaine and Wills made some key observations. London, they said, had become 'a major centre for migration'. Of 341 low-paid workers selected at random by the team a startling 90 per cent were economic migrants, evidencing 'the very significant reliance of the London economy on migrant workers'. Some sectors had become heavily dependent on migrant labour. For example 58 per cent of London Underground's contract cleaners came from Nigeria or Ghana, while 27 per cent of those who worked in the hospitality sector came from eastern Europe. The team commented: 'Such concentrations seem to be at least partly the result of strong migrant networks. Nearly two thirds of people had found their current job through friends and family'.[191] It would be interesting to investigate what impact these relatively new yet robust networks have had on London's sense of community. Do such networks promote or erode social cohesion? Is London society becoming more or less Balkanised? Are Londoners more or less willing to pull together?

The prospects for migrant workers were not good. The survey showed that 'migrant workers had experienced high levels of de-skilling and downward social mobility'[192] and that 90 per cent of migrant workers earned less than the GLA's Living Wage for London (which in 2005 stood at £6.70 per hour). Sixty per cent of migrant workers 'received no maternity or paternity leave... half had no annual pay rise and a third had never had a pay rise. Half of all workers lost pay for taking time off for emergencies, and just over half... did not receive sick pay.... Over two thirds... had no access to a company pension scheme'.[193] Contrary to tabloid depictions few economic migrants lived off the State: '94% of people paid tax and National Insurance, whilst fewer than 1 in 5 (16%) claimed any kind of state benefits'.[194] Many worked in sectors with high levels of turnover. Sub-contracting was commonplace. Regarding migrant workers' home life Evans et al. noted:

> Contrary to stereotypes of lone male migrant workers, the majority of people lived with other members of their family – whether partners, parents or children. A third were responsible for dependent children (children under the age of 16) in the UK. A third also had dependants living abroad, and two thirds regularly sent money overseas.[195]

The sending of money overseas by London's economic migrants has important repercussions for migrants, the recipients of remittances and the London economy in general.[196] Clearly low-paid workers who send remittances to relatives and friends are going to be in an even worse position economically. London is an expensive city. Those who live on the cusp of poverty cannot afford to give money away. Yet many do. Analysing the global picture, Datta et al. note:

> [R]emittances have been dramatically increasing in volume. A recent World Bank (2006) study reports that officially recorded remittances to the developing world in 2005 were US$167 billion, a dramatic increase from US$31.2 billion in 1990. As such, remittances are the second largest capital flow behind Foreign Direct Investment (FDI) and ahead of ODA [Official Development Assistance] (which it overtook in 1995). Indeed, the true volume of remittances is possibly 50 or even 100 per cent higher than official data indicates... due to the widespread use of informal channels to remit in the form of informal remittance transfer schemes (IRTS), the use of private courier services and other gifts disguised as gifts and bill payments.[197]

Datta et al. comment that when it comes to international development, remittances are a double-edged sword: while they may benefit individual recipients they make it less likely that first world countries will donate 0.7 per cent of their GDP to third world countries. Ironically migrant workers' sacrifices and sense of social responsibility may serve to erode the UN's efforts to boost third world development. Less development spending by first world countries increases the pressure on economic migrants to send money home. As the number of economic migrants – and therefore the volume of remittances – increases there is less incentive for first world countries to meet their international obligations.

In *London in the Twentieth Century. A City and Its People* Jerry White passed this judgement on Britain's capital city at the end of the twentieth century:

> A new world had risen from the collapse of the city's industrial base in its long depression from the mid-1960s to the mid-1990s. Work was increasingly polarised between low-wage low-skill service-sector jobs and high-skilled office and professional work, with rewards in financial services satisfying Croesus at his most unquenchable.... There were far fewer opportunities for low-skilled Londoners to earn a decent living in the new economy than the old.[198]

Given that London's fate is today so intimately tied to that of international capital, Londoners would do well to understand the nature of the New Millennium Corporation (NMC). The NMC's most salient feature is its mobility. For Albert Dunlap the NMC is obligated only to its shareholders: 'The company belongs to people who invest in it – not to its employees, suppliers, nor the locality in which it is situated'.[199] [200] In *Globalisation. The Human Consequences* Bauman analyses the spatial liberation of NMCs (and of the privileged world-citizens who run them).

Bauman describes international capital as 'unanchored power'[201] disassociated from locale or sentiment:

> It is up to [shareholders] to move the company wherever they spy out or anticipate a chance of higher dividends, leaving to all others – locally bound as they are – the task of wound-licking, damage-repair and waste-disposal. The company is free to move; but the consequences of the move are bound to stay. Whoever is free to run away from the locality, is free to run away from the consequences. These are the most important spoils of victorious space war.[202]

Bauman considers modern capitalistic enterprise to be without conscience: 'Capital can always move away to more peaceful sites if the engagement with "otherness" requires a costly application of force or tiresome negotiations. No need to engage, if avoidance will do'.[203] Governments perform a facilitative role for private enterprise, says Bauman (by, for example, addressing issues of criminality and antisocial behaviour and by acquiescing in the privatisation of public space).[204] One of the consequences of governments' cultivation of capitalistic enterprise, claims Bauman, is the increasing inability of national governments to control their own destinies. He talks of 'the growing experience of weakness, indeed of impotence, of the habitual, taken-for-granted ordering agencies [national governments and other traditional loci of power and influence]',[205] of the 'unruly and self-propelled character of world affairs' and notes 'the absence of a centre, of a controlling desk'.[206] This generates a 'feeling of unease' which, suggests Bauman, is 'an expectable response to a situation without obvious levers of control'.[207]

Only time will tell if Bauman's pessimistic vision of the nation state and of social security is correct. One thing is clear, however. Capitalistic enterprise will continue to move backwards and forwards across the globe, ever watchful for new openings and helpful governments (like those of China and India).[208] And what of the masses? They would do well to remember that what international capital gives, international capital can take away.

Endnotes

1   Port Talbot steelworker Owen Reynolds quoted by Ian Jack in his book *Before the Oil Ran Out: Britain in the Brutal Years*. See page eighty-three.

2   The term Londonland is used to emphasise the *disjunctive* quality of Britain's capital city. London is markedly different to other British conurbations. In its size, demography, geography, economy, government and overall political and economic import it is unique. London is Britain's only World City (a fact confirmed by London's hosting of the 2012 Olympics).

3   In August 2005 the Home Office observed: 'Accession workers are continuing to go where the work is, helping to fill gaps in our labour market'. In October 2005 the *International Herald Tribune* described Britain's influx of migrant workers as 'one of the

great migrations of recent decades.... The incoming workers took jobs in a broad range of fields... with maids, farmhands, waiters, cleaners, sales assistants and kitchen staff topping the list'. See Fuller (2005). At the end of 2006 the *Guardian*'s economics editor reported: 'Half the employers in London are relying on migrant workers to plug the gaps left by an acute shortage of skilled labour'. See Elliott (2006). In March 2007 the Labour government pondered ways of getting Britain's long-term benefit claimants back into work. In January 2008 right-wing lobby group Migrationwatch warned that economic migrants were creating a 'new underclass' amongst Britain's indigenous population (Johnston, 2008).

4   Teather (2006)

5   Cited in Teather (2006)

6   *BBC News* (2006). By 2008 house price inflation seemed to be slowing (Balakrishnan, 2008).

7   Teather (2006)

8   By March 2008 the average price of a dwelling had fallen to £179, 358 (Balakrishnan, 2008).

9   Bates (2007)

10   O'Grady cited in Seager (2006)

11   Harman cited in Teather (2006)

12   *Daily Mail* (2006)

13   Correspondents cited in the *Guardian* (2006)

14   Lansley cited in Teather (2006)

15   Balls cited in Teather (2006)

16   Cited in Teather (2006)

17   Hodges cited in Teather (2006)

18   In 2006, despite nearly ten years of Labour government, Thatcherism (that is, monetarism and fiscal prudence) remained the dominant economic discourse.

19   By 2008 the world seemed to be heading for recession (Guha, 2008). In Britain the Centre for Economic and Business Research (CEBR) warned that the financial sector would shed 6,500 jobs (Wachman, 2007). The normally taciturn International Monetary Fund (IMF) urged nations to make contingency plans for any recession that might occur (Davis, 2008). In March 2008 the US Federal Reserve attempted to rescue America's fifth-largest investment bank, Bear Stearns (Mortished, 2008). Bear Stearns was eventually bought by a rival at a knock-down price.

20   Citizens Advice London (2003)

21   Centerprise Trust (1977) pp. 15–17

22   Centerprise Trust (1977) p. 18

23   Campbell (1984) p. 124. Northern steeplejack Fred Dibnah made numerous TV programmes about his own and other crafts. Dibnah demonstrated workers' 'pleasure in the skill of manufacturing'.

24   Campbell (1984) pp. 122–3

25   Campbell (1984) p. 119

26   Campbell (1984) pp. 118–19

27   In *The Road to Wigan Pier* George Orwell ventured that working people did not act

– rather, they were acted upon: 'This business of petty inconvenience and indignity, of being kept waiting about, of having to do everything at people's convenience, is inherent in working-class life. A thousand influences constantly press a working man down into a *passive* role. He does not act, he is acted upon' (Orwell cited in Campbell, 1984, p. 116).

28   Campbell (1984) p. 121

29   Citizens Advice London (2003) p. 14

30   Citizens Advice London (2003) p. 13

31   In his work on risk perception and communication Kasperson (1992) noted how some social institutions (like newspapers) acted to amplify risk messages, while others acted to attenuate them. Kasperson's amplification/attenuation dynamic can be observed in other areas of social action (like legislation). Some agencies act to support and embed (amplify) legislation. Others act to reduce (attenuate) its impact.

32   Knight (2005)

33   Given that it is always cheaper to pay up front for goods, those without surplus cash are *inherently* disadvantaged.

34   Davies (2005)

35   Steven (1995)

36   In July 1976 the Greater London Council (GLC) and Docklands boroughs (which together constituted the Docklands Joint Committee) published a strategic plan for the locale. The plan failed. Between 1975 and 1980 Docklands lost 8,500 jobs. Given the economic and technological forces in play at the time (containerisation and the use of much larger vessels, for example) it is quite possible that the Docklands Joint Committee would have failed *whatever* it had done. See Al Naib (2001) p. 31 and Humphries and Taylor (1986) pp. 19–20.

37   In 1997 the chief executive of the (now-defunct) Tyne and Wear Development Corporation (TWDC) claimed that the Thatcher government's Urban Development Corporations (UDCs) pursued a 'hands on, comprehensive approach to regeneration' (Balls cited in Tighe, 1997).

38   Cited in Dovkants (1995)

39   Cited in Dovkants (1995)

40   Rosen cited in Dovkants (1995)

41   Taylor (1995)

42   Jacobson cited in Taylor (1995)

43   Steven (1995)

44   The Jarman Index was applied to 403 local authority areas. The London Borough of Tower Hamlets was ranked 403rd – the most deprived area in Britain.

45   Taylor (1995)

46   This was one of the LDDC's final communications.

47   LDDC (1998) p. 1

48   Heseltine cited in Tagg and Pickard (1995)

49   According to journalist Chris Tighe, TWDC 'anxious not to create social tension… emphasised consultation with locals in its pursuit of "social regeneration"'. The UDCs' unelected status (they were actually quangos (quasi-autonomous non-governmental organisations)) could create tensions with those seeking democratic accountability.

50 LDDC (1998) p. 1

51 LDDC (1998) p. 5

52 The LDDC's programme represented a major state-initiated intervention in the British economy. Tax revenues were admixed with private equity to generate social benefits – like employment opportunities for indigenous residents, community projects, environmental improvement and a modern transport infrastructure (something Docklands communities had always lacked).

53 By the time of their abolition in 1998 TWDC and Teesside Development Corporation (TDC) had 'injected about £800m in public money into the region and triggered almost £3bn in private sector investment. Shipyards, colliery and port land, vast industrial sites and redundant docks have been transformed with universities, football stadia, smart offices, bijou housing, arts and leisure facilities, shopping malls and industrial units'. See Tighe (1997).

54 LDDC (1998) p. 4

55 LDDC (1998) p. 6

56 LDDC (1998) p. 2

57 LDDC (1998) p. 2

58 Tagg and Pickard (1995)

59 Tagg and Pickard (1995)

60 Dovkants (1995)

61 The *interconnectedness* of the residents of London's working class districts is a feature of films like *Waterloo Road* (that starred John Mills as a soldier trying to save his marriage).

62 Young and Willmott (1966) p. 41 and p. 45

63 Britain's economy reached its nadir in the 1970s when Denis Healey, Labour's chancellor of the exchequer, had to go cap in hand to the International Monetary Fund (IMF). Decades of private under-investment, badly judged state investment (fast-breeder reactors, Concorde, the Advanced Passenger Train, the TSR-2 strike aircraft and the like), low productivity and short-termism had finally caught up with the British economy. See Hutton (1995) pp. 10–11.

64 In 1890 General Booth noted the emergence of a 'Darker England' within a 'Greater England'. Benjamin Disraeli spoke of 'Two Nations': The Privileged and The People. See Hudson and Williams (1989) p. 3. Beatrice Webb described the East End as a 'bottomless pit of decaying life'. Novelist Henry James described London as 'an ogress who devours human flesh to keep herself alive to do her tremendous work'. See Cox (1994) p. 152. In 1899 Charles Booth produced a schematic representation of wealth and poverty in Hackney and Bethnal Green. Booth's colour-coded map (today entrusted to the Museum of London) analysed each terrace and square according to the economic status of its residents. The map's key had seven elements: 'Wealthy; Well-to-do; Comfortable; Poor & Comfortable (Mixed); Poor; Very Poor; Semi-Criminal'. In Booth's day 'poverty was widely seen as the fault of the individual – with some people in poverty categorised as being "criminally poor"'. See *BBC News* (2007a).

65 Hudson and Williams (1989) pp. 2–3

66 *BBC News* (2007a)

67 UNDP cited in Lean and Ball (1996)
68 Lean and Ball (1996)
69 *New Internationalist* (1996) p. 19
70 *New Internationalist* (1996) p. 19
71 *New Internationalist* (1996) p. 19
72 *Economist* (2000) p. 31
73 Seabrook (1983) p. xiii. A 2008 rise in the number of reported cases of domestic violence in the UK was partly attributed to the economic slow-down and its associated fears (unemployment, loss of income, loss of status, homelessness, disenfranchisement, alienation, etc.).
74 IFS cited in Elliott (2004)
75 Elliott (2004)
76 Between 1997 and 2002 Tony Blair's government managed to reduce the number of people living in poverty by 7%. In 2001 there were 13 million people living in poverty in Britain. See Batty (2002).
77 As mentioned earlier social and economic schism is a long-standing feature of British life. Hudson and Williams (1989) noted: 'Persistent if changing inequalities are enduring features of life in the UK'. See Hudson and Williams (1989) p. 3.
78 Office for National Statistics (2005) p. 63
79 Office for National Statistics (2005) p. 70
80 *Economist* (2008d)
81 *Financial Times* (1997) p. 16
82 Dornan cited in *BBC News* (2004)
83 Teather (2006)
84 Hutton (1995) p. 14
85 Ward (1997)
86 Hutton (1995) pp. 6–10
87 Prince Harry's return from the Afghan conflict in 2008 received extensive television, radio and newspaper coverage, with the main television channels broadcasting 'specials' on the young Royal's front-line deployment. The BBC was later criticised for its intense reporting of Harry's deployment and return. Newsworthy stories at the time included the government's rescue of a failed bank (Brown's nationalisation of Northern Rock) and the deepening economic gloom (which led, for example, to some people having their credit cards withdrawn).
88 *New Internationalist* (1996) p. 19
89 See Theobald (1994) pp. 137–8 for a detailed description of the structure of Britain's late/post-industrial labour market.
90 Bauman (1998) p. 112
91 When Prime Minister Tony Blair's leading election slogan was 'Education, Education, Education'. The Blair government invested heavily in secondary education and encouraged the university sector to dramatically increase the number of undergraduates.
92 Dubiniec (2006)
93 Frost cited in Stewart (2007)

94   Stewart (2007)
95   Green cited in Johnston (2008)
96   The data used by Migrationwatch could be presented in another way, of course: it could be argued that indigenous workers are excluding *themselves* from paid employment by choosing a life on benefits over a life in work (albeit poorly paid work). It would seem that the work ethic is not especially strong amongst some of Britain's working class.
97   Johnston (2008)
98   The mother of one of the migrant workers 'had paid 190,000 yuan (£13,600) and put her house up as security to snakehead gangs to ensure her son's passage to Europe'. See Carter, Pai and Butt (2006).
99   Carter, Pai and Butt (2006)
100   Pai (2004)
101   Qin cited in Pai (2004)
102   Zhang cited in Pai (2004)
103   The Blair government responded to the havoc wreaked by some unscrupulous gangmasters by setting up the Gangmasters Licensing Authority (GLA). The GLA aimed to eradicate the exploitation of workers in the shellfish-gathering, horticulture and agriculture sectors. The GLA licensing system was applied to the shellfish-gathering sector from April 2007.
104   Little (2007)
105   Little (2007)
106   Maxwell cited in *BBC News* (2007b)
107   Morris (2008)
108   Whitehouse cited in Morris (2008)
109   In Poland, for example, as many as 25% of recent graduates are unemployed. Students' good English makes them attractive to UK employers. See Dubiniec (2006).
110   Low-cost carriers like Ryanair, easyJet and Poland's Wizz Air make working away from home affordable and tolerable. Thanks to low-cost carriers economic migrants are no longer marooned in their host countries.
111   Zhang cited in Pai (2004)
112   UNICEF cited in Radnedge (2007)
113   Reitemeier cited in Radnedge (2007)
114   According to Hudson and Williams (1989) relative poverty can be defined as the inability 'to participate in the consumption of material and non-material goods and activities to the level which forms the expected standard of living in any time and place. Therefore the poorest may become better off in an absolute sense while becoming impoverished in a relative sense'. See Hudson and Williams (1989) p. 3.
115   Cited in Radnedge (2007)
116   At the end of March 2007 the government confirmed that the number of children living in poverty in 2005–6 had actually risen by 100,000. Barnardo's chief executive called the lapse a 'moral disgrace' while the shadow chancellor noted 'that poverty is increasing, inequality is rising and the incomes of the poorest fifth are in decline'. Narey and Osborne cited in Bennett (2007).
117   Gillan (2007) pp. 14–15

118 As far as the British press is concerned Britain is plagued by loutish behaviour. Alcohol is perceived to be responsible for Britain's 'yob culture' (a tabloid term used to describe antisocial behaviour).

119 Cheal (2004)

120 Cheal (2004)

121 *BBC News* (2006)

122 Wales cited in *BBC News* (2006)

123 Robins (2006)

124 Welsh cited in Nicoll (2005)

125 Nicoll (2005)

126 In the 1960s the Labour government offered financial incentives to local authorities to build towers. System-built tower blocks often developed structural faults that allowed water to enter the flats. Sometimes there were too-few lifts. Lifts were prone to breakdown. Repairs could take days. Elevated walkways and poor lighting facilitated petty crime. Poor public transport served to isolate those without cars. Edge estates developed an island quality. The partial collapse of the just-erected London tower block Ronan Point in 1968 and spiralling social problems proved terminal: politicians and people rejected high-rise living. Local authorities began demolishing towers, replacing them with low-rise blocks and houses with gardens and garages. The notorious North Peckham estate in London, built between 1969 and 1975, lasted less than thirty years. It had been razed by 2005. See Glancey (2005).

127 Solihull Metropolitan Borough Council's own director of public health confirmed that Solihull was the most socially polarised local authority area in England.

128 Taken from an edited extract of Lynsey Hanley's book *Estates: An Intimate History*. The extract was published in the *Guardian* (2007).

129 Treneman (1999)

130 Completed in 1977, by 1991 one sixth of the Jubilee's properties were empty.

131 Cited in Campbell (1993) pp. 183–4

132 In her book *Wigan Pier Revisited* Beatrix Campbell addressed one of the limitations of investigative journalism – subjectivity – by quoting George Orwell's analysis of his own middle-class bias: 'All my notions – notions of good or evil, of pleasant and unpleasant… of ugly and beautiful are essentially *middle class* notions…. I have got to suppress not merely my private snobbishness, but most of my other tastes and prejudices as well'. Orwell's notion that journalists and writers can never fully escape their own class sensibilities (and prejudices) is as germane today as it was when he wrote *The Road to Wigan Pier*. Writers who are open about their biases are more credible than those who are not. Credibility is (partly) a function of reflexivity (self-awareness). See Orwell cited in Campbell (1984) p. 1.

133 Speaking at the Conservative Party's spring conference in March 2008 Cameron emphasised the role of the family in building stable and prosperous communities.

134 Cameron cited in Woodward and Muir (2007) p. 4

135 Blair cited in Woodward and Muir (2007) p. 4

136 *Guardian* (2007) p. 30

137 Hain cited in the *Daily Mail* (2007). Note the similarity between Hain's 2007 comments

about the close proximity of money and deprivation and those made by the *Standard*'s editor Stewart Steven in 1995.

138   Things did not look as rosy in 2007–8, however. City bonuses were predicted to fall by a couple of billion pounds from their 2006 high of £8.8 billion (Wachman, 2007).

139   Sheffield was known as Steel City. The combined impact of low productivity (due in part to under-investment), globalisation, rationalisation, de-industrialisation and Thatcherism took a heavy toll. One Sheffield steelworks saw its workforce decline from 18,000 to 3,500 during the 1970s. The British film *The Full Monty* chronicled some of the effects of this reversal of fortune.

140   Young and Willmott (1966) p. 147

141   Young and Willmott (1966) pp. 132–3

142   Young and Willmott (1966) p. 150

143   In Bethnal Green there had been one public house for every 400 people. On the estate there was one pub for 5,000 people. There was no cinema.

144   In her 1992 book *Affluent Workers Revisited: Privatisation and the Working Class* Fiona Devine noted of her 62 interviewees (families who worked at the Vauxhall plant in Luton, Bedfordshire (now closed)) that their lives were not exclusively home-centred. Revisiting her research two years later she wrote: '[B]oth the men and women interviewees enjoyed the company of their colleagues from work inside and outside the workplace.... The interviewees [did not] lead exclusively privatised styles of life'. See Devine (1994) pp. 7–9.

145   In 2007 some 12 per cent of the British population lived in local authority-owned housing (in 1979, the year of Mrs Thatcher's election, nearly half the population lived in local authority-owned houses and flats). See Morrison (2007). Of course many of those who owned their own homes in 2007 still lived in a *council-built house* on a council estate (with all its attendant problems).

146   Weaver (2007)

147   Glancey (2005)

148   Morrison (2007)

149   Moore (2007)

150   McRae (2007)

151   *Independent* (2007)

152   Stubbs cited in Willis (2007)

153   Carvel (2005)

154   Schifferes (2003)

155   Kaletsky (2005) p. 34

156   Lawson (2007)

157   Until the spectacular crash of September 2008, the Square Mile had almost as much financial clout as Wall Street. Indeed in some domains (outreach to, and business links with Asia, for example) it was ahead. See McGeehan (2008).

158   London's economy benefited from the Commonwealth Preference System 'which allowed free trade within the Commonwealth and erected high tariff barriers to discourage trade with other countries'. See Humphries and Taylor (1986) p. 5.

159   The companies' art-deco style office complexes along the Great West Road were a stylish

addition to the cityscape.

160 Ailsby cited in Humphries and Taylor (1986) p. 10

161 Passingham cited in Humphries and Taylor (1986) p. 11

162 Beynon (1973) p. 53

163 Passingham cited in Humphries and Taylor (1986) p. 11

164 Teachers and politicians produce the same rhetoric today, even as school and university-leavers take mundane and poorly paid jobs in Britain's burgeoning service sector. Does working in a call centre really require a degree? What workaday insights does a degree in media studies or history give a trainee supermarket or fast-food restaurant manager?

165 Cited in Beynon (1973) p. 114

166 Beynon (1973) p. 109

167 Beynon (1973) p. 18

168 Beynon (1973) p. 61

169 Cited in Beynon (1973) pp. 61–2

170 Humphries and Taylor (1986) p. 12

171 See, for example, Hall and Jacques (1989)

172 White (2001) p. 48

173 White (2001) p. 55

174 It is important to consider how Londoners of the time might have felt about the new architecture. It is possible that many welcomed the clean lines, rationality and comfort of the new glass and concrete boxes. And in any case even an anonymous box was preferable to a weed and rat-infested bomb site frequented by gangs of out-of-control children (it is often forgotten how lawless post-war London was). London's war wounds had to be healed. Critics of London's modernist experiment (like Prince Charles) should perhaps show a little more understanding of London's predicament in the immediate post-war period.

175 White (2001) p. 49

176 Humphries and Taylor (1986) pp. 118–20

177 Cox (1994) p. 143

178 Cox (1994) p. 171

179 Cox (1994) p. 14

180 White (2001) p. 206

181 White (2001) p. 206

182 Humphries and Taylor (1986) p. 20

183 Humphries and Taylor (1986) p. 21

184 White (2001) p. 207

185 Like any other British city London had its fair share of large-scale industry. During the Great War, for example, 'more than 28,000 women and girls were filling shells and bullets at Woolwich Arsenal.... Of Britain's net increase of 644 factories employing twenty-five or more persons in the years 1932 to 1937, 532 or 83 per cent were located in Greater London'. See White (2001) p. 188.

186 Humphries and Taylor (1986) p. 18

187 The electronic trading era was launched by the 'Big Bang'.

188 White (2001) p. 211

189　White (2001) p. 81
190　White (2001) p. 215
191　Evans et al. (2005) p. 5
192　A case in point was the degree-holding inhabitant of the Thetford house. He intended to give his son, an undergraduate, every opportunity to succeed. Given the fate of the father one wonders how realistic a hope this was?
193　Evans et al. (2005) p. 4
194　Evans et al. (2005) p. 5
195　Evans et al. (2005) p. 5
196　Datta et al. (2006) pp. 1–5
197　Datta et al. (2006) p. 3
198　White (2001) p. 406
199　Dunlap cited in Bauman (1998) p. 6
200　In some companies (UK low-cost airline easyJet, for example) many employees are also shareholders.
201　Bauman (1998) p. 9
202　Bauman (1998) pp. 8–9
203　Bauman (1998) p. 11
204　The replacement of the traditional British high street with shopping malls is an example of the privatisation of public space. Malls are privately owned, privately policed zones of consumption and control. Some years ago the Bluewater shopping mall in east London banned young people from wearing 'hoodies'. Public houses with internal cameras sometimes request drinkers to remove their head-gear (so an accurate record of customers can be maintained). Britain has one of the highest concentrations of surveillance cameras in the world.
205　Bauman (1998) p. 60
206　Bauman (1998) p. 59
207　Bauman (1998) p. 57
208　The collapse of MG Rover in 2005 and purchase of Rover's plant by China's Nanjing Automobile evidences the dynamic and rootless character of international capitalistic enterprise. Nanjing relocated Rover's plant to China, producing its first MG sports car in March 2007. Rover's collapse cost Britain's economy over 20,000 jobs (but provided a new source of labour for the peripheral economy of part-time, semi- or unskilled work). See Harrison (2005).

CHAPTER THREE

Workers' stories

There is no greater modern illusion, even fraud, than the use of the single term *work* to cover what for some is… dreary, painful or socially demeaning and what for others is enjoyable, socially reputable and economically rewarding.[1]

THE sixteen interviews reproduced here are the core of this book. This is where a few Londoners get the chance to tell their own stories. Actually, too few Londoners. Despite the author's best efforts many of those contacted were reluctant to 'go public'. Some of those who agreed to be interviewed subsequently declined to talk to me. Many seemed suspicious (despite me establishing my bona fides with my university business card and a letter typed on university notepaper). I made several appointments to interview a car-repairer from eastern Europe. He never showed. I went to his garage. He made another appointment. When I turned up at the garage as arranged it was shut. I made an appointment to interview a London Underground employee. We arranged to meet at a Docklands tube station. He never showed. When I called his mobile number his handset was switched off. I arranged to interview a female Metropolitan Police officer. I was given her e-mail address by her Division. I e-mailed her. She never replied, despite initially agreeing to be interviewed. I arranged to interview a Turkish shop-owner who knew me as a customer. He withdrew the offer of an interview. An old friend of mine said he would get me an interview with a builder and an electrician. Nothing happened. I talked to a Member of Parliament for whose campaign team I had worked. He promised to publicise my research. No-one came forward. *Not a single constituent.* And so it went on. Some arrangements worked. Some promises were kept. Others not. What follows, therefore, is absolutely the best I could do in the time available. The sample is not as ethnically diverse as I would have liked. And it is not as representative of the world of work as I would have liked.[2] It is, however, an honest attempt to get under the skin of Londonland's workforce.

For those readers who have not read the two original WEA/Centerprise volumes (which is probably most of you) I reproduce below a list of the people and trades featured in *Working Lives. Volume One 1905–45* and *Working Lives. Volume Two 1945–77*.

Emily Bishop, embroiderer
Ida Rex, schoolteacher
John Welch, demolition worker
Mary Welch, leather worker
Albert Moseley, cartage contractor
Mark Simons, tailor
Alfred Dedman, lighterman
Paul Martinson, cabinet-maker
Betty Ferry, boot and shoe-maker
Lew Lessen, barber
Myrtle Mae Green, hairdresser
George Wood, mortuary technician
Joy Hendry, health visitor
Ken Jacobs, postman
Dave Boldinger, shop assistant
Annie Spike, housewife/night-cleaner
Ron Barnes, taxi driver
Mike Christou, fish-and-chip man
Brian Simons, teacher
Mrs Folanho, machinist
Tony Kyriakides, curate

1. The bus driver

Ali, who was born in Turkey in 1984, had lived in London for seventeen years. After doing some GCSEs and a City and Guilds in computing and information and communications technology Ali had a succession of jobs, most of which he did not enjoy: 'I have had lots of jobs.... IKEA... really bad place, unorganised [sic], I'll tell you that.... supermarket jobs... minor jobs, but I don't count them'. The worst job he ever had was 'working in a Turkish supermarket. Very long hours and very low pay'. The best job was his current job of bus driving, although it had its irritations: 'I love driving... it's good to drive... it's one of my interests, but the problem is in London the traffic. The traffic is a nightmare here. Other road users treat you with disrespect. Road tax, congestion charges, fines... if you take them off it is very good to drive, but with them it is a nightmare'.

Ali was on a permanent contract with a major operator. He was based in north London (Tottenham) and worked full-time. Getting the job was not without its hurdles: 'You have to do your health check... you have to apply for a new licence... go to Stamford Hill garage and they train you for a couple of weeks... if they find you are good enough they test you and if you pass they put you into type training and that's for the ticket machines... there are written tests... route learning... I know six routes at Tottenham garage so far...'. Ali described his terms and conditions at the Tottenham garage: '[I do a] minimum fifty hours a week. I used to do over eighty or ninety... which is very high pay... we didn't drive for ninety hours... we do an eight-hour shift driving but some eight-hour shifts they pay twelve hours.... When you do overtime it's double pay.... Currently we do fifty-five to seventy hours'. He got a minimum of forty-five minutes for lunch: 'Some duties we get one hour, some duties we get over an hour, some you get a very short break, and that's forty-five minutes. For EC rules we have to have that break'.

Ali was ambitious. He wanted to climb the management ladder: 'After six months, after you pass probation, you can also, if there is one available, you can apply for Controller. [As a Controller] you organise the buses and keep them to time because some buses are late... you make sure buses are not together... leave two minutes, five minutes gap in between.... That [job] pays better, but it's more stress because you have got calculation... time calculation is a very stressful job... sometimes the traffic out there is a nightmare. [If there is a Controller job available] I'm going to apply because my aim is to rise up. I don't want to stay as a driver'.

Ali was happy at the Tottenham garage. He liked his workmates: 'I find all my colleagues in Tottenham really good. I communicate really well with them and they all know me. Really nice people, they are. Different nationalities, it's very good'. Asked what he thought they thought of him he said: 'I don't think they're thinking the same as I'm thinking to them. They think I'm too hyperactive, too much energy, which I am. I have too much energy inside. I can't sit still and they complain for that. And I always use bad words. They complain about that. Mainly they are jealous because of my age because I am the youngest driver in Tottenham. I started this job at the age of twenty-one. And now I'm twenty-three and they are jealous because I'm too young. And too good for them'. Despite describing his colleagues as 'really good' Ali said they could be jealous: 'What bugs me is the other drivers... they can't take each other... they are back-stabbing each other... they are not hand-to-hand... one hand is somewhere else... they are not supporting each other... that's the only reason why I don't like this place... not just this place, every garage they have the same problem... too much jealousy... they can't take each other's success... that's how they are...'.

Despite being reasonably contented with his lot at the garage, being out on the road could be stressful. Difficult passengers and thoughtless drivers were especially annoying: 'The worst argument is with passengers and other road users. They don't have no respect. In law the big vehicle always has priority, but nowadays... it's not English drivers, I'm not being no racist now, it is the foreign drivers, they have no respect whatsoever. That's including the black people, Turkish people, my people. I mean, they have no respect... it's like they took the licence from butchers.... They swear a lot, the passengers, especially the kids, these kids are the worst nightmare. Years ago we were respecting the drivers. Now kids have free pass, free travel, and they are taking the piss. They are vandalising the buses. They are disrespecting the old people. It's really bad'. Ali said he had been threatened at work and seemed frustrated that he was forbidden to react: '[I have been threatened] plenty of times, from kids. But we could not do nothing. We just have to, like, hush our mouth and sit down in the cab. Hiding under a skirt'. Asked whether anyone had ever pulled a knife on him he said: 'No, nothing like that's happened so far... if you argue with them more it gets worse and worse... someone has to shut their mouth, and I suggest it should be us... to keep the job, to look after your family, you have to shut your mouth for the job. Because on the contract, when we started, it said these regulations, and we accepted it. So we have to'.

The job had its compensations, however, like a variable shift pattern (although the mid-day to ten o'clock 'middle shift' was not much liked): '[I like] seeing different people... your shifts, they change... we don't always work in the mornings... your rota changes... sometimes you do early shifts which start at four in the morning and finish at one o'clock, sometimes you start at twelve o'clock in the afternoon and finish at ten... everyone hates the middle shift because you don't have time with your family or for your socialising... the late shift starts at three o'clock and finishes at one o'clock [one a.m.] and you still have time with your family [in the morning]...'. Asked what he thought of his line-manager Ali said: 'My boss is a wonderful man... we changed managers this year... our new manager is a perfect, wonderful man, he helps everybody. Only one thing – you must never lie to him, he hates lying, and that's the best thing I like about him, same as me, I hate lying... gossiping, lying and spite, I hate. The manager is just my type'. Ali believed himself to be well-regarded by management: '[My manager] thinks I am a real gentle person. As I said, too much energy. They see me as the baby over here... they feel good about me because I have had success in this garage... I have been in the competition for Driver of the Year... the garage are getting complements about my driving, and I have been commended a lot of times and that's why the manager loves me...'. Regarding the bus company Ali felt it paid a fair rate for the job and that it was well-run. 'It is highly well managed... it is one of the best companies' he said.

Regarding the state of the country Ali was especially concerned about crime and immigration: 'Right now we don't have safety... people are running away from London because of pick-pockets, stabbers, you know... all these criminal things just happen in London... this really upsets everybody... the worse thing is immigration... they immigrate a lot of people from other places and they are unuseful [sic]... and the tax you pay... it really upsets me that you are paying to those kind of worthless people who drink alcohol, does nothing, gambling, they should not have brought those kind of people here... because it's messing up London... slowly, slowly it's killing people here...'. Asked what three things he would do if he were mayor of London Ali's thoughts again drifted onto the subject of crime and immigration: 'First, I would... that's a really biting question... maybe I'd make education much better...

more security... employ more police officers... invest money in parks and make them more attractive for people with their families... right now, in Turkey, when you go out with your girlfriend you have plenty of places to go out... it's lovely.... If I had plenty, tons, of money the first thing I would do is stop immigration... I would send the unworthy people back to their homeland... and make this place a really good place to live and everyone across the world when they hear "London" would put their heads up. But right now it's embarrassing, because English people are leaving their homeland and going to Spain... they are leaving London, they are leaving their home to foreign people. I think they should support their home.... In Turkey, that's how it is, if they don't like the person they are exiled straight away, send them back to their home, and that's what they should do, and if I was the mayor that's what I would do... no matter how many tears that person had.... Me and my brother and family are working hard, working hard, but all we're doing is paying for people who don't deserve it, that's my only concern...'.

Ali had become cynical about politics and politicians: '[Voting] doesn't really change anything, everyone is the same, they smile at your face, they think they are your good friend, but they're not... they have got bigger friends... it's the money... money has power, mate'. Ali felt the government could help him and other workers by reducing the tax burden: 'Tax is too high, we are paying too much tax, and we do not get any benefit at all, and that really upsets us... God help us all...'. Asked to comment on Ken Livingstone's record as mayor of London Ali accused him of avarice. He also revisited the 'issue' of immigration: 'Maybe some things he's doing are good... but all he's doing is getting money, getting money, getting money, that's all... the thing he's forgotten is that the money he's getting foreign people are taking to their country, so it's a big mistake opening the gates.... He has messed up the traffic totally with the Congestion Charge... traffic cameras... really he's not thinking about peoples' safety, its about money... it's like robbery... it's not happening in the outer suburbs, only in the inner suburbs...'. If Ali was cynical about politicians he was also cynical about trades unions. He criticised his own union: 'I am paying three pounds something per week, but we don't get help from the union... we pay our money and they just hush their mouth, because they get money from the big people... the T&G...'. Ali seemed disaffected with and alienated from the political process: 'I used to vote, but I am not going to vote unless I have to, that's a different story, but other than that I'm not going to vote, it doesn't make any changes anyway, so there's no point, you're wasting your time...'.

Regarding London as a place to live Ali liked some parts but despised others (even his own neighbourhood of Tottenham): 'If you go to the City, the City is a wonderful place... but it's a really expensive place to live.... If you live in Tottenham, like us, I'm sorry it's junk, it's a shit-hole, where we're living here. If you have got the money the best place to live is in the City because there are respectable, reliable people who have honour.... Here there is no-one like that... it's not easy to live here...' (Ali lived a 15-minute walk away from the Tottenham garage). Although he thought the 2012 Olympic Games would be 'very good' for London he did not plan to go: 'Well I really don't like athletics very much.... If it was football it would be a different story, I love football... I go to football, I support Tottenham...'. Asked to describe London in one word, he gave this response: 'It's Great. It's worth me leaving my homeland and coming here to work, it's really good.... I just love London... maybe because of my friends... it's really good...'.

Ali's somewhat extended one-word description of his adopted city marked the end of the interview. By this time both of us were getting quite wet as I had interviewed him outside his work's canteen and it had started to rain. I went home for tea and Ali clocked on.

Verstehen

I lived in Tottenham for sixteen years, first with my wife, then, after she left, alone. It's not a glamorous neighbourhood. It consists of a large volume of Edwardian and Victorian housing that is all decaying (rotting?) at the same rate. The roads are grimy and the pavements uneven, despite the best efforts of Haringey Council. Tottenham High Road wears a patina of decay and poverty. The shops are, for the most part, cheap and the owners suspicious. The area around Seven Sisters Tube is overwhelmed with noisy, choking traffic. On match days the High Road is swamped by police, many on foot. That's something you rarely see in Tottenham – police officers on foot patrol. The coppers descend like an invading army. I have been told that few live in the areas they police; that they hunker down in the suburbs or home counties, safe; that they commute in, do their shift, then vacate. How do you police an area effectively if you are not part of its social fabric? How can you understand London's lightning-quick and impactful social transformations if you don't experience them personally as a private citizen? Food for thought, Commissioner. The road that links Seven Sisters to West Green is lined with cheap restaurants. Behind these restaurants there is a car park and access road. I wonder whether people would eat in those restaurants if they had seen what I have seen from that access road... the litter, the overflowing bins, the syringes, the condoms, the rats, the pools of fetid water that never seem to drain. Every Londoner should take a walk down that access road. It's an education. Dickens would recognise it.

2. The social entrepreneur

Steve, who was born in Islington, London in 1962, lived in Stamford Hill with his long-term partner (who worked in the media and had travelled widely). Steve had had numerous jobs, including school laboratory technician, accounts administrator, labourer, social worker and house-husband. At the time of the interview he was working as a social entrepreneur directing a company that provided cycle training for school children. Steve, who left the state education system with GCSEs and a technical college certificate in biochemistry, described his kaleidoscopic employment history thus: 'On leaving school the job I talked my way into on the strength of getting some A-levels was a lab-tech position working in a school which I did for two and a half years. I was doing a day-release and as soon as I got my day-release qualification which committed me to working for the borough – Haringey – I actually resigned. They let me go and didn't charge me for my course. I was very happy about that. That all came about because I had come across some other interests in life that made me realise there was more to work... so I left there and went off travelling to Europe... that was the first time I had left the country, in fact the first time I had got out of London.... I came back and worked for some chartered accountants in admin. At the time people were being trained to be Rank Xerox operators. So I became the company Rank Xerox operator. That was quite interesting... but I did that to get money to go travelling... went off to India and travelled around for about six months. I came back and took a while to settle down because it was a very mind-opening experience. I suppose I came back with quite a lot of confidence. I think travel does that'.

On his return to the UK Steve tried self-employment: 'On coming back from India and doing a bit of social work I had a period where I was self-employed... I spent quite a lot of time self-employed... working for friends who were architects. I did a bit of painting and decorating and building... manual labour. Although I wasn't that skilled I had enough nous to be able to work out how to get the jobs done. Having done a few jobs directed by them... rooms to strip that haven't been stripped for thirty years... you end up picking up a little bit more than if you were just working on a site. At the same time I knew someone whose father restored church icons... he had some building work he had to do... I did some work with him in Spitalfields on the houses down there... that was quite fun. We in fact did some work for Gilbert and George, restoring one of their panels in their lovely Spitalfields home. That is one of the fascinating things about being in a city like London... you do have these sorts of crossovers all the time. Again through one of the architects I worked with an Italian bricklayer... about fifty years old, still lived with his mum... quite an odd sort of cove... but at the same time had all of these wonderful connections, again with Gilbert and George and with other artists, because he just happened to be a fantastic bricklayer. Working with someone who on the surface was not very bright but as a craftsman was just incredible was enjoyable. So all of that was very interesting, quite enjoyed it, it was a very easy way to work...'. Steve relied on state benefits to supplement his unsteady income: 'Like many people around me I was living communally with other people and working as it suited. The whole unemployment benefit system was in a kind of melt-down... it meant that you could quite happily work while signing on.... When I was signed on in Islington you had to sign on once every three months which did not really encourage you to sign off... so it supplemented your wage. That was quite a nice period, living communally and doing all of that'.

Steve came to social work through working as a cleaner: 'I worked part-time as a cleaner just because it was an easy way to get some money and while doing that ended up working at a children's nursery.... The woman running the nursery said "Look... what are you doing cleaning? Come and work in my nursery". So I made a switch into what was then the beginnings of becoming a social worker. So I worked in an under-fives nursery... did a child psychology course while I was there... and quite enjoyed that...'.

Having begun to build a career in education Steve engineered another career change: 'I went to work for a restaurateur... quite an exclusive restaurant in which I became the barman. A way a lot of small businesses exist is that they attract quite a lot of quality people not because they are paying them a huge amount of money but because there is a social scene that is interesting... the work becomes secondary to the social scene... so I did that for a while. I really enjoyed working in the restaurant, although it does become your life... your evening out starts at one in the morning... you end up in dodgy Soho clubs until six in the morning... sleep in the day and enter London's nocturnal life which is a whole new gambit...'.

Eventually Steve returned to the state sector: 'I moved into social work and managed to talk my way into a job working in an Independence Training Unit.... I did that until I was deputy of the unit.... Then I managed to squash a disk in my back and this coincided with my partner expecting children and I think a realisation for me that although I quite enjoyed social work it is a job you can only really do if you do not have children of your own. It is very demanding. Most of the clients I was working with were very needy'. The coincidence of Steve's injury, his partner's pregnancy and his relatively low wage persuaded him to become a house-husband: 'When I squashed my disk I was earning about half of what my partner was earning... so it made much more sense for me to stop work.... So I gave up work and became the housewife... I claim the term "housewife".... At the time if you were a house-husband you had to explain what that meant... but everyone knew what a housewife did.... We did adopt very traditional roles... we gender changed... I did all of the cooking, shopping, washing, cleaning, looking after the kids. It was a fantastic experience. As a man at home you are pretty much guaranteed that when your partner comes home they want to have the children. You are a suspicious character in some ways because you are a bloke doing it and because you are generally in the company of other women, many of whom had husbands who were out working... I can remember some uncomfortable moments.... I started getting involved with PTAs... became a school governor... got involved with swimming coaching... then started a business that delivers cycle training. I have slowly grown that business'.

The cycle training business was a source of pride for Steve: 'It started off with wanting to run a bit of cycle training for children at the schools my children were at. I very quickly realised that the training they were getting was great and the people who delivered it were great but they were really not in any way representative of the children they were training, in so much as they were well-educated, white and middle-class. They liked cycling, they were enthusiastic about cycling... but as role models for the children they were training... it still made cycling aspirational in some ways but also out of reach... not something the children were going to aspire to because they were not aspiring to be those people. We also realised that this was quite an expensive way to get your cycle training because your skill – your resource – was not in the local community. London Cycle Campaign got some money so we put the money towards training trainers from the local community. The trainers are now the core of the business delivering most of the cycle training. We also had to work out how we got to people. In communities all over the world cycling is associated with poverty and having a car is associated with success. How do you break that relationship? We had to get to the children when they were very young. By training children who are six or seven it is much easier to grab the parents because they realise very quickly that they can't accompany their children because they are moving too quickly. So you say "we can cycle train you". We are slowly getting to them.... I seem to have become not a cycle trainer but the financial director and manager which is something I feel happy doing. Some of our trainers were on supplementary benefit but you can create enough work to raise them out of that... they are able to work PAYE. We can give them a wage that allows them to step out of that horrible trap of being a single parent trapped on benefit. You can see someone blossom from being this single parent mum trapped on benefit with no prospects to being a cycle trainer working with other peoples' kids getting a lot of respect and getting a decent wage'. Asked if he would describe himself as a social entrepreneur Steve said: 'I'd call myself a facilitator. People come with ideas and I can make them function, work, put in practical systems and support – this is the concept, here is the money, this is what we can actually do. We can create a product to sell to people...'.

Asked which was the worst job he had ever had Steve picked labouring and demolition, although it did have its compensations: 'I'll qualify it slightly... one of the biggest pluses has been the opportunity to do some quite tough jobs, physically hard... but that is always possible if you know you are not stuck there... demolition was a horrible, horrible job, and invariably you are working with people who are not protected. Certainly at the time when I was doing it, masks, helmets, health and safety just did not exist... we are talking not that long ago... beginning of the Eighties. Quite a lot of work was carried out in an ad-hoc fashion. If you know you are just doing a job for a short while, passing through, you can observe people doing it and you can say "this is a dreadful job". One demolition job involved carrying breeze blocks up stairs and rubble down for two days... there were no chutes... just physically draining and mind-killing... but we were doing it at a sort of run with student heads thinking it was a bit of a challenge. The old boys who had been doing it for years thought we were mad... which we were'.

If labouring and demolition was the most physically stressful job he had done, social work was the most psychologically stressful: 'Mentally, stress-wise, probably the worst job was social work... working with emotionally damaged youth... with young people who had been brought up in the care system. I suppose my position was slightly informed by being in care myself as a kid so I had some direct experience of where they were. The job constantly reinforced me with this sense of how dreadfully the state had done in looking after them. It had taken them out of a situation which apparently was not good and then done the most dismal job. One had very few resources. You had very little to offer them in the way of a future. But you were in a position of having to get them to accept what was on offer. They were probably going to become homeless or end up in prison or fulfil all of the other stereotypes...'.

Steve was in no doubt about the best job he had ever had: 'Being a housewife has been the best job... the most rewarding.... Although you have issues of status, at least you get noticed.... They say the most invisible person in the street is a woman with a push-chair, but if you are a man with a push-chair, when I was doing it in the early 1990s, people do notice. There is nothing worse than being a man and making a judgement when your child falls over "You are not hurt so get up and get some comfort" only to have a woman run in to rescue your child from this inadequate fathering. A lot of interesting things happened in that area. Women feel they can come and interfere with your children in a way they would never do with another woman, even if they thought she was not up to the task'. Asked if he considered such interference a kind of reverse sexism Steve said: 'Absolutely!... I know now without any doubt that I did create in my children a sense of adventure... they did climb trees and go to heights that other parents were not happy about...'.

Steve had lived in London all his life, in a variety of circumstances: 'I lived with my parents, moved out of there into a squat... I stayed there for three years... met another group of people who shared a house just down the road here in Hackney... I met my present partner there...'. He and his partner and their children now shared a large, comfortable four-bedroomed house in the north London neighbourhood of Stamford Hill. The house had a rear garden and was in a reasonable state of repair (in the author's judgement). Steve was especially enamoured with the living space, both internal and external: 'This house gives you space... the house goes up around a central turret with a room on each floor, but that means that between the bottom of the house and top of the house there is a lot of room which means you can be away from people. That is quite important. Togetherness is important but one must also be able to get away into a space of one's own. The garden is fantastic. An important aspect is we like being in the garden and doing the garden. When we are away we spend time in the country... a bit of outside space is quite important and for the children it is absolutely essential.... We felt especially lucky with this house because to go from a flat into this house was a big leap... it was almost outside of what we could afford. It wasn't in great condition and it isn't in great condition now'.

Stamford Hill has been home to London's Hasidic Jews for many years. There are Jewish schools, shops and community centres (many of which have been vandalised). Stamford Hill today is an ethnically diverse, if somewhat tatty, neighbourhood: 'There is a predominant group here which is the Hasidic Jews... with whom I get along very well... [although] one has one's mutual enjoyments and frustrations.... Over and above that this is an area where there are many other cultures with no other defining group.... Poles... Romanians... everybody is here. I think it is very difficult to live multiculturally where you are culturally outnumbered to the point where you feel you are a minority in your own community. One could say that that is possible with the Hasidic community, but they impact differently on life in general.... There is a genuine mixing and melding here that makes life comfortable.... I also like the fact that this is an area where there is a lot of street life... lots of people walking on the street, children, mothers, fathers...'.

Although he felt comfortable in Stamford Hill, the area, like most of London, could feel menacing: 'The worst aspect is almost the same as the best. You live in an area where there is poverty, deprivation, estates, people living in difficult circumstances. What that tends to generate is a sense of disenfranchisement... people who don't feel part of the community see it as a resource that they can prey on. I'm not directly affected by that. I create a large figure on the street [Steve was quite tall and seemed to keep himself fit] and I am not an obvious victim, and I am aware of that, but I know people who are possible victims. I find that quite concerning, whether it is my mother who is seventy-eight and lives around the corner being robbed of her pension or my son being mugged for his mobile telephone. These are things that have happened to us. I find that aspect the most difficult. How do you create a sense of community where it is not alright to rob someone? [There is something wrong] where you have to walk down the street and engage the "thousand yard stare" when you are going to get your Sunday newspaper. Maybe I should go in the car so I can avoid that...'.

As usual the interview concluded with a discussion about politics – personal, local and national. Steve praised the Labour government's record on employment: 'The most significant change under Blair is that, certainly in London, there is employment for all. I know there is always going to be a percentage of the population that is trapped in poverty, trapped not by a lack of jobs, but by the lack of their ability to move themselves out of the position they are in. Ten, fifteen years ago there was a likelihood, especially for youth, that there would be no job...'.

On the subject of how jobs are best created Steve believed in self-help – in entrepreneurship: 'What the government can't seem to do politically is to realise that the areas where you have innovation, where things are actually created, is at a grass-roots level. Business can spring from communities that seem hopeless, but you have actually got to trust the people within that community to grow businesses. Transport for London have a great idea: they want to have some cycle training. They say "OK, we'll give the money to your local authority... because they can manage the money... because they know what they are doing". But they don't know what they are doing. It is just an easy way for government to pass the money down. The money comes from central government... Transport for London get it... local government gets it... they all take a bite for managing the money as it comes down. Eventually it comes down to an organisation like our cycle training scheme where we then have to jump through all sorts of hoops and provide all sorts of paperwork and justification for what we are doing. But having done this we are still put in a position where the local authority – even though it has no knowledge of cycle training – feels it should dictate what cycle training takes place. This comes from people who are not grass roots in the community; people who are not seeing what is happening on the ground; people who are not seeing the benefits of training local people to be skilled, and keeping that skill in the community. They are looking at what they think is important: "Is this profitable?"; "Surely we should buy in the skills because it is cheaper?" The fact that it takes money away from the community does not seem to hit home. We must get away from the "bums-on-seats" attitude'.

Steve, who always voted, did not feel that voting changed the lot of the poor: 'I know from my roots, from where I come from, that when you are poor elections don't change your lot. At the end of the day you are still going to have to get up and do that crappy job. Whether or not there is an extra couple of pence on a loaf of bread actually does not make any difference. All of the political promises made by parties, on the whole, go straight over your head. What keeps the masses down is the fact that there is not starvation... there is generally accommodation to be had... so you are not exposed to the elements. There *is* a place to fall to that is worse than what you have got, but the majority is saved from that.... So they keep us nicely boxed in this little area.[3] When Kinnock lost his last general election I was devastated. I could not believe that the population could not see that we needed change. It was unbelievable on every level that Major got voted in. The need for political change was great. We had this great long Conservative run... we had a long period of Blairism. Long periods of stability do seem to benefit us in some ways but they all run their course in the end. On a local government level it is absolutely clear to me that the worst thing that can happen to any local government area is that you end up with a council that feel that they are never, ever going to be voted out...'.

Regarding the trades unions Steve felt they had not moved with the times: 'I used to be a NALGO rep when I was a laboratory technician. My politics were left of Labour. I believed that trades unions were essential, that workers rights had to be protected. I still believe that what trades unions did on some levels was right and had a big impact on workers' rights and protecting workers in the workplace... and offering more security. But there is no question in my mind that public services were damaged by the unions. I believe that when it became very clear that the unions had to work with the employers rather than against them they missed the boat. They believed they had to fight government... and they lost. I don't know whether the trades unions can recapture for me a sense that they have a real value. There is a need for a body that can protect workers and work with management, and in public services that needs to happen...'.

Steve felt that migrant labourers required protection: 'Some workers are protected by the fact that they have a value in the labour market. Then there is a whole underclass of workers who are just turned over. They are mainly immigrants, they are poorly paid, their conditions are appalling and the job they are doing is appalling. When we look at public services and we say our hospitals are not clean, they are not clean because we have a constant turnover of workers who don't really know what they are supposed to be doing... there is no sense of ownership of where they are working... they are not going to be enthused'.

Steve believed London to be special: 'As a Londoner I have no doubt at all that it is special. It is a place where I see a greater mix of people'. Asked to describe London in one word he said: 'I am stuck somewhere between awesome and comfortable'. He elaborated: 'It has an international status. Everybody knows someone who lives in London'. On this note I said goodbye to the Islington lad who used to hike down to the City to watch the Barbican's reconstruction with his street-mates.

Verstehen

London is a physical text that can be read in an infinite number of ways. It can be read as a dirty, noisy, shambles of a city. Ugly, greasy, rotting, rainy, sweaty, stinking, hopeless – like the metropolis in *Blade Runner*. It can be read as a baroque centre of privilege, with castles and palaces and parades and gold carriages and coppers in white gloves. It can be read as a symbol of defiance. Defiance of the vilest credo ever to infect the human spirit – Nazism. What is both alarming and intoxicating is that it can be read in all of these ways in a single day. Take a bus down the old Roman road from, say, Tottenham to the City. When you get into town go and stand on Westminster Bridge. Then reflect on what you have witnessed and how you felt about it. Try to sort your emotions out. Difficult? You bet.

3. The artisan

Cassandra, born in Epsom,[4] Surrey in 1968, lived with her long-term partner in Upper Tooting, south London. Divorced, she had lived in London for about eight years. After working for a housing association she moved into fundraising, working for a cancer charity and the Alzheimer's Society. Her time at the cancer charity was not especially happy: 'It was a lovely organisation. The people were wonderful. But when I joined the organisation it was in its final throes. Their major funder was withdrawing. It was a demoralising time there, really. It was taken over by another, larger charity'. When interviewed, Cassandra had two jobs. She dabbled in fundraising. She also worked with stained glass, which she found both challenging and rewarding: 'I wear two hats. My main job is making stained glass, leaded lights, glass lamps. I have my own small business, very small, just me. I do that working from home. I do some fundraising still for a charity I used to work for, many years ago, and I do that on a freelance basis'. Asked to describe her stained glass work in more detail Cassandra said: 'My workshop is in the cellar of the house I share with my partner. It's a bit grim, really. Unfortunately the cellar is a bit damp at the moment because of the rise in the water level of the Thames. It has flooded the cellar. I also have an office upstairs which is quite self-contained'. Cassandra had avoided hiring others to help out, even in busy periods: 'The only time I have ever used people is to fit the leaded panels. I don't fit the panels myself'. Asked if she had ever turned work away Cassandra said: 'I have not had to do that yet, although it is getting near to that state. I have to be very realistic when I am telling people about timescales. I leave it up to them. If they are prepared to wait that long, fine. It is now August and I'm telling people I won't be able to start their work until November, so they take it or leave it, really. But no, I have not actually had to turn anything down yet'. Asked if she had ever been tempted to hire staff Cassandra said: 'I haven't. As I work from home I don't like the idea of having employees coming to the house, really. And to be honest the business has not been financially viable enough to be able to pay people. The first few months of the year [2007] were very, very quiet. There was hardly any work coming in at all. I was just starting to panic and then the phone calls started. You start getting work again. But it is very unpredictable, so to hire anyone on a long-term basis would not be fair, really'. Asked how many hours a day she worked on her stained glass panels and lights Cassandra said: 'The days seem to be getting longer, actually. I would say probably nine to ten hours per day. It can be a lot less than that when it's quieter. I did have a very large contract a couple of years ago. I had to complete a lot of work within a very tight timescale. I was probably doing fourteen hours per day... I was living, eating and sleeping glass for about five weeks'.

Working from home and being her own boss appealed to Cassandra: 'Working from home is the best aspect of the job. I do work perhaps longer hours than when I was employed, but at least you can work the hours you want to work. So if you want to start later and finish later you can, or vice-versa. It's having that freedom and flexibility. If you have got an appointment in the middle of the day it doesn't matter. You don't have to book time off work. You can book appointments around work. My mother is quite elderly so having the flexibility to go down any day of the week without having to check with the boss weeks in advance is good. So I enjoy being my own boss'.

Despite the attractions of self-employment she sometimes felt vulnerable: 'The worst aspect is that you are quite reliant on yourself the whole time. Obviously if you are sick there is no-one else to do it for you. Fortunately I have not had any long-term sickness, so I've been OK. It can be a worry. If I was ill I obviously would not be earning. And also you are having to do everything: the administration, the book-keeping, as well as the actual job in hand. It was quite daunting when I started off. But when you get used to it it's OK. So the worst thing is that there is no back-up'. Asked if she had ever lost sleep over a job Cassandra said: 'Only once. That is going back to that time I had the large contract a couple of years ago. It was an awful lot of work. Also it was quite daunting because it involved working on a building site.[5] Being female you do feel a bit.... As it was it was absolutely fine. They were a great bunch of people. The day before my first day working on site I did probably lose quite a bit of sleep'.

Asked whether she felt she was paid a fair rate for her work she replied: 'I think so. When I started off I probably under-charged, because I wanted to get the work coming in. I don't make the lamps very often now, I just make them for myself, because you can't charge a fair rate – there are so many cheaper replicas being imported. You can't compete with the prices. I think I charge a fair rate for the leaded lights. Some take me a lot longer than I anticipated, so perhaps I lose out a little bit there. I think on the whole I have now got my pricing structure right'. Asked if the leaded glass industry was a competitive industry Cassandra said: 'I think it is. There are a lot of stained glass businesses around, especially in south-west London. But on the other hand there is a lot of business to be had, there being a lot of period houses in the area. A lot of them are being refurbished, original features are being reinstated, and there is also repair work. On the whole we are good at passing work on. I've had other people pass work on if they have been too busy. We all seem to rub along'.

Regarding their accommodation Cassandra and her partner lived in a large period four-bedroomed house that her partner had been refurbishing since the day he bought it. Its unfinished state was a minor irritation to her: 'There's a lot of work to do on the place, and it would be nice to one day have lights in the hall and have the proper floor down and just things like that, really. It would be nice to have the luxuries of life'. Cassandra did not think it likely her partner would ever bring somebody in to finish the house off: 'No, probably not. He claims to enjoy it as a hobby'. 'One day it will be a very nice house' she said.

The house itself, although terraced, was spacious: 'It is a four-bedroomed Victorian house with cellar, currently under water, kitchen, lounge, dining room, bathroom, en-suite, and a converted loft'. There was also a roof terrace, small front garden and medium-sized rear garden. The best feature was 'the space. There is room to have an office which you can shut off. It's handy for shops. When it is all finished it will be a rather stunning house'. Asked when she thought the refurbishment might be completed she replied: 'How long is a piece of string? My partner likes to call it a hobby'.

Despite being an 'incomer' Cassandra liked living in Upper Tooting: 'There are lots of great shops nearby. You do not have to go into town. It is also nice that we are very near to the common so you have got that open green space, which I enjoy, because I like to cycle. People on the whole are jolly nice. There are plenty of places to eat and drink'. The area did have some drawbacks, however. Traffic was a big problem: 'Traffic is the one thing that does annoy me, because I cycle a lot. The Chelsea tractors. There are so many of them around here. Apparently Wandsworth has more four-by-fours than anywhere else in the country. That can be a bit irksome'. Despite some near-misses (including one that could have been fatal) she did feel that the mayor of London had done much for cyclists: 'I cycle to my clients. It's a lot easier and quicker. Ken Livingstone has done a lot to improve the cycle routes. I think the number of cyclists has gone up by 125 per cent since he's been mayor, and he's had an awful lot to do with that. I know it is controversial, but I am all for the Congestion Charge.[6] I think it is great to reduce the amount of traffic in the centre of London'. As to the furthest she would cycle to a client Cassandra said: 'We are not talking huge distances. East Dulwich. I have a folding cycle so I can take that on the train. I cycle in all weathers, snow, hail'. Despite liking her neighbourhood Cassandra felt a time would come when she would leave London: 'I've not really lived here that long. I have never really felt that London was completely my home. And also I prefer to live more in the countryside. Somewhere a bit more rural, near the sea. My partner has now bought a cottage near the sea, so I think I will stick with him. Our long-term plan is to move out and live down there, to move out gradually over the next few years'.

Although she had never been a member of a trades union, Cassandra thought unions did a good job: 'I agree with unionism. It's just that I've never been in a profession that has had its own union as such. It's important to know there's someone there by your side if you need it'. She always voted at elections: 'I have never not voted. I believe you should vote. Especially being a woman. So many women fought for the right to vote. Some people do get lazy and say there is no point. But I think it is important. If you do not vote and you are not happy with what is going on you have no right to complain because you have not tried to have your say'. Asked whether she thought voters were given a real choice at election time she replied: 'If you mean if the parties have all melted into one, probably they have. They have blurred their boundaries and they are all getting very similar on the surface. Fundamentally there are differences. It's quite easy for the tabloids to say they are all the same. But if you scratch the surface there are fundamental differences which are important'. Cassandra praised the minimum wage (introduced by the Blair government) but felt more should be done for women who either worked or wanted to work: 'More could be done for women with children. Better and cheaper child care. Often you hear of women who want to go back to work but by the time they have paid for the child care it is not worth their while'. Asked whether the government should do more to help micro-businesses like her own she replied: 'It's not really something I've thought about'. Asked what she would improve if she were mayor of London she mentioned public transport and the lot of cyclists: 'I'd abolish four-by-fours. I'd do more to improve public transport. A lot has been done and a lot is ongoing. But somehow we need to make the tube more pleasant. More carriages. More space. Make the carriages more airy. Not having so many speed bumps would be quite nice as well. When you are going down a hill over speed bumps it's quite unnerving.... I haven't tried taking my folding cycle on the tube yet. I'm not sure you are allowed to. That's something I'd have to check out'.

The 2012 London Olympics would have good and bad impacts she thought: 'I'm in two minds about the Olympics. It is a great achievement that we were awarded it, especially as we beat the French. The good thing is it will help get things like transport improved, which I like to think would have been done anyway, but this has just accelerated things a bit. I'm a bit distressed to hear that current sports facilities used by community groups are being demolished to make way for facilities for the Olympics. I hope facilities will have a life beyond the Olympics. I find the major overspend and under-budgeting that has taken place quite alarming. We are all paying for it so I'd like to think we'll get fair use out of the new facilities'. Asked if she thought the money being spent on the Olympics would have a bigger impact if it was spent directly on regeneration she replied: 'I think there's a lot to be said for that. You hear stories of school playing fields being sold off to make way for other things. You hear of a lack of investment in sports in schools. We have to try to find enough Olympians. How are they supposed to train in the meantime? From a tourism kind of angle the Olympics are a good thing. There will be a lot of people coming over and staying in London. Visiting other attractions as well. Other places will benefit. The sailing is taking place off Weymouth. So I'm sitting on the fence over it, really. One day I feel one way, and another day I feel another way. They're controversial, I think'.

Cassandra felt London's cultural and ethnic diversity made it a special place: 'What is special is that there are so many diverse nationalities and cultures. On the whole we all tend to rub along pretty well together. I am conscious of other areas where there is perhaps more racism, and communities are not so integrated'. Asked why London seemed to be a fairly harmonious city Cassandra said: 'Being a large city with a large population you are quite anonymous. That can work both ways. It is not a tight-knit community where you would have to get along with everyone very well. Perhaps it is just that people do not have to have so much to do with each other. London has had a long, long history of mixed communities going back over hundreds of years, so it may be a historical thing'. Her one-word description of London was 'cosmopolitan'.

4. The cabbie

Michael, born in 1952, had lived in London all his life. Single, he had no children 'that I know of'. After leaving comprehensive school at sixteen years of age he had a succession of jobs – twenty in all. The worst job was 'Working in a factory that made leather slippers for Marks and Spencers... they had the concession for it... in Walthamstow'. Michael disliked the job 'Because it was the most boring thing I have ever done.... It was virtually a production line... God-awful... I did it because I had to'. His best job was 'Possibly in the rag trade. I had a nice job. I was a cutter, manager, whatever, making coats, making different things. That was probably my best field of work'. He liked it because it was varied and creative: 'It was interesting, you had created something at the end of it, there was a finished article, a coat, a shirt, a tie, whatever. It was because you created something at the end of it, really...'. In the early 1990s Michael fell on hard times. Unable to find a job he turned to taxiing: 'I had to do it because I had been made redundant.... I was about forty, thrown on the scrap-heap, could not get a job, so I thought I would have to do something like this and I've been doing this for ten years now...'. On average he worked a ten-hour day and took time off 'When I can afford it'. The working day was pretty hectic. A proper lunchtime was a luxury: 'I don't really take lunch... ten minutes if you want to get a roll. I'll eat it then I'm off again'. His only other breaks from driving were taken 'between fares'.

Michael worked from a cab rank located opposite a tube and railway station in north London. His cab was one of several parked in a line waiting for a fare. Traffic could make getting to work difficult: 'When the schools are on it could take me forty-five minutes [to get to the rank]. When the schools are not on it should take me fifteen...'. Asked what he thought of his fellow black cab drivers he said: 'Most of them are fine, some of them are not, there's a minority that are not... untrustworthy... maybe that's enough for now... apart from the slang words for it'. Asked what he thought his colleagues thought of him he said: 'I think they trust me. I think they think I'm OK. I have a level of seniority on the rank because I am one of the earlier drivers on the rank so people do tend to think well, he may know what he's on about a little. I don't stitch anybody up... there's a level of trust where they think "yes, he's quite straight", you know. I think... they might tell you otherwise...'. His worst argument at work was due to 'Another driver stitching me up... nicking jobs off of me... knowing full well... doing it blatantly in my face, you know...'. The job's best aspect was its 'freedom' – as a black cab driver Michael was more or less self-employed. Being self-employed did have its disadvantages, however: 'The unpredictability of the money [is a problem]. You can be out for eight hours and earn very, very little money... you can be out for those eight or nine hours and earn OK money. Trade is down, there is more drivers, we are being flooded with drivers.... [There's] competition with minicabs or private hire and I'm earning half what I was earning when I got out here ten years ago on the same rank, you know, so that's not good. It's probably one of the things I dislike about it'. Asked whether he felt black cab drivers were paid a fair rate for the job he replied: 'When you have a customer yes I think we are paid a fair rate... I can't argue with that.... It's just there are not enough of the customers, that's the problem. We charge customers good money to get into a cab and we deserve to give them a good service. Basically you have to know where you are going. The rate we charge them is more than adequate, really'. Michael felt that black cab drivers were sometimes put upon, as in the case of disabled access: 'We have to have this facility, it's a must, part of your driving test, part of your knowledge when you go to be a cab driver, you have to show that you can use a wheelchair, get it in, fit it in. If you didn't pass that part of the test you would fail so you wouldn't get your badge. You'd have to take it again, and so on'. Asked when the wheelchair requirement came in Michael said: 'That's been in for some years. When I got out ten years ago they were leading that way. There were other black cabs that were not wheelchair-compatible. The first cab I had wasn't wheelchair-compatible, which was OK, but within three to six months of my getting out they brought in new legislation. All old cabs had to be converted, so we had to change our cabs and go on to these purpose-built cabs... or have your cab converted at a cost.... It didn't cost me but at the time the drivers were paying an average of two grand out of their own pocket. This has never been subsidised, like the buses are, not at all.... I know that some cab drivers who did have their cabs converted for that kind of cost had their cabs taken off the road a year or two later.... They had to go and get a different purpose-built cab, a "wheelchair-compatible" cab'.

Despite feeling put upon Michael had decided against joining a union: 'I'm not in a union. Some drivers are... a lot of drivers on the radio circuit are. I am on one circuit but I am not compelled to be in a union. Some of the drivers on different circuits are. I wouldn't join because I don't really like them. I have been in them before, but no I'm not at the moment'. Asked what he thought of the trades unions in general he replied: 'I'm indifferent to a point. When they were powerful they kind of ruled the roost and it's like anything they just sell out to their own back pocket. I just don't trust them. They rarely look after the people within their shelter, as it were. We tried to get that minicab office not put in here [Michael's cab rank competed with a minicab office located inside the tube and railway station]. It's madness having that minicab office. We have been here for years, this cab rank. We left it to the union. "We'll sort it out" said they. Didn't do a thing. I knew they wouldn't but I left it to the others,

the powers that be. Now that's in there it's taken half of our work. Madness. That
was the London Taxi Drivers' Association which is a subsidiary of Computercab or
Comcab or whatever they call themselves now.... Maybe the Transport and General
or a few others like that... maybe they're a bit better, you know.... The Association
could probably help you with a solicitor if you had a speeding ticket. I've heard they
are pretty good with that. I've not had that one yet... I've handled that one myself'.

Asked what he thought was the best thing the government had done for
working people he replied: 'I can't think of anything'. Michael did, however, feel the
government should address issues like 'Tax, red tape and political correctness'. He
held political correctness in deep contempt: 'It's absurd, obscene even. [They need
to] stop us – white middle England – becoming the minority, the put-upon people.
They could do that, but they won't.... The racial political correctness is what we need
to change.... I feel there are lots of people, white, middle-England, working-class
people that are prisoners in their own country at the moment through this political
correctness rubbish'. Michael seemed disillusioned with politics. Asked whether he
voted he said: 'In recent years, no. I would always vote and I still would vote, because
if I don't vote then I can't complain, you know, but recently I get the feeling that
things have been so fragmented and diluted I could, you know, fiddle twenty votes
and this mob [Labour] would still get in'. Michael was no fan of London's Labour
mayor, Ken Livingstone: 'I am not happy with what he is doing. He doesn't like black
cab drivers. He will argue that until he is blue in the face. He doesn't like black cab
drivers. He likes his buses and his private hire. That's his little baby. He has actually
been on this rank with his oppos [colleagues] about three years ago and got minicabs
up to where he needed to go. But at the same time, which is not known to everybody,
he has a Gold Account with Computercab, so when it's late and he needs to get home
to Kilburn or wherever it is he lives he won't trust those boys [minicab drivers]...
he wants one of these boys who knows what he's doing. The man is two-faced. He
doesn't like us. He will get us off the road before long. Ten years, if he's still in, this
will be such a small little affair, you know. He keeps giving us rises... he's pricing us
out of the market.... And I don't like his Congestion Charge... so...'.

Asked what three things he would change if he were mayor of London, Michael
replied: 'I really, really don't know. That's a tall order. I'd spend a lot of money trying
to clean up crime. Crime is running amok. But their figures won't tell you that'.
Asked if he suffered harassment while cabbying Michael said: 'Luckily enough we
don't get that many. I have had about three or four in the ten years, which is very
good. I know other lads that have had more. It's the luck of the draw. Or you get
people who say "I'm not paying you". "Well, OK, I'll take you to the police station".
Then they suddenly throw the money at you. Usually speaking if somebody wants to
get out and get away with it, it's not worth engaging them. I could engage in fisticuffs,
but for what – five, six, seven pounds – what's the point? I could get hurt. If I hit him
or her the chances are I'll lose my badge. They'll get away with it. The law tends to be

a lot in favour of the perpetrator at the moment, or that's the way you feel. You can't always get a copper when you want him'.

Michael was asked to comment on claims by Ken Livingstone and the Metropolitan Police that there were more police on the street: 'There are part-time bobbies on the beat who can't even make an arrest. I don't think there are more police on the beat. They are still shackled. Any copper you talk to... they are not happy with it. They are stifled. There was a guy on the TV one morning this week... he was a CID-type guy... he was talking about this stabbing in Luton [a police officer had been stabbed and killed in Luton town centre]... he said down here just the other week he engaged a guy with a gun – and he emphasised it was a black guy. He is off-duty this copper. He has commandeered a push-bike and given chase. He has 'phoned in with his number, whatever, to get armed back-up which didn't appear for half an hour. So what chance have I got down here? The crime is out of order. We get threatened over here... we get cut up on the road... people pull knives out... and they say "no, no, our figures don't show this". Well I'd like them to come out at midnight and go on the top of one of the double-decker buses around Tottenham and places like that and see how much they like it or send their wife out and get harassed by the hoodies that's in and around the area, but they won't do that will they? Their figures don't show that. Makes you a bit bitter, doesn't it? Don't get too old and bitter and twisted! They are tied up with paperwork. That's why they don't come out. I wouldn't be a copper for all the money in the world at the moment because it is such a thankless task. It would be so frustrating. You'd think "I've got to let these people go".... Minor criminals, major criminals, they get away on technicalities and the political correctness thing. You know... public transport, people are still frightened to get on public transport after certain times.... You wouldn't go on the top of a bus because you'll get stabbed, mugged. It's happening all of the time. I'd probably improve the transport system if I could, not necessarily just black cabs but the whole lot because it is in a little bit of disarray... and maybe bring the prices down on the buses and tubes to a reasonable figure... maybe I'd improve the education'.

Michael felt that London was no longer a special place: 'There used to be something special about it... I don't think there is now... I think it is a dirty place. It is very multicultural, but I don't honestly think that that works. It's great when you get the tourists over here, that's wonderful, you see all sorts of different people.... The actual people that live in and around it... no. And it's quite unclean I feel... expensive beyond belief. It used to be special, because you had things like Carnaby Street as a fashion whatever and stores like that.... I used to go and shop there myself in the Seventies, but now I wouldn't bother'. Michael was ambivalent about the London Olympics: 'It's a double-edged sword... I think people will learn out of it for those three or four weeks, but after that we'll have empty stadiums. I'm worried in my profession because I think there'll be loads of black cab drivers pushed through for that because his [Ken Livingstone's] idea is to get everybody from Kings Cross to the

Olympic stadium in about three and a half minutes, so he'll put loads of bus lanes in and when that's all over we'll all be looking around for a job'. Asked whether he could sum London up in one word he initially said: 'Probably not... I wouldn't be doing it justice'. Then he recanted and offered 'lively'. With that I thanked him for his time and exited the back of his cab to catch a bus home.

5. The company director

Lance was born in 1968 in Tokyo. He was very much a global citizen having lived in seven countries before settling in England (he had lived in Japan, Ireland, America, Mexico, Israel, Germany and Scotland). He was well qualified, having an MA in history and a degree in law. During his fifteen years in London he had held five jobs: 'My first one was working as a graduate trainee, an account executive for a small PR company for about a year and a half. Then I moved to one of the world's largest PR companies and I worked there for about two years. Then I moved to an agency that during the late 1990s won all the awards on the PR scene. I was there for about four years and became an associate director. Then during the last dot-com boom I was head of communications for an Internet-based trade company. Then about six years ago I started my own agency with my business partner'. His worst job had been 'Washing dishes in a hotel in Germany when I was a student'. As to why this was his worst job he said: 'Extremely long hours. Unpleasant people. Very heavy manual labour'. His best job was his current job 'because I run my own company'.

Lance described his current job with pride: 'I am one of the partners in a medium-sized London PR agency. I run the business along with my business partner. We have thirty-five people working for us. We built it up from just two of us with a £10,000 loan to a two-million pound turnover. We have been short-listed for, or have won, thirty awards in the past five years. Our client list includes Google, Burger King, General Motors, Heinz, Bandai and Jetex... so we are quite well known in our industry. I handle accounts there, I run the business, I look after personnel, I do finance... and various things like that'. Asked how he came to be in a position to run his own business he said: 'Coincidence, actually. I had read a book called *Open Mind* by somebody called Andy Law. He described an advertising agency called St Lukes which was quite famous in the late 1990s and that kind of spurred the idea that I would like to do something similar in the public relations field. Nothing ever came of it. Then when I was doing my dot-com job I met someone in a pub who told me that a former colleague of mine was thinking about setting up an agency and that spurred me to contact her and suggest that we do it together'. Asked if it was unusual to have a female partner in the PR business Lance said: 'I would not say so, no... we have perhaps twenty-six, twenty-seven women and eight or nine men... a lot of agencies have even more women'. Asked how many hours a week he worked he said: 'That's quite a difficult question because my actual office hours are not that bad...

sixty hours each week is probably a good guess... but in the office probably not more than forty-two, forty-three'. Working at home was more difficult these days because his partner had just given birth.

Asked what he thought of his staff he said: 'I think we have built up quite a young agency... the average age is twenty-five, twenty-six, so it's quite a lively atmosphere. By and large I am privileged to work with a talented group of people. Not everyone is so, but that's the same in any company you would come across. I think by and large we are fairly fortunate with the people we have got working with us. One of the associate directors has taken on the hiring process quite a lot'. Asked what he thought his staff thought of him he said: 'That's a very good question. I have no idea. Last year in a survey we were ranked number one in our industry on whether people trust management to do the right thing. The people who have just joined us can see that we are very different in terms of atmosphere and the way we treat people. When people have been with us for a while they tend to forget what other agencies are like, and they then start to see more faults rather than plus sides, if you see what I mean'. Staff could discuss issues at regular company meetings: 'We have bi-weekly breakfast meetings and we have bi-monthly company meetings as well. Everyone is invited. They attend if they are around'.

Lance admitted that running the company could be stressful. Asked if he could recall the worst argument he had ever had at work he said: 'That was probably with my business partner when I was first starting up... over small things, really. It is quite a stressful environment when you put your livelihood on the line. There is a lot of potential for misunderstanding. So we did have pretty bad arguments at the beginning, but when you look back at it they were about things that were not very significant in the scale of things.... Normally a bit of shouting was involved, and then after a cooling-off period things settled back by themselves'.

Asked whether he felt he received a fair reward for all the effort he had put in to the company he said: 'No I do not. I am now paid a market rate. But for the first five years I wasn't, so in a sense I am playing catch-up for what happened in the first five years. I could have made a lot more money had I stayed working for someone else. I would say that for most of the five years I was paid about a third less'. Asked if he thought all his hard work and sacrifice had been worth it Lance said: 'I suppose you make a trade-off, don't you? I suppose you get the satisfaction of running your own company. I do expect to see a financial return on it at some point. Now I am paid more than I was in my last job... but it has taken us a while to get there'. Asked if he thought he would stick with his current job or move on Lance said: 'PR is very much a young person's game and I think that both I and my business partner are approaching the end of our shelf life and I think that when we have been doing this for ten years, in about four years time, it will be time for us to move on. I don't know exactly what we'll be doing but we'll have to find something else to do'. Asked if he thought he might move out of PR altogether Lance said: 'Perhaps, but I don't know what that is yet. Actually my business partner and myself did seriously look at buying a place in Marrakech and doing it up and renting it out as a hotel. For various reasons that never saw the light of day. I have to say I think the market has overtaken us. It's just got too expensive. It was going to be like a project on the side. Maybe something like that – a special project – is a possibility'.

As to his London lifestyle Lance and his wife lived in a two-up, two-down maisonette in Greenwich. 'We used to own a house in Belsize Park in Hampstead, and probably given a choice we would move back there' he noted. Greenwich had its plus and minus points: 'I like Greenwich a lot. There's a nice neighbourhood, a nice community feel with our street... but at the risk of sounding like some sort of conservative sixty-year-old there are gangs of hooded teenagers wandering along the street'. Asked whether he would like to move out of London he said: 'I am of two minds about it. I am not sure whether I would want my son growing up here when it is time to go to school'. Lance's commute to work was spectacular: 'I take the boat from Greenwich to the City and then I walk... that journey takes one hour. The best thing about the boat is that I always get a seat and it's always on time ... and the view is a lot better'.

Lance did not feel the Labour government had done much for working people. 'Nothing stands out' he said. Asked whether he felt the government could do more for business entrepreneurs he said: 'There is this talk about tightening up maternity and paternity rules... making employers give more. Even as a new dad[7] I think that, for small businesses, that's a nightmare. We have people with us at the moment who have been gone for almost a year. We have to take them back after a year even though their jobs may no longer be available. Now if you are a large Plc with thousands of people that is all very well. If you are a small company with thirty-five people, having to create an extra job for someone when their job has been filled is quite difficult. I've never actually voted Conservative in my life but I cannot think of a single thing that this government has done to make the lives of small businesses easier. Frankly they have made it more difficult, because Gordon Brown raised the rate of corporation tax for small businesses from nineteen to twenty-two per cent, which is crazy. What the government should be doing is supporting people like us and taxing the large Plcs'. In Lance's opinion New Labour were far from being the party of small business, despite the political rhetoric: 'I think that they are the party of large corporations, and not the party of small businesses. I think they are the party of the City. They are the party of Canary Wharf... the party of the Plc... but they are not the party of small business'. Asked if he thought the present Conservative Party's policies were better for his size of business Lance said: 'They probably are but I still wouldn't vote for them'.

Lance felt the unions could be manipulated by cliques: 'It's difficult to comment because I work in an industry where they are not really relevant. I think the problem with trades unions is they don't reflect their membership base, and then it's a small group of activists which gets involved and which fill the top positions, which is not representative of the members. I'll take your union to start off with [the university lecturers' union]. One thing I have been reading about is the Israel boycott decision which I personally think... I'm not a fan of the Israeli government, there are a lot of things they do which I disagree with, but I think that this decision was wrong, and from what I understand I am not sure whether the people who made that decision are representative of the people who are actually members of that union. I think that's a prime example of activists who are not representative of the union membership making decisions which I don't believe are in the union's best interests'.

As for the democratic process's capacity to articulate the popular will Lance said: 'Yes I think it can change things. If you look at the changes that came in after 1979 that was people voting in an election. I also think it's a civic duty for people to vote, and I always make a point of voting in elections, because I know that people around the world have died for the right to vote. I happen to agree with countries like Switzerland where it is a civic duty to vote'. Asked if he thought voters had a real choice at election time Lance said: 'There is a choice. I'm not sure there's a real choice. I suppose one of the things about democratic politics is they tend to converge into the centre anyway. That is a reality of life. Actually I do think there is a real choice. If you take policies towards Europe, for example, then there is clearly a real choice. On other issues, there isn't.... I think the Conservatives are probably better for small businesses... but I wouldn't vote for them'.

Lance found Ken Livingstone's mayorship something of a curate's egg: 'Sometimes it's good. Sometimes bad. I think there was a great quote by Dan Johnson, the leader of the Greens in the London Assembly, who said that Ken Livingstone is only radical about things he has no power over. So he grandstands a lot about Iraq or George Bush, etc., etc., but in the areas he has policy decisions he is not radical at all, and there has been a lot of talk about him being in the pockets of property developers, so again favouring big business.... I think the Congestion Charge was a good thing, actually, because I think something had to be done to take a mass of cars out of central London. I believe that eighty per cent of people who drive in central London each day do not need to'.

Asked if he thought there was something special about London Lance replied: 'Yeah I know that Ken Livingstone has this thing about London being almost a city state. I think it's very different to the rest of the UK. I think that social attitudes and a spirit of inclusiveness are a lot better. It is a much more diverse place. A much more varied place. I think that is a good thing. London is like Singapore or Hong Kong. It is almost like an enclosed economy in its own right. The City here serves not just the UK but Europe and the world, and the same with a lot of other industries that are based here... they are based in the UK but they don't serve the UK'. Asked if he thought that London was more connected to Paris, New York and Rome than to England and Britain Lance said: 'Absolutely. I would say because of the large proportion of the foreign-born population, I would say the social make-up, I would say in the sense that it is quite outward-looking. It is not as insular as the rest of England is. To give you an example, there has been a lot of talk about the number of eastern Europeans coming to the UK. I happen to think this is a very good thing, because I think they are hard-working people. It is good for the economy, and good luck to them. However, I know that that view is not very widely shared.... Most of the negative comment I hear is from outside London... I think if you are a Pole or Romanian you will fit in better here than if you move out to a small English town'.

Asked what three things he would change if he were mayor of London he replied: 'Gosh. The Congestion Charge should cover zones one and two.... Related to that I would make a massive investment in the tube, so services actually run the way that they're meant to. I'd have them running all night as well, a twenty-four-hour service... other cities manage it'. Asked why he thought Britain was still very much a 'close-at-midnight' kind of place Lance replied: 'I don't think London is.... In terms of the public transport system it's just historical. Lack of investment in the infrastructure. Livingstone was right to oppose this public–private partnership business for the tube.... He wanted to raise bonds on the market like New York has done which has worked out cheaper than the current arrangement, so the whole set-up is a lot more expensive than it needed to be and it isn't working. I would abolish council tax and replace it with a London-wide income tax'. Asked if he thought a local income tax would be more equitable Lance replied: 'I do think it would be more equitable... I also think it would probably be more efficient'.

Lance was very positive about the 2012 Olympic Games: 'They'll be a good thing for London without a doubt. Because I think there is an enormous amount of prestige attached to it. It's good for the regeneration of London's East End. I think it'll put us on the map even more'. Asked to comment on the argument that the money would have a bigger impact if it were spent directly on social amenities Lance said: 'If you took that argument to its logical conclusion we wouldn't be doing anything except spending money on housing, health and education.... Big projects like the 2012 Olympics kind of give us a momentum. This intangible feelgood factor that it gives us, you can't really quantify it but it does have an effect. The positives will outweigh the negatives'. Asked whether taxpayers' money should subsidise things like opera and theatre, traditionally the preserve of the middle classes, Lance replied 'Absolutely'. He described those who argued against state subsidies for middle-class pursuits as 'killjoys'. 'Unique' was Lance's one-word summation of London.

The interview over, Lance headed back to his partner and their new offspring. I finished my expensive coffee in the expensive coffee house that had been our venue then departed the curtain-walled towers of Canary Wharf for the unglamorous realities of north London. From skinny latte to deadly kebab in sixty minutes (on a good day).

6. The tube driver

Geoff, born in 1955 and married with three children, lived in Watford. Educated at a Catholic comprehensive school run by nuns Geoff had left at the age of seventeen, half-way through his A-levels. Since leaving school he had seen 'Three main stretches of employment. Ten years with the Post Office. Ten years self-employed as a taxi driver in Watford. Seven years with the underground'. His worst job was 'Working in a factory on a press, making specialist cutting blades for metalwork. That was the most boring six weeks of my life. It was the most boring thing. Standing at a press all day. Not piece rate, but almost... so many per hour. Forty hours a week. I was really moving from one job to another, just doing a bit of a search, really... I thought I'd try factory work, but it wasn't for me'.

Working for the Post Office was secure but boring: 'Maggie Thatcher came to power... I was going to get married and I was looking for a secure job. The Post Office was suggested to me.... Unemployment rose, it was quite a tough time, those early years, but I was in a secure job earning good money. As the pressures disappeared slightly, we got on top of our mortgage. But I couldn't face the thought of another ten years. That ten years hadn't qualified me to do anything in particular. I was very qualified in the Post Office, I had done well, ended up as an inspector there, but I couldn't face thirty more years of it.... People were retiring and dying...'.

Not wanting to get trapped Geoff took the plunge and became self-employed: 'I became a self-employed taxi driver because I had friends who were doing it and it was an escape, a complete change from the Post Office's protected environment. I really enjoyed the freedom of being a taxi driver, I was self-employed, never late for work, took holidays when I wanted. Security is what I didn't have as a taxi driver, sick pay, paid holiday... as a taxi driver I always had to pay for my holiday twice... put money aside to pay the bills when I was away and pay for the holiday. With the underground the cheque arrives while I'm on holiday regardless. But I enjoyed the freedom of being self-employed. I enjoyed working for myself, getting the rewards, however much I put in I got out. I enjoyed trying to balance when to work and when not to work. Learning when the work was going to be there and not trying to flog a dead horse, you know. It was a sharp learning curve but I enjoyed that. After ten years of driving the age started to tell, however. I was looking for a private pension and they were incredibly expensive at the time. A friend of mine suggested the underground. I'd worked in London for a year when I was about twenty, and I'd travel up on the Tube. It was a different world in those days, nothing like it is now, the pressure wasn't there, there were no queues, you could get on a tube at nine in the morning. He said there's a job fayre in Watford Town Hall and London Underground were recruiting... so I said to Sue [Geoff's wife] if I pass the tests I'll take the job. If I don't I'll stay taxi driving. It's done us well up until now and I'll work out a pension. Maybe I'll have to work longer or whatever but we'll make it. But the underground has been a great experience. It provides security'.

Asked to describe a typical day's work as a tube driver Geoff said: 'A typical day's work is very untypical. The shifts are very varied. Anything from eight to four hours. It's a thirty-six-hour working week, but that is an average over twelve weeks. So you could end up doing forty-odd hours one week and then just over thirty the next, so you could do three days of eight hours, one of six, whatever. It is very imbalanced [*sic*]. Yesterday I did nearly eight hours, tomorrow my working day is six hours. It could vary from a quarter to five in the morning to as late as a five o'clock start in the evening, finishing at one, one-thirty in the morning, and any variation in between. The shifts start every fifteen minutes. Say tomorrow my job is to take a train out of Neasden Depot, take it empty to Stanmore sidings, and about fifteen minutes later start off at Canons Park and take that train to West Ham, empty it, and take it away to Stratford Market Depot, for some strange reason, then make my way to North Greenwich to have my breakfast... there is a canteen facility there. Now I don't quite understand why I take a train from Neasden Depot and almost do just one trip on it and put it away at Stratford Market Depot. I have not been there long enough to understand why. It obviously works for London Underground, but it does seem a very strange arrangement. The maximum you can drive is four hours fifteen minutes in any one stint, actually sitting in the chair, then you have to have a break. You are not allowed to do any overtime at all, but you can book overtime, obviously, if a train breaks down, but you can't volunteer to work a rest day for safety reasons'. After working a block of four hours and fifteen minutes drivers had to take a thirty minute break: 'Thirty minutes minimum, but usually they schedule it to be about an hour or so...'. Asked what he thought about the limited notice period for rostered duty Geoff said: 'Well at the moment I'm on the reserve, so I know roughly what I'm doing in the next twenty-eight days. If I was rostered, I think a roster is about one hundred and thirty weeks long... I could tell you what I'm doing in about ten years time. Hopefully in three or four months I'll be on the roster, and I'll have that choice. If you are a driver there is a third choice... you can join what they call the Mafia, which is a euphemism for a group of about one hundred guys who come together and they hand their duties to the Mafia Man and he looks after himself first so he gives himself whatever he wants.... London Underground are almost thinking of making it official, it works so well... you tell him roughly what you would like to do'.

Asked if there was a split or division between the underground's operational and commercial side Geoff said: 'Yes. I'd say it's a three-way split[8]... the drivers are not really operational. The station side are more face-to-face. The drivers are operational but all they do really is drive the trains. They call the drivers "knuckle-draggers"... you watch them get out of one end of the train then drag themselves up to the other end and then drive it off in the other direction. A lot of people say that drivers are there because they don't want to have that interaction with customers. Most of them are smart guys... but there is that element of them not understanding how the station works... a lot of them are direct recruits from the old days so they haven't got railway experience... a lot of them are limited to the line they are driving. Jubilee drivers can't drive the District Line. It's a different stock, so to move you have to go through another training course. If there is somebody ill on the train the basic thing is get them off the train. Get the train moving. So the driver goes that way and the station staff deal with the ambulance. The third side of the underground is the administration, which is IT, advertising. I saw more of it as a station supervisor. As a train driver it doesn't really impinge on your job. Administrators work mostly nine to five, Monday to Friday. That's most obvious at Christmas... the admin side disappears some time before Christmas and comes back two weeks later... then you get a torrent of work over the e-mail system...'. Asked if he felt there was any tension between the three cultures Geoff said: 'I think there's a certain amount of ignorance. A lot of the drivers have come from the station side so they understand that, but some of the drivers don't, they were direct recruits. The station side don't understand the pressures on a driver until they actually drive a train. It's a one-man business. Unless you've actually been in front of the train and understood what happens, you know, it is completely unique'. Asked if he thought his understanding of drivers had changed since he moved from station management Geoff commented: 'To understand the pressure they are under, yes. There are different pressures from the train itself. If you put it out of service because there is something wrong with it, it's your call, you know... you are the eyes and ears of the line controller... you can report what happens... you can have a discussion about it... but in the end they are going to put a train out of service on your say-so. Even running up and down the line a couple of times in the front doesn't give you that feel of what the pressure is really like. The admin side doesn't really understand how the service works at all. I've spoken to people on courses from, say, the IT section, and they ask "what does a line controller do?" They don't understand it. They don't need to, really'. Asked if he thought the whole thing would come together better if employees knew more about each others jobs Geoff said: 'I think any knowledge helps. Ignorance is a bad thing. I think it's difficult from the health and safety aspect to get that knowledge across. But anything would help. At the moment the underground has got a professional set of managers. They have gone towards recruiting graduates and trying to bring them in further up the line... they are moving around the company. Whether you can replace that London Underground knowledge with professional experience from outside I don't know. But the more the people in the company know about what everybody else does the better'.

Asked how time-served drivers viewed someone who had moved from station management into driving Geoff said: 'I'm a bit unique. Station supervisors wear a white shirt so the first thing I did was I went and got myself a blue shirt, so I didn't stand out in the crowd. It's very much what people see, isn't it? So they see somebody in the correct uniform who looks about the right age so I don't get asked too many questions, but obviously when the subject comes up I do tell them "I've only been doing this for a month or so", you know. I'm a slightly strange hybrid... I look as though I fit... so when you look around the canteen I look like one of the experienced hands... and I know how to look... but obviously I stand out because I'm looking for knowledge at the moment. I'm asking people questions. People are helpful. The first thing I learned on the underground is that you'll always find people telling you how to do the job... they might not want to help you do the job, but they'll always tell you how to do it. And, of course, people like to show their expertise. "What do you do when you're approaching Westminster station, you know, where do you start braking?" People are always prepared to help'. Asked if he would describe tube drivers as craftsmen Geoff said: 'Yes, I would guess so. It's not the sort of job you can pick up easily. Some people can't do it. Other people try and fail. At the moment it's quite a difficult job. Quite pressurised. You've got an awful lot of people's lives in your hands. If you make a wrong call you have got a lot of people you are going to have to answer to. Not many people can take that pressure and do the job. I think once you get used to it you forget it. That initial training does find people out. People have tried and failed. But there is a certain skill to bringing in two hundred tons minus the passengers when it's wet and raining and the thing has got to stop. The trainers tell you you've only got so much contact per wheel, fifty-six wheels per train, so you have got the area of a piece of A4 touching the rails as you are coming in to a station. So you have to know what you are doing, and do it properly. It's very easy just to shoot through the other side, you know. When it was six cars it was one hundred and eighty six tons. It's now seven cars – the Jubilee now has the extra carriage – so we are figuring it's two hundred and ten'.

Although Geoff was still learning the job he had thought about promotion, although he wanted to stay in train operations: 'The step up from station supervisor is duty station manager. The step up from train operator is duty manager trains. I was never interested in being the duty manager on the station side. I saw the job intimately... and didn't like it. It's more political. Very little actual power. They have got a lot of responsibility. They run the stations. It's one of these jobs where you seem to be in the middle. Duty manager trains, however, is a very specific job. You are much more involved in the day-to-day running of the railway. You handle major incidents, what we call "one unders", which is a big part of the job. It's less politics. It's more "let's get this train moving". It's more hands-on. "How are we going to get the service back and running?" I always fancied that, chancing my arm, getting as high as I could. I like change. I enjoy it. I never enjoy going for the interviews, though. I never enjoy the tests. But I do enjoy the change. Maybe I'll try for that in three years time. I'm not somebody to tell someone else to do a job I can't do myself... I'm fifty-two now. Thank God they've made the Age Discrimination Act, you know. I'm going to test that to its limit. I think it did help me get the training for this job, you know. They are very inclusive, the underground, I'll give them that. They don't just pay equal opportunities lip service'. Asked if he had encountered a macho culture on the underground Geoff said: 'I've heard of it... personality clashes, and stuff like that... I've never experienced it. My take on it was that it was people who couldn't do the job telling you to do the job. There's a fair amount of people who are, shall we say, misfits for the job, who have taken the job for its salary alone. I always dealt with that in a non-confrontational manner. I never saw the point in going head-to-head with people. You don't have to go confrontational'.

Asked to recall his worst argument at work Geoff eventually described a confrontation when he worked at a tube station: 'I've had plenty of arguments. I have gone home lots of times thinking I wish I hadn't said this. I have tried to work them out and let them go. When I was taxi driving it was always about money. When I've looked at arguments, sometimes I have been right, sometimes I have been wrong. You know, I've tried to square them away. I'll give you an example. I was training as a ticket seller at Northwood station – this is one I try and laugh at – first day on the job behind the counter. Now I don't know what I look like but I do understand what the London Underground glare looks like: "Leave me alone" sort of thing. They all practice it and they can all do it really well. A lady came up, and whatever I'd said, she said: "Do you know you underground staff are the rudest, most unhelpful people I've ever met". It wasn't that I hadn't given her a ticket. It was probably just the way I looked and somebody in London Underground somewhere along the line had messed her up. Obviously if she had seen my point of view, she would have understood a little bit more. I was looking uncomfortable – scared about doing the wrong thing. It wasn't "Why are you troubling me for a ticket", you know, the way she interpreted it. I think most arguments come from misunderstandings. When I worked at Baker Street, a big interchange station, I always thought that London Underground had done something to people – packed them in like sardines, sweated them and then thrown them out at Baker Street in a bad mood. But when I went to Northwood I met people for the first time at the start of their journey. They were like that when they started... the one per cent. It wasn't the underground that did it... maybe it was the stress of their job, of what they had to do to earn a living'.

For Geoff one of the best aspects of train driving was that at the end of his shift the job was over. There was nothing that would drag on into the next day: 'As a station supervisor I was stuck until someone came to relieve me. If there was nothing to do you did nothing. If there was something to do you had to do it. With the driving I like the idea of knowing what I'm going to be doing tomorrow. I like the idea that when I get to Wembley I'm finished. As you are going along you are just knocking off the stations. When I get to Wembley I just hand the train over to somebody else and walk out of the door. As a supervisor you never quite put the job down because stuff you were dealing with today might last for months. You know, work to be done on the station. I don't look at the clock and think "another three hours to go". I just think "when I finish this run I'm finished for the day". It's been a refreshing change. I've enjoyed the training. After three years of doing the same job this has been a real breath of fresh air to me. I started off as a station assistant in Baker Street, I was then a reserve ticket seller, moving from station to station where I was needed. Then I was a station supervisor at Canons Park, a one-man station'. Asked whether he ever brought his driving job home with him Geoff said: 'Not the actual work. I'm pretty good at picking up mechanical things. I've a feel for mechanical things. You know, to drive a train... can you feel it? Can you feel if there is something wrong with your car? I have found myself pleasantly surprised. I'm good at it. The money can be attractive to some people. You can get yourself trapped in a job where you are only doing it for the money. You don't really enjoy it. I knew what I was getting in to'.

Asked if he ever brought his work home when he was station-managing Geoff said: 'I don't think so, no. London Underground is a strange organisation in that way. So long as you have done the right thing you are OK. I wouldn't really get stressed about things. As a station supervisor you go in and you put repair jobs out. If something is wrong you just ring up somebody and say I want this sorted. If you are on holiday the world goes on. I would not say it's cynicism because people take pride in their jobs, but there is an element of "What do you expect from London Underground, you know". They pay an absolute fortune out for the work and it is never done that brilliantly. Certainly it doesn't match the price, I imagine. Stress-wise, I wasn't cynical about it. I took pride in my work, but I didn't let it get to me. I didn't let customers get to me. I mean, you can't not have arguments with people, but I used to try and do it as best I could. I learned to stand back. With train driving, it's stressful actually doing the job. You've got a thousand people or whatever on your train... but I just do the best I can. If something has gone wrong I just try and get by it – and do the next one right. You can't let things affect you. You are going to make mistakes. As long as you get yourself out of it as best you can and do the next one right you're OK. The underground is like nothing I have ever done before. Ninety-nine per cent of commuters you never speak to... because they know what they are doing, and they understand the system. Your job really is just dealing with the one per cent of people who are either panicking, or they don't understand, or they are very unhappy... but most commuters understand the system. Like the underground staff they just know what's going on'.

Geoff thought that London Underground was generally well-managed: 'Yes I think it is well managed. For the actual job it does, it's very well run. I think people vote with their feet. When I was at Canons Park travellers would come in at half past eight in the morning. They wouldn't come in at half past seven. They'd expect a train. They'd get a train. If there weren't seats in the train as they came in they'd look up and see one due in two minutes and stand back if they wanted a seat. I always thought that was them putting their faith in the system, if you know what I mean. They weren't jumping on the train saying "I've got to get on now". It wasn't "You only send one train every fifteen minutes". It's one train every two minutes in the peak, you know. London Underground really does do a fantastic job. But it's at its limits. It can't take any more. On the Jubilee we have a contract to put twenty-four trains per hour through Canary Wharf. Whoever built Canary Wharf paid a big lump of money to London Underground to build the Jubilee Line extension. The deal is they put twenty-four trains per hour through Canary Wharf in the morning and evening peak. Putting the seventh car on and running twenty-four trains per hour is as much as they can physically do. When it goes automatic they'll get rid of the signals and have a moving signals system so the trains can run closer together. I believe the actual capacity will be thirty-three but they are going to aim for thirty or thirty-one trains per hour. And that is it then. You can't add another carriage. You have gone automatic. You have got as many trains per hour through Canary Wharf as you can. They are building three more office blocks in Canary Wharf at the moment, God knows how many in the future. We'll be all right maybe for the Olympics, but that'll be it then. Unless you build Crossrail. Unless you build more lines, they physically can't take any more... the only thing is to be like Japan and have those guys cramming them into the trains'. Asked whether building more lines would help, Geoff said: 'I'm not sure. Will London keep sucking businesses in, like we said at the start, or will that go somewhere else? The City is bringing in more and more work... if that is the case they'll have to build Crossrail... the sensible answer would be to move some of it somewhere else.... If we could go back we'd build double tracks, bigger tunnels, you'd do it all differently. Bigger everything, you know. But we are stuck with what we've got. We have already gone beyond the point of cars in London. In fairness to him, I think Ken Livingstone understands what to do – what we need to build to keep London going'.

The best thing the government had done, said Geoff, was to make the Bank of England directly responsible for monetary policy: 'I'd say their best move was letting the Bank of England deal with inflation, letting go... letting the chips fall where they lie'. For Geoff pensions and prestige projects were an issue: 'The government should look after people's pensions and regulate things like that better. I don't think that governments can run big projects.... I don't think they can get involved in bankrolling projects. I can understand the problem the government has with Crossrail... Wembley Stadium... the Millennium Dome... it's very difficult to get governments to run projects. I think the best thing Thatcher did was to stay out of the Channel Tunnel project. I think they can be more transparent about pensions and what people are doing with people's money. They should concentrate on things they can do, like pensions. But it's very difficult, realising what they can or cannot do... that's half the problem'. Geoff's advice to government was, in effect, realise your limitations.

Geoff was a committed trade unionist: 'I was in the RMT. When I was a station assistant I was in TESSA. Now I'm in ASLEF. In my job trades unions are completely necessary. You definitely need union representation. It's a very complex job to do. You need to be aware of the rules. You need to be aware that the responsibility you carry could lead you into places where you need professional help and advice. I think all the working conditions we've got in this country were won by unions. I don't think any organisation will give rights to workers without a fight. I think they have laid the basis for all of our modern working practices'.

Despite his enthusiasm for trade unionism Geoff was alert to abuses: 'They do get a bit out of hand. Arthur Scargill and the likes wielding their power when it wasn't needed. I couldn't stand the old RMT with Bob sending his letter about stuff around the world rather than just concentrating on terms and conditions. I think their power has been misused in the past. The RMT is turning out now to be a very powerful trade union for the reasons we said – London needs the tube. But then you can easily abuse that power and strike for all sorts of different causes that have got nothing to do with us...'. Asked if he thought the balance of power between unions and government was wrong at the time of the Winter of Discontent Geoff said: 'Well, I think they were trying to protect things that were worthwhile. I think the Thatcher government saw it the opposite way. I think there were two extremes there.... They destroyed the coal industry between them.[9] Now it looks as though we need a viable coal industry. I think everybody in the country recognised the extremes... I think we lost something there in the middle'.

For Geoff elections were still important: 'I think we should vote. I think if we all voted we'd get a better result. I'd almost be in favour of compulsory voting. It was a hard-won right. People died for it. It's worth having. If more people voted those opinions would be better expressed, you know'. Asked if he thought he was given a real choice at election time Geoff said: 'I think you have a real choice but I think our elections are getting more presidential, so the choice is not a choice of policies or political persuasion, it's a choice of personalities. I think you have a real choice but not what we intended it to be, if you see what I mean. We are not really in a real debate any more, I think. Our politics has become presidential. I think we should call it the presidential election'. Geoff believed the two main parties had converged: 'I think they're almost indistinguishable in policies. Maybe not in style. But I think it's presidential'. Geoff believed the primary choice at the next general election would be between David Cameron and Gordon Brown 'because that's who you are handing the real power to, I think. Because I think Tony Blair has proved that. I think Margaret Thatcher proved that as well. I think that's how our government is run now. The papers portray it that way. They are after the top man all the time. I think the prime minister has always had more power than the president. They can do a lot more immediately than the president. I don't think people understand the manifestos or even really believe them, now, you know'.

Of Ken Livingstone Geoff said: 'I think he's doing a good job. I don't agree with a lot of his policies. I've been reading the *Evening Standard* long enough to remember Red Ken, and all that, but I think at the moment the guy has got a grasp of London, what it is, what it needs. I don't think he wins all his battles but I think he understands. If you took over from him would you get rid of what he has done? That's the question. I don't think anybody would. I think the Congestion Charge has been a success. I think it brings in revenue, which no organisation can do without, and I think it has kept people off the roads. He's putting things in place, like the Oyster Card... he's coshed the local railways, the franchises, into using Oyster Cards. I don't think they'll unpick what he's done. You might disagree with his politics but I think he does understand London, you know. For a left-winger... he's allowed the gherkin and the shard of glass, and all that. He's welcoming business. He does seem to understand what is needed.... But I think he knows that the Olympics and PPP[10] on the underground won't work... we'll have a massive bill afterwards. I think the cost overruns on the Olympics will be just like they were at Wembley, you know'.

London was a special city, said Geoff: 'I think there is something special about it. I read Peter Ackroyd's book about London. Both my parents were Irish, they were immigrants in the 1940s. There were signs up "No blacks or Irish", but they used to laugh about that. I think it's the same today, Polish people coming here, Asian people. London just seems to absorb all sorts, and I think it absorbs people without too much racial tension. Lots of friends have been to Germany and places like that and say it's not quite the same there, and so I think London is unique in that way. It does seem to be a melting pot. I just went in to Watford today to get some things and there was an Asian guy in full outfit with a Muslim sort of head dress and two people in front of me... there was a man and woman in their sixties and they were talking Italian. That was just going into Watford, and I thought "fair play", we just seem to do it and nobody really seems to notice. There are some stresses and strains but I think most of the problems seem to be due to youths rather than any ingrained hatred. We don't seem to have ghettos. We have areas where there are a lot of people... Edgware, Canons Park, a heavily Jewish population, but you don't really notice it as such apart from the businesses. You don't have ghettos as such. London seems to have been doing it for ever...'.

Asked what he would change if he were mayor of London he said: 'I'd improve the tube, but I'm not sure we should build more lines. If money was no object you could rebuild the whole thing properly. Also I'm a great fan of the environment. Small things. If we could improve litter and people's respect for the place... but I don't want to go as far as they do in Singapore where they get birched, and all that. We should improve people's sense of where they are. I've been to Austria recently on holiday. The place is immaculate. I'd make all the museums and art galleries free. I think education is the only way we can go with everybody, all the extremists. The only way you can go is to educate people. Get people to understand where some ideas are right and some ideas are wrong. For example, Muslims will never get their point of view heard in this country because we only hear the extreme bit... just try and get everybody understanding'. 'London... it is London' was Geoff's summation of his city. That was the end of the interview. I packed up my tools – tape recorder, spare batteries, list of questions, note pad – thanked Geoff for his time and coffee and biscuits then departed his immaculate terraced house to get a tube to Baker Street. The tube departed and arrived on time and was clean and comfortable. My ticket, however, was expensive.

7. City worker

Samantha, born in Bury St Edmunds in Suffolk in 1978, had lived in London for ten years. Both she and her partner worked in financial services, her partner for Deloitte and Samantha for a Japanese investment bank. The bank's offices were located very near St Paul's Cathedral. Samantha's educational career ended with a degree at Brunel University in west London: 'I went to prep school, then to a private school to do my GCSEs, then I left there and went to a comprehensive to do my A-levels, then went to Brunel University, Uxbridge and finished with a BA in English Literature.... I lived in Richmond and Twickenham, so I was in London, but quite far out'. Like many of those who attend a London university she decided to stay in the capital and get a job: 'I have had four different jobs since I've been here. When I was at University I worked in a restaurant in Richmond. Then I stayed there for a short time after I graduated. Then I worked briefly at the BBC. Then I worked as a "moves and changes" consultant mainly around the City. Then I worked in my current job as a team assistant at an investment bank'. Samantha described the BBC job as a bit of a curate's egg: 'It was very strange... I was a sort of hospitality coordinator so I would organise events and hospitality sessions – like drinks, after-show parties, that sort of thing'. Samantha had met quite a few celebrities through her work: 'We used to do all the hospitality for Top Gear, and all the sports programmes, so we met Gary Lineker, Jeremy Clarkson, a lot of newsreaders as well, so it was fairly interesting, actually'. On the down side Samantha could find herself getting blamed for things that were out of her control: 'It sounds very glamorous and exciting. It was actually very hard work. People were not terribly friendly or cooperative. It was the sort of job where you were only noticed if something went wrong. So it wasn't altogether a pleasant experience, which is why I only stayed there for about six months'.

Samantha felt her current job to be the best she had had since graduating: 'Although it is not a particularly exciting job, it is challenging. I have met some really interesting people through it, and I feel that I am appreciated, whereas in other roles I feel I probably wasn't. I think that's the biggest thing for me, so that's probably why I like it'. She described her work for the Japanese investment bank: 'I am a team assistant in Corporate Finance... we basically deal with clients. We sometimes bring them to the market. We might carry out an IPO [initial public offering] for them on the main market, and sometimes on other foreign exchanges as well. My responsibility is to ensure that the office runs smoothly, that people turn up when and where they are meant to, that I book travel for them, organise meetings within the office. We also have a lot of regulation to follow from the FSA [Financial Services Authority] so we have to ensure that all our documentation is up to date. We organise events, and all sorts of other ad-hoc things that might happen. We also do a lot of work on Excel [a database and spread-sheet program]. We have lots of presentations to prepare'. Samantha saw the investment bank job as a definite step-up from her job as a moves consultant: 'I was working as a consultant and I was doing really large moves and changes for investment banks and it was very stressful. I worked very long hours and I wasn't getting paid a lot of money and I realised people working for banks were doing less stressful jobs and having more time to themselves and getting paid loads more than me. To be honest I wanted to pursue other things later in life and I realised I needed money to do that. So I decided to change careers slightly. So it's purely for the money, to be honest'. Asked what she would really like to do if she had ample funds Samantha said: 'Well I'm hoping fairly soon now to be able to start my own shop so I'm saving rapidly, well, sort of, to do that. I'll probably sell women's wear... a mixture of casual and smart'.

As with most City jobs the hours could be long: 'My contractual hours are nine to five, but the hours I actually work are eight to six. Depending on how busy we are it can often be a lot longer than that. It's a bit different to what we are meant to work'. Samantha's longest working week was 'probably in the region of seventy hours when things get really busy'. Samantha did not get overtime for working longer than her contracted hours. A proper lunchtime break was almost unknown: 'To be honest none of us really take lunch as such. Every now and then when it's quiet in the summer we all go out and meet friends for lunch, but generally it's a culture of eating at your desk and just getting on with it. I don't really take lunch'. Asked how she compensated for not taking a lunch break Samantha said: 'Well I try to eat healthily and drink lots of water during the day, which often doesn't happen. If I have time I go to yoga once a week during the day as well which is quite nice. But often, again, work gets in the way of that, unfortunately'. Samantha said that if it wasn't for coffee breaks staff would be at their desks all day: 'We take it in turns to come out of the office to get coffee. So if it's your turn to do that you get a five minute respite whilst you go and buy coffee. But otherwise no, we'll be at our desks all day'. Samantha said she would find it difficult to get promoted at the bank. She was not unduly bothered by this, however: 'I'm an assistant so I can't just start doing corporate financing because I'm not an economist. I don't have an MBA... or any of that sort of thing. But I have been given a lot more responsibility. But to be honest, for me it's a means to an end. I didn't go there to be promoted. I went there for the money. So I'm not too bothered about that for the time being'.

Samantha could find her workmates somewhat irritating: 'To be honest a lot of the time I find them fairly irritating. They are obviously all very intelligent. They work very hard and they do earn a lot of money. But I think sometimes it goes to their heads, and they spend a lot of time congratulating themselves and that sort of thing.

But generally they are decent people. For the most part they are fine. Just every now and then when stresses run high they can be a bit irritating'. Samantha's employer was not the highest payer in the City: 'I would say that our salaries are relatively low compared to other banks because we started off as a sort of separate team which was started up by my boss and was then acquired by the bank. I'd say the top people earn about £200,000 [2007 salary level]. They rely more on their bonuses than actual salary to invest'. Asked to comment on the bonuses paid by her bank Samantha said: 'I do know, actually, because I'm privy to all information. I happen to know that one year our managing director received a £500,000 bonus. I'm sure that's the highest bonus that's been given out'.

Asked what she thought her colleagues thought of her Samantha said: 'I think sometimes they think I'm fairly stupid. That's the impression that they give off, anyway. I think, though, that sometimes I am oversensitive, and I don't think they actually mean it, because there are times when I know that they value my opinion. We talk about what we do in our social lives, so there is some sort of rapport'. Asked why her colleagues sometimes thought her 'fairly stupid' when she had a degree from a good British university Samantha said: 'I don't know. I think that sort of thing [Samantha's degree in English Literature] is often forgotten, because everyone I work with is either a lawyer or a doctor, so they have gone a lot further in education than I chose to, so it's slightly different I suppose in that way. I think generally they think I'm a hard-working, pleasant person, so they like me... I think'. Samantha dealt with work-place angst by 'bottling it up': 'I have never had an argument with anyone in my current job. I generally prefer to bottle it up and go home and talk to my boyfriend or friends about it. It's not really that sort of environment, thankfully'.

Samantha was clearly intelligent. It was unsurprising, therefore, to hear that she sometimes felt she was under-achieving at the bank: 'It sounds a bit arrogant but I sometimes feel that the job is beneath me, because I know that I'm more intelligent than some of the things I end up doing. But I just have to focus on what I want to achieve in the future. That helps'. Asked if she was ambitious Samantha said: 'I think I am but not in the same way that other people are. For instance I decided... I realised I didn't want to continue in academia any more after my degree because I realised it wasn't for me. But I'm definitely ambitious in other ways, sort of in an entrepreneurial way'.

It seemed that academia had conspired to alienate Samantha from her love – English literature: 'I think it was the fact that I did a degree in English literature that turned me off academia. Although I really enjoyed the degree, I think I probably went into it not really having given it too much consideration. I think I did it because I was always good at English, and I enjoyed it. But with hindsight that probably wasn't the most sensible choice. I realised as well that it was taking my enjoyment of literature away. In my final year I did a lot of work on Charles Dickens. At one point I was having to read one Dickens novel a week. If anything it became a chore rather than an enjoyment, and I just realised that my heart wasn't in it. That's why I decided that academia was not for me'. Asked if she had fallen back in love with literature Samantha said: 'Yes. It took about a year. I found it was quite difficult to ask for help at university, because I have always felt that asking for help was a sign of weakness, so I must admit that I felt very isolated from lecturers at university... I didn't really feel that I needed any help particularly, so I never went to them, so I think I probably missed out on a lot – guidance-wise from lecturers – which was probably a mistake on my part. I probably contributed to it'.

Returning to the subject of work Samantha described her boss: 'I think he's a really kind man, actually, which is quite surprising in the City. He's not the normal type of person that works there. He's very laid-back. He's got lots of children and dogs. He's obviously very fond of them, which is nice.[11] He's quite good fun to go out with. He likes a drink. He smokes like a chimney. He's quite politically incorrect, which is quite refreshing sometimes. He can be quite funny. And he's a very kind person. I know that a couple of years ago he didn't take a bonus himself so the rest of the team could benefit. I found that out through someone else, so I'm pretty sure it's true. So I respect him. He's very smart as well'. Samantha thought her boss liked her: 'I think he likes me. I'm pretty sure that he thinks I'm sometimes too quiet, and other people make a big fuss about things and get their own way, and he feels I should make more of a fuss about things. He has told me that, actually'.

Samantha thought the bank was generally well managed: 'I do think it's well run. Having worked for a small family business before this, people are listened to and content. We don't actually have appraisals. My boss doesn't like doing them. So we're a bit abnormal in that respect. If anyone has a problem we all have people we can speak to, and most of the team have been working together for quite some time so there's quite a good rapport between people. It seems to work very well'. Asked about the size of the enterprise Samantha said: 'There are about two thousand in the bank's London office and there are thirty-two in our team.... Lehman Brothers have seven thousand in London alone, so when you think of it like that our office is really small'. Remuneration was something of an issue for Samantha: 'Well actually no, I guess I'm not paid a fair rate. It all rather hinges on what bonus we get every year, because obviously we don't get overtime. We work very long hours, and there have been times when I've worked weekends. But I don't mind doing that because I know that I'll hopefully get remunerated in a nice way. Last year was pretty good, but unfortunately this year everyone is quite concerned that it's not going to be the same. We all feel that we've put in a lot of hard work this year and we probably won't see any benefit from it. I think my basic salary is perfectly acceptable, though'.

Samantha had always lived in rented accommodation. At the time of the interview she was renting a one-bedroomed flat in Putney with her partner: 'It's a garden flat. We've got one bedroom, a kitchen, sitting room, toilet and garden, and a cellar. Because there are two of us sharing a small flat we were able to afford something quite nice. It's nicely decorated. It's clean, has a garden so we've got outdoor space. We've got room to put all my books, all our accumulated belongings, which makes a lot of difference. Putney is a nice area. Friendly people and close to amenities, that sort of thing. I like Putney's outdoor spaces, like the river. It's quite pretty. It doesn't feel too dirty or "inner-city" like other places I have lived in. It's peaceful and it feels fairly safe as well'. Asked which was the worst locale she had lived in Samantha said: 'Stoke Newington. But I think a lot of that was due to the fact that I didn't like who I was living with. It was a horrible flat as well, I'm sure that had an impact. This was a few years ago, and I think it has become a lot more trendy now and it seems to be a place where a lot of young couples buy houses. I'm sure it's a very nice place but I didn't enjoy my time there'. Samantha's ideal locale was south-east London: 'I just moved recently from Blackheath and I really liked living there, again because of the park and the heath. I am the outdoor type so I would probably buy somewhere there if I had the money. My dad's family came from Limehouse originally so I don't know whether that has something to do with it. And he's in the Navy, so perhaps there's a connection there'.

Samantha's pastimes included long-distance running and shopping: 'I have some hobbies. I love ballet, so I go to the ballet quite a lot. I'm also quite a keen runner. I have just done the marathon and I have got a half-marathon coming up soon. I'm constantly running, training for those. And I also enjoy shopping, which is a bit shallow, but I quite enjoy it'. Asked why she had taken up running Samantha said: 'Originally because I wanted to give up smoking, and also because I was never any good at sport at school and I wanted to prove to myself that I could do it and I actually really enjoy it now, surprisingly... I kept at it'. Asked if she thought there was anything special about the London Marathon she said: 'I think there is. I've done other runs where you run around a town and there's no-one watching... I think it's quite special to run around parts of London that you wouldn't normally get to run on, like main roads. And the crowds, especially in the East End, are amazing. They really spur you on, so it's quite moving, actually. I think that's probably why it is so enjoyable'.

Samantha thought the government had done some good things for working people, like regulation of hours worked, but felt the government could do more for women: 'They could do a lot more to help women go back to work after they have had children... perhaps single mothers as well.... I think a lot of women don't fulfil their potential because they can't afford to go back to work. So I think that would be something the government could do'. Asked what practical steps the government could take Samantha said: 'I don't know where they would get the money from, to be honest, but I suppose some sort of crèche scheme. In an ideal world it could be sponsored by large corporations. I think there's a lot of wasted talent, and I think a lot of people, women in particular, get stuck in a rut, and don't ever manage to get out of it, so I feel for them. Having said that I don't know how easy it would be to implement'. Asked whether getting stuck in a rut with children was something she feared Samantha said: 'Yes, definitely. I don't think I would like that at all. I would like to have children, but I don't think I would have them until I had managed to make sure I was in a place where I was happy to have a break from'.

Samantha, who was not in a trades union, had some issues with the movement: 'The only impression I get of them at the moment is the transport unions [Samantha caught a tube to work]. They seem to make a lot of fuss out of nothing. I don't know if it's true but I heard a couple of years ago that they were threatening to go on strike because they felt they were working too long underground, which seems completely ridiculous. I would say most people think the transport unions make a lot of fuss out of nothing, but I don't really know about other unions, I must admit'.

Ken Livingstone had done some good work, thought Samantha: 'Although I sometimes find him a bit irritating I think he's done a really good thing with the Congestion Charge because I'm quite anti-car, and I think that's fantastic... I've never had a car, actually. I appreciate that for some people the charge has made things very difficult, like businesses, people with children, but I think it's for a greater good, to be honest, for the city as well as for the environment.... Other than that I must admit I don't know an awful lot about what he has done. I think there are more buses, and I think they are more frequent, although I do miss the Routemasters... they were a lot quicker. Although they were a lot smaller, you could just jump on and jump off. They were just more fun. I do miss them, although they were quite dangerous. I have fallen off one before'.

Samantha thought there was something special about London: 'I would definitely say there was something special about it. I know that I deliberately chose my degree course to be on the outskirts of London because I wanted to live here. I just think it's a fascinating melting pot of all sorts of people. And I think that for me the most interesting thing is that it is so ancient as well. Wherever you look there are so many different styles of architecture.... I think it is completely unique, in that sense, to any other city I have ever visited'. Asked whether she thought of London as more of a city state than the capital of Britain Samantha said: 'I think to a certain extent it is quite insular because I think people within London, especially people who work here – especially in the City – sort of think that everyone outside London is pretty much unimportant. They don't contribute a lot to the economy. I think people who live here have a certain attitude... a slight snobbishness, almost, that it's a superior place to live and work'.

Samantha was bothered by antisocial behaviour and crime: 'If I was mayor I would encourage people to stop dropping litter. I would have some sort of compulsory tutorial in manners, because I think that people are really, really rude. I think it has a bad knock-on effect. If someone is rude to you I think you can get quite angry. I don't know why, I think you get too embroiled in it, and then you pass that on. I don't know how you could change that. Possibly by having opera played on the tube. I've heard that that works. And I think I'd like to help teenagers who seem to have no hope. I don't know how easy it would be but I think I would like to go a long way to helping them to realise they have potential and that there is more that they can do… I feel they are the future. It seems to be a real problem with young black men… they don't seem to feel they have a place in society, a valid place'. Asked why she thought a section of society was being left behind Samantha said: 'I don't really know. I think a lot of it has to do with their parenting. I don't necessarily blame their parents. But I think, having spoken to friends who are teachers in inner-city schools, they don't really have any discipline at home. And they don't have role models, perhaps, which obviously isn't their fault. I also think that we learn from our parents, and if your parents don't go to work, there's nothing for you to aim for, and, conversely, if people are really spoilt as teenagers they have nothing to aim for either, so I think that has a lot to do with it. I also think that just the places that they live are pretty grim. I have a friend who works in Bermondsey, and a lot of her pupils come from an estate nearby, and it just feels a really desolate and forgotten place. I think living there must affect you. I also think there's a lot of fear which drives young men to carry weapons because they are afraid for their safety. And I suppose it all comes down to drug culture as well, which is why people are more likely to carry weapons. I don't really know what can be done about that, but I am sure that's one of the causes of all the problems'. Asked if she had ever been a victim of crime Samantha said: 'I have, a few times. I used to live in Highbury with a friend of mine. We lived in a really posh road, and we had a lovely flat… her dad owned it. I was coming home one night, I think it was January, and I had a hat on, and I think I was followed all the way down my road by two men who pulled my bag off me. It was quite late actually. I followed them up the road. I was quite badly injured as well because unfortunately I wouldn't let them take it at first. I called the police and all the rest of it. I got my bag back the next day because they had literally taken out a few bits of change and thrown it over someone's wall, and actually last week I had my wallet stolen on the tube, so I have had a few experiences of crime. But I think it was partly my own carelessness being out late at night alone. Also it's just an opportunist thing. I have never been particularly bothered by it but I've been more careful about my own safety since then'. Asked if the episode had affected her outlook and confidence Samantha said: 'No. A lot of people have asked me since… because I was mugged by two black men… "Do you find yourself wary around certain people?" To be honest, not at all. It is just I wouldn't like to be out late at night and be in the vicinity of anyone I didn't know, to be honest'.

Samantha believed that politics still mattered and that one should always vote: 'Yes one should vote. I think it's really important that you make your voice heard, especially for women, because people went to a lot of trouble to make sure we got the vote. I really think it's down to us to make the effort to go down there and vote, even if we don't necessarily know a lot about it. I think it's important to read the literature you get given beforehand and make some effort'. Asked if she thought she was offered a real choice at election times Samantha said: 'I must admit I do feel a bit apathetic at the moment about politics. I don't really see a lot of difference between many of the parties or the people standing. I don't know if that's my fault for not making enough effort to get to know about it or if it's just badly communicated. I'm not entirely sure, actually'. Asked if she had become cynical about politics Samantha said: 'Yes, possibly a little bit. But I think it's more the fact that there seems to be so much red tape, especially in London, just to get anything done. Getting a parking permit can take months. Getting a doctor's appointment seems to be nigh on impossible. It's quite frustrating'.

Despite being frustrated by certain aspects of London life Samantha was looking forward to the 2012 Olympics: 'I think it will be a good thing in the sense that hopefully some areas in the East End will be regenerated... I think jobs will be very welcome if that does happen. But I wonder what will happen after the Olympics is over, actually, and what will happen to those people and all the buildings? I also feel it's a shame that they are knocking down quite a lot of interesting buildings, although a lot of those communities were broken up anyway after the Blitz. I hope it will be a good thing, but I'm a bit sceptical'.

I had conducted the interview in a City coffee bar, its clientele a mixture of gawking tourists and suits. Inevitably the staff was mostly from mainland Europe. The coffee was drinkable but pretentious and expensive – an allegory for New Labour's Britain, perhaps?

Verstehen

One of the most glaring deficiencies in British public administration is the capital-revenue trap. Central and local government can be very good at finding money for grandiose and generally useful projects. At the same time the authorities can be very bad at securing long-term revenue funding for their upkeep. It is one thing to build a thoughtfully designed, well-served, mixed-tenancy housing estate. It is quite another to secure adequate revenue funding for its maintenance and, indeed, long-term development and improvement. We seem to have a knack of throwing money at a problem without thinking through the long-term consequences of our initial interest in that problem (whether it be tackling drug abuse, replacing antisocial tower blocks or beautifying cityscapes with trees, flower beds and new street furniture). I am in the habit of cycling around London. It's a great way of getting under the skin of our capital city. You see so much more than you do from a bus, train or car. You not only see London. You hear and smell it. You perceive its texture. I have cycled up and down the Lea Valley, a long ribbon of green space and water that stretches from the capital's northern boundary to the Thames. Like most of London's open spaces the Lea Valley is peppered with industrial and leisure developments. Many of these developments are in a state of significant disrepair. The trading estates are shabby. They are vandalised. They are dark (often because their street lights have been shot out). They are used for illegal dumping. They are used for prostitution. The leisure developments are unpainted and dilapidated. Why? Why is it that managing agents and councils and government departments feel they can get away with doing so little? Is it because they believe Londoners won't notice? Or that Londoners don't care? Would business people, councillors and civil servants be as disrespectful of their own neighbourhoods? Why do they feel they can behave exactly as they want in places like the Lea Valley?

8. The London Underground manager

Derek was born in 1950 in Walthamstow. Married with three children, his partner worked as a health visitor. After leaving school with A-levels he went into banking where he took the Institute of Bankers Examinations with Barclays Bank. He then worked in the brewing industry and on London Underground. As a trade union health and safety representative with the Transport and Salaried Staff Association (TSSA) he was taking various health and safety qualifications. 'I'm on the third level TUC health and safety course at the moment' he said.

Derek described his careers in banking, the brewing industry and public transport: 'I worked for Barclays Bank between eighteen and twenty-one. When I went to the Middle East it did not quite turn out as I expected it to, so after my spell there – I worked in Abu Dhabi between 1971 and 1973 for the British Bank of the Middle East – I asked to rejoin Barclays Bank. I was with them from 1973 until 1995, when they said that they were getting rid of staff. There was a huge cull of staff especially in my grade, and you could see that the industry was being dramatically re-shaped. I worked for them in West End offices until 1995 when I became what was euphemistically called a voluntary leaver. So I decided to jump rather than be pushed. Part of the deal was that I went to an out-placement agency, and they helped you to find jobs. They are not an employment agency as such, but they help you to shape CVs and write letters, and gain skills for interviews and so on and so forth. I was there for a week. While I was there I met a chap who was a surveyor for Allied Domecq. His offices were relocating from Buckinghamshire to Leeds. He did not want to go. So he had gone to this agency because it was part of their deal. And I was talking to him and he asked me about my hobbies. I said my main one is making beer at home. He said Allied had got the Firkin Brewery and asked me if I'd be interested in a contact name and number? I jumped at the chance. I called this person. I was out of work for six weeks from Barclays Bank until I got my job with the Firkin Brewery. I was brewing beer for them for about two and a half years. But it was a very dirty, messy job, and it was quite tiring as well because you were expected to run the place on your own. You did the whole process from start to finish on your own. Making the beer. Casking it. Filling all the forms out to sell it to the pubs. If anything was wrong you would have to go to the pub which had a problem with the beer. It was quite difficult, hard and heavy work. I was looking around. It was just before the Jubilee Line extension was opened. It was 1998. They were actually recruiting staff then for the underground, specifically for the line. I had an interview with London Underground. I must say it was really overkill because they did assessments on mathematics, English and how to communicate. We even had an exercise where we sat around a table and we had to problem-solve. I realised from the outset it wasn't the task they wanted you to complete it was how you interacted with other people. I got the job and started working with London Underground in 1998. I'm now a station supervisor... I'm on the highest grade there is at the moment, SS1'.

Derek's worst work experience occurred towards the end of his time with Barclays: 'It was just before my final departure from Barclays. This was in 1995. I opted to take the severance package. It included a year's salary as a cash lump sum, and the option to have a pension at the age of 50 and several other things. The drawbacks were that I had to repay or reschedule any personal loans I had. After about four months they said to me "we are going to take you off what you are doing at the moment. We would like you to archive a lot of paperwork and boxes to go to our archiving storehouse." I said "Well I can't do that during the week because there are people working. It is really a weekend job." They said "don't worry we'll pay you whatever overtime you put in." So I did this archive work with another chap. We worked in two locations. The first was 137 Brompton Road, opposite Harrods. We were working in those cellars you see under the pavements. You know the sort, with glass plates in the pavement... we could see vague shadows passing overhead. I could not stretch to full height under there. We were stooping trying to get these boxes out. They were filthy. There had been damp in there. Cobwebs. Dirt. Dust. At the end of a stint if you blew your nose you would have like black gunge coming out. I went down there in rough clothes every morning, and when I got there changed into even rougher clothes. I did all this work for them, archiving, putting labels on boxes, and what have you. I felt really upset that I'd reached a certain level, sort of managerial level in the bank, and they had pulled me out and asked me to do this. Well I did it anyway. The saving grace was that because I said I was doing weekend work we used to inflate the hours and my final net salary in December 1995 was £3,000. I was doing this with another guy. One weekend I said to him – because I was absolutely pooped doing this. It was heavy work, pushing trolleys around, stacking stuff up, putting stuff that needed to be binned in bags, and so on and so forth – I said to him why don't we just claim for this weekend and we won't bother to go in? We'll start again the following week. And he said "that's fine". So we put the chit in, and it all got accepted. I felt as though I was getting my own back for them making me redundant. That final job for Barclays was really awful, filthy work. It was worse than working in the brewery'. The best job, said Derek, was working for the British Bank of the Middle East: 'The best job was working for the British Bank in their London office, because I was getting orientation there. I was a spare body, and I was able to go to departments just to sit in, not actually to do any work, just to listen and gather information. They encouraged me to study for the Institute of Bankers examinations. They gave me several mornings per week just to study for my examinations...'.

Derek described his current job: 'London Underground has "Centurion" managers. They are in charge of a group of stations. There are six stations in the Wembley Park Group. As a reserve supervisor I get to manage a station in turn. Sometimes when there's a surplus of people you do what we call spare duties. You go to a station and try to find something to do. You tend to go from feast to famine. At the moment we are in the summer holiday period and we get three weeks summer leave. We get our holidays imposed on us. We get two weeks for spring. Three weeks in the summer, two weeks in autumn. Then there is another two odd weeks later on in the year. You have to bear in mind the only bank holiday we get off is Christmas Day. We work bank holidays and Saturdays and Sundays. It's tit for tat. At Wembley Park I could have up to fifteen people working under me. Wembley Park is a big station. And now the new Wembley Stadium has opened we are dealing with events. If you have an event team you are talking about thirty staff, and then you have got all the police. My main concern at Wembley Park would be to do TRANSEC checks. Because of the bombings we are expected to check large stations once an hour. We are expected to make sure the service is running properly. We'd have to assist in de-training trains… do paperwork. The other stations are slightly different in that they are scaled down and they'd expect the supervisor to sell tickets and do everything else as well. At somewhere like Neasden you'd be working with a ticket seller, and a station assistant, so there would only be three of you on duty at any one time. At night time we have night supervisors who work from eleven until seven in the morning. That's to book on contractors who work during engineering hours. You'd be on your own. You'd be seeing the last trains out. But you could have drunks in the station, weirdos. A supervisor was assaulted the other day by a bloke who was not only drunk, he was on drugs and he was taking medication for being schizophrenic. It is something we have to look at in our health and safety meeting. The job can be fraught with difficulty. When I worked at the bank, I was dealing with a fair number of people, but they all came from pretty much the same background. The staff at London Underground come from all races, gender types, and what-not, so it's more difficult. You have a huge spectrum to deal with. Then you have the people who use the service. They range from being a well-heeled businessman to a vagrant. If there is something that needs to be done to maintain the service, that takes priority.'

The shift pattern and overtime could be tiring and stressful, said Derek: 'At the moment because they are short-staffed they will probably ask people to work overtime. The union has gained a thirty-five-hour week. But on our shift patterns you cannot work that. You have three men working through twenty-four hours which means eight hours each. You get a thirty-minute unpaid meal break, so that's seven and a half hours. You will find that most people who work for the public services have an unpaid meal break. The unions have pressed management to have it paid but the company are loath to do that. You are supposed to have a half-hour undisturbed meal break, but more often than not someone will bang on the door. Because you are the supervisor you have got to deal with whatever problem it is and try and go back to your sandwiches or shut your eyes for ten minutes. It is very, very tiring work, very tiring. Shift patterns? For rostered staff it's normally from 07:00 to 15:00, then 15:00 to 23:00, then the night-man comes in. The problem with this is that you have to have very good administrative staff with their eye on the ball to organise it. Unfortunately for the last couple of years we haven't had the staff. So you could be working and it's getting on for half past two. You look and see who your relief is. "Oh, there isn't one. I wonder if someone is going to turn up?" You ring your duty manager... and you ask "Who is coming in to relieve me?" Then you get "Oh they haven't put anything down. Can you stay on for a few hours?" So you are geared up to go, and then you have the rug pulled from underneath your feet. Some people can be extremely bolshie. They say "Look, my contracted hours are until 15:00. I'll leave the keys with somebody on the station and you can sort it out yourself". A lot of people are not as bloody-minded as that, and they will try to accommodate. But it seems to be happening so often on our group that the morale is pretty low. We have lost some administrative staff who were very good at rostering. They understood the roster patterns. They understood that if there was a problem at short notice – say someone went sick – who they could pull in to fill the gap. We had a guy a couple of years ago. He didn't have his eye on the ball. He had me working on three consecutive days. He had me doing an early shift. Then I went the following day onto a late shift. Then he wanted me to do a night shift as a favour. When you have to get up at 05:00 to do an early turn, the following day your sleep pattern is all over the place. You tend to get up early. When you are on "earlies" you tend to get up at the same time every morning. For example, I woke up at five this morning. I have been on earlies. I tried to go back to sleep until six, but I couldn't sleep any more. And to go from one shift pattern to another like that, bang, bang, bang, I felt absolutely drained at the end of it, and I swore I would never do it again. I get this kind of grinding noise in my ears. It is like when you are under the water... I don't know if you have ever heard that sound of the sand sliding around. Sometimes I get that in my ears. It's lack of sleep and stress. Sometimes you are sitting in a chair at work and your eyes close, and you'll hear a noise and you'll wake up with a start. You have just dropped off to sleep. It just happens like that. All of a sudden you will hear the phone... so you have to shuffle out and deal with something. Shift working is really difficult. We jump from one shift pattern to another – you do a week of earlies, then lates, then nights. They say it takes years off your life, doing shift work, and I can believe it. It is very stressful and tiring. So when I got my annual leave I just flaked out. I tried to recharge my batteries'.

Derek generally got on well with his London Underground colleagues: 'They come from all parts of society. I've got a lot of respect for the guy who works for the RMT. He does health and safety with me. He's very keen. People come from all over the place. By and large they are very easy to get on with. We are all in the same boat. We all work shitty hours. You get a kind of camaraderie. You do get the odd person. There is one guy – he is a real mickey-taker. He's been working for the company for about six or seven years, and he's always had Christmas off, because he's always gone sick'. Derek thought he was generally liked. He'd started at the bottom of his third profession: 'I would like to think that they think of me as being relaxed and laid back and fair with them. When I started this job in 1998 I started as a station assistant, which is the lowest grade. So I started from the bottom again. Some of the supervisors were very good to me'. Derek had doubts about seeking further promotion: 'Several of my colleagues have tried to get promoted to duty manager. I would not like to do that. As a supervisor I stay in my position until I want to work somewhere else on the network. At the moment I don't want to go anywhere else. If I'm asked to work extra hours I get paid for it.... In Barclays they expected you to do extra work and they didn't pay you for it. The unions are quite strong on the underground, and they weren't in the Bank. On the underground if you work overtime you get paid for it. You actually have a lever there. If you are running a station and it's only you there, you can turn around and say "I'm sorry, my contracted hours are this and I'm not working any more. I'll give the keys to somebody". So duty managers can be dealing with some very bolshie staff. We also have some people who mickey-take – who play the rules. As a supervisor you are where you want to be. The pay is very, very good. But the pay is compensation for the dreadful hours and non-existent social life. Apparently there's a fifty per cent turnover of raw recruits in the first year. You do see this. They come in and they say "I can't do this. I haven't got time for my girlfriend or boyfriend. I can't go out in the evening". They tend to drift away. Older employees are the more stable ones. People whose children have left home, you know, who have got teenaged kids, and what not. I'm very interested in the health and safety aspects. That is a lever against the managers because health and safety law is enshrined. If I see something that is contrary to the Health and Safety at Work Act I will tell management they are breaking the law. The strange thing is I get lots of training on this and "paid release" to do it. The managers have very scant training on it. So I probably know a lot more than they do, which is rather odd'. Derek was absolutely determined not to become a duty manager: 'Managers are told where they work, so they don't have a choice. That's why I don't want to become a manager. They can work extra time and don't get paid overtime for it. I knew one once who went twenty-four hours without a break because there was no cover. Fat chance I'd do that. You have to actually manage people. So if you became a duty manager you would not want to work with the group where you'd been a supervisor, because people look at you in a completely different way. Truth to tell their pay isn't much better than mine with overtime. So it's a no-brainer'.

Derek tried to avoid arguing with colleagues, although his superiors could sometimes be abrasive: 'I always try to get round arguing with people. The managers we have got have come up through the ranks, like anybody else. A lot of them don't have any school qualifications. I think their man-management skills are appalling. They tend to dictate to you. Sometimes when you can get your own back without them knowing you do it. I have done this. Revenge is sweet. I've had rows with customers as well. Sometimes they swear at you, and normally I just shy away from it. But sometimes if you've had a bad day, you'll start back at them and that's when it flares up. It's the worst thing you can do'. The best thing about the job was the pay: 'The money, first of all. That's the best thing. Plus, now that we've got this extra leave, the fact that I can have time off. The only down side is that they tell you which weeks you will have off. If you want to change your holiday you've actually got to approach somebody and swap with them…. So the pay and holidays are good, but that is balanced by the fact that shift work is shitty and the hours are shitty'. For Derek the worst thing about his job was 'the stress of shift work and appalling hours. Getting up at 05:00 is especially bad in the winter when it's cold. You have icy road conditions. It's pitch black. So you're stomping around a freezing cold station, the office is cold, and what not'. As with many city jobs the journey to work could be problematic: 'I have had problems because I drive on the North Circular… I do tend to leave extra early, because the journey time is normally an hour, so I'll generally give myself an hour and ten minutes to be there early. I have known it to take an hour and a half. However, if I'm up at five to be out of the house by half past five I can get there in thirty-five minutes, because there's no traffic on the road. I know where all the speed cameras are, so I know which bits I can speed on. I have done eighty on the North Circular. When there's no traffic it's wonderful'.

Derek's time in work was not made any easier by his troubled relationship with his boss: 'My boss is a duty manager seconded as a group manager. I find him particularly obnoxious because of the spin he puts on things when he's doing his job. He's always looking at the more positive aspects of what the company are pushing out, and he won't say anything about the pitfalls. He's very difficult to deal with… but a lot of managers are like that. When we had health and safety meetings his predecessor used to say "no problem, no problem, just put it down on paper and we'll have a look at it". You'd put it down on paper and wait and wait and wait and nothing got done. That was another technique. Give me what you've got, and I'll just sit on it'. As to what Derek thought his boss thought of him he said: 'Probably not a lot. He thinks I'm a bolshie troublemaker. Someone who's always stirring up trouble. He's been pretty short with me, on more than one occasion. That's what he thinks of me'.

Derek thought London Underground's size could make it difficult to manage and adapt to changing circumstances: 'London Underground is like a supertanker. You have got this huge body that is going at a particular pace and it's difficult to turn it around. That's why they brought these Americans in…. We have this all-singing, all-dancing Oyster Card. Whilst it's a reasonably good product, they've brought in some things. For example, if you've got pre-paid where you put money on the card, if you don't touch in and touch out [Oyster Cards must be scanned at the beginning and conclusion of every journey] it charges you the maximum cash ticket fare. Don't forget there are a lot of immigrants who can't properly read and speak English. I had one woman who came up to me one day who said "This card is so expensive". But I saw that she had made three incomplete journeys in a week. The company has launched this thing and we are having to deal with it. When we have events at Wembley Park our managers encourage us to flog Oyster Cards to visitors. My RMT colleague said "If Manchester United are playing Coventry how many are going to be interested in having an Oyster Card? They are going to be as much use to visiting supporters as a chocolate tea pot." So I wrote to our general manager and explained the problems. Managers just don't listen to people at grass-roots level – and I actually mean listen, not just hear. They hear stuff and don't do anything about it'.

All things considered Derek thought he was paid a fair rate for the job, although working for London Underground was no bed of roses: 'I think it's the appropriate rate... not a lot of people can hack shift work... your social life is deplorable. People say we are overpaid. I have actually sat with a driver. It's one of the most boring jobs in the world. They are working an eight-hour shift and they can't afford to lose concentration for one second – despite the fact they might have got up at four o'clock that morning and started driving a train at five. If they lose their concentration they may get a SPAD [signal passed at danger]. Then they get disciplined. I have seen drivers who have had problems of that nature. If they hit two in six months, they get stood down. Very often they'll be asked to work as a station assistant. They call it being "dipped". They lose their driver's pay, so they go from £34,000 [2007 wage levels] down to about £17,500. I've seen marriages break up because of it. One driver got dipped because of a couple of problems he'd had. He was told he may be reinstated in about nine months. His wife left him. He was living up to his income. It's not all a bed of roses'.

At the time of the interview Derek lived in a comfortable, well-maintained and tastefully decorated house in Seven Kings in north-east London. The London boy had not always had it so easy, however: 'I lived at home from six to twenty-eight when I got married. In that time my parents were scrimping and scraping to pay off a mortgage they got from Redbridge Council. When my mother and father got married in 1949 they lived in the house my grandfather had rented in Walthamstow. They had me in 1950 and my brother in 1952. But they only shared two rooms there. There was a bedroom for all four of us. My grandfather had the rest of the house. The kitchen was shared. The toilet was an outside privy. I remember when I was a kid I wanted to go to the toilet one evening in the winter time and I wanted to do a number two. I can remember going into this really dark yard and opening the door and it was absolutely freezing. It was the middle of winter. And I was just sitting there looking at the clouds going past the moon above the gap in the door. My mother used to wash with a "copper". She used to boil the clothes in a copper, and then she used to put them through the old hand-wound mangle. We used to have to share the bath water. We had an old tin bath. It used to hang outside in the yard on a nail. Sometimes the cats had urinated in there so mum had to rinse it out with carbolic just to get rid of the smell. Then we'd have a bath one after the other. In 1956 we moved to Woodford Bridge from Walthamstow. I was six. I've never lived in rented accommodation. I lived with my parents, then when I got married I moved into a house that my wife had got mortgaged. I took the mortgage over because I was with the bank, and so on. Then we moved here about twenty-three years ago, to this house'. Derek and his wife had put money into their long-term residence: 'We had this house extended some years ago because with three kids we felt we needed an extra toilet and shower room, so we extended it at the back... you could say it's a four-bedroomed house'. Derek was proud of his post code: 'This is Newbury Park. It's adjacent to Seven Kings, but we always say Newbury Park because it sounds posher'. According to Derek Newbury Park *aka* Seven Kings 'was convenient for London. It has excellent transport. The underground station and national rail are just down the road. Plenty of buses. The number 25 goes straight into central London. Some years ago they decided to stop the M11 at Redbridge, so consequently in the rush hour you get loads of traffic coming from north to south hitting the Redbridge roundabout. It has to fan out somewhere so it causes a lot of congestion in this part of the borough'.

Although Derek liked the physical proximity to London he felt the area was changing: 'The accommodation is fine. It is just that the area has changed somewhat. My wife and I are thinking of moving away, possibly with me taking early retirement at sixty, in three years time, and moving out of London. By and large I've been quite happy here'. Later in the interview Derek was more forthcoming about the changes he was seeing and what he thought of them: 'This community has changed so much in recent years. Redbridge Borough Council adopted a policy of taking in asylum seekers from other boroughs. The poorer part of Ilford, the Loxford area, which is in south Ilford, has been flooded. There's been a huge influx over the past few years of a mixed Asian population. I now almost feel alienated when I go to Ilford. It's like the Tower of Babel. You hear so many languages you feel like a foreigner in your own country. My wife and I just had a few days in east Sussex. It's a beautiful part of the world. I think if I retired I'd move down there if I could. It's virtually unspoilt. Beautiful countryside. It's like I remember England about thirty or forty years ago'. Asked where in London he would most like to live Derek said: 'I think somewhere like Totteridge Lane. If I won the lottery I would buy a house there, or in Mill Hill, because there are some sweeping panoramic views there. It is still relatively unspoilt. Also Carshalton'.

Working on the underground had a major impact on Derek's social life. Asked how many nights out he would have in a week Derek answered: 'Probably none. I normally have about one night out a month, when I go to my union branch meeting. I went to one yesterday in Euston. I don't really go out that much in the evening at all, by virtue of the fact that I do shift work. London Underground has a no alcohol policy, so that prohibits... puts a real crimp on my social life... the nature of my job virtually prohibits me from making any plans. I'm also what they call a reserve supervisor, which means I could go on any one of six stations, so I'm not permanently at any one place. I cover for people who are sick, on holiday, and so on. We are supposed to have twenty-eight days notice of duties in advance, so you can see that I can't plan ahead. I actually put a grievance in with the company because they are not giving us enough advanced notice. At the moment I am only getting two weeks notice. I certainly would not go into central London unless I could help it. I had enough of that when I worked for Barclays. I commuted for twenty-four years'. Derek had no personal hobbies. His spare time seemed to be taken up with work-related activities: 'My union activities and my health and safety work are my hobbies. I gave up making my own beer because it is now cheaper to buy it. I have not got the time to do it. I do some DIY though. In London it is now difficult to get people to do small jobs for you'. Derek described his experience of immigrant labour: 'We did have some Kosovans – this fellow and his brother – to do some tiling and put a kitchen in. We asked them if they were able to do that, and they said "yes, we've done it before". We took them at their word. They seemed to have so much work it was very difficult for them to plan ahead. I did notice that two of them started the tiling, but the following day only one appeared, because one of them had gone off to do another job. Basically they see London as a gold mine. They can do as much work as they can handle. I think they want to make as much money as they can then go back to wherever they come from with a nest egg. I got the impression they were trying to do as much work as they could. Because of that they were spreading their resources around'.

On the subject of national politics Derek praised the government's national minimum wage policy: 'I think the minimum wage is the best thing they've done. I've been to Brick Lane and seen Bengalis working in leather sweat-shops and the conditions were appalling. Having said that, I went about twenty-five years ago, and I went quite recently and all these places have disappeared. They are all restaurants. The guys who were working in these shops... the complexion has changed completely now.... When you think that the East End area of Brick Lane used to be home to Russian and Polish Jews after the Pogroms in the nineteenth century. Previous to that you have French street names from when the Huguenots were displaced... now you've got the Bengalis moving in. One wave of immigrants displaces another. But the area is still grindingly poor'.

Verstehen

During my time in London I have lived in numerous locales. I've lived in Brixton, Pinner, Uxbridge, South Ealing, Ealing Green, Tottenham, Enfield and, I am proud to say, the East End, specifically Plaistow. It's true what they say about the East End – there's nowhere else like it in the Great Wen. It has a feel all of its own. It's difficult to define, but I'll try. The East End is a hard-edged place. It isn't pretty. Hitler and post-war university-educated town planners saw to that. It isn't particularly friendly. Crime, alienation, racism and mutual distrust see to that. But it is likeable. I liked the bleakness of it. I liked the tracts of urban desolation, especially in Docklands. In Docklands you had a horizon. In Docklands you could stand under a big sky. In Docklands you could feel a bitter wind – even at the height of summer. You weren't so much in a city as in a vast urban plain. I learned a lot from my landlord Mr Schwartz. I learned how to judge situations and people. I learned to be pragmatic. I learned when to jump in and when not. I grew up. There's a beauty in brick and concrete. It's hard to explain. But you know it when you find it. The East End is my spiritual home.

Derek felt the government could do more to promote health and safety in the workplace: 'I'm a health and safety representative. The TUC has been pushing for a number of changes to be made in health and safety legislation. I am very conscious of the number of accidents that take place each year at workplaces that are avoidable'. Derek believed the underground to be a safe place to work, however: 'On the underground we have a really, really strict safety regime, so I would say that the safety regime on the underground is second to none. That's only because the unions have insisted on having the appropriate number of health and safety representatives and the unions are very strong. It's in places like construction. A short while ago a crane collapsed and two guys lost their lives. This kind of thing should not be allowed to happen. A lot of people who were working on the new Wembley Stadium were Russian and Polish. Because of the language difficulties they do not appreciate the health and safety regime that applies in this country. Of course some of them would be afraid to lose their jobs if they spoke out. I feel there's a lot more that could be done for health and safety. In Australia safety reps can issue a notice to their employer to say that they're doing something wrong, and it ought to be addressed. The TUC is pushing for this, but the government does not want to know. In past years the HSE has been diluted. They have lost representatives who go out and look at the workplace... they are trying to dilute the health and safety laws we have in this country. Another thing they have in Australia are Roving Representatives. At the moment I'm only allowed to be a health and safety representative in my workplace. In Australia – and I believe in Sweden as well – health and safety representatives are allowed to visit other workplaces by invitation to put forward their ideas on what sort of health and safety regime a company should have. I think the government could introduce legislation to that end. The working man should expect to come home without loss of life or limb. They really should bring Corporate Manslaughter in [corporate manslaughter legislation was introduced in 2008]. If managers don't know what their staff are doing, what sort of managers are they? Someone said to me that this government is the best Conservative government this country has ever had'.

Derek was ambivalent about the political process. His faith in it had reduced: 'You never really know whether the party will carry out what it said on its election platform.... The present Labour Party stole the Conservative Party's clothes, and because of that they've been running around like headless chickens. They've had a succession of leaders who have not performed. I think Tony Blair was a consummate actor, I voted for him... a couple of years later you ask what have they done so far? I was reading an article about stealth taxes. They have disincentivised a lot of people including myself. I left the Labour Party when they brought in fees for kids to go to university. All three of my children went to university. I worked out the other day that sending my children to university must have cost me £90,000 one way or another. The fees were the last straw... I despair. I was a Young Socialist at school, and I've been a card carrying member for thirty years or so.... After four years of Tony Blair I thought this bloke is just a slick lawyer. I thought he's actually leading people up the garden path. After a while I started to not believe him. Sometimes when he appeared on TV before he left I felt like putting my foot through the screen. Yet he managed to inveigle a lot of people with what he was doing. But I believe that he was only acting. It's very much like Princess Diana. She managed to appeal to a lot of people, because she appeared to be nice and cuddly. Whether she actually was or not is another thing. But she managed to present herself in such a manner that a lot of people were taken in by her'.

Derek gave the mayor of London short shrift: 'I think Livingstone is his own greatest self-publicist.... He's a horrible man. I hate him'. Derek's three suggestions for improving London were pedestrianisation, planning and a pigeon cull: 'I would try and pedestrianise more of the centre. I would try to get an integrated road structure. Road works cause an awful lot of problems. They should be planned better. With planning traffic could be diverted, and everybody knows in advance. Better planning. I'd get an integrated plan for road works. I'd eliminate all the pigeons. They're rats with wings'. Unsurprisingly Derek considered London to be a special place: 'Historically London is a special city. I think that the River Thames has a lot to do with it. London was heaving with workers. On the Isle of Dogs you had rows and rows of terraced houses and it was only dockers who worked there. Very often they would throw coins in the road and the man who got the coin would get the job and he'd go off to work. Historically London has been the focal point of the whole UK. In some ways that's probably wrong. I wish that more was devolved from London, because London was never meant for all the road traffic it takes. London's is the oldest metro service in the world, and it needs radically overhauling. It is being done, but gradually. So you have this creaking infrastructure in London. It has a lot of historical things going for it, a lot of quirky things. Changing of the guard. Buckingham Palace and a lot of things tourists are interested in... but it groans and creaks along. I don't know what effect the Olympics will have. I was hoping that we wouldn't get them. I was hoping they'd go to France because I don't know how we are going to cope, to be honest. I know my council tax is going to shoot sky-high. In Canada they had the Winter Olympics in Montreal. They are still paying for that. The Greeks are saddled with debt. They have all these show-case places. Some of them are actually empty now. It's hopeless. They are going to try to regenerate east London. I wonder what the standard of the new housing is going to be?' Derek's one-word appraisal of his birthplace was 'Congested'.

I enjoyed my visit to Seven Kings. I enjoy exploring London's peripheral places. I enjoy London's urban sprawl (much more than the City itself which I find hackneyed and claustrophobic). On arriving at Seven Kings I got hopelessly lost, despite having an A-Z. I ended up outside a mosque trying to re-orientate myself. Prayers had just ended and the mosque's congregation was spilling into the road. On seeing me consulting my A-Z several men came over and offered directions. They were open, friendly and helpful. I found Derek's house in no time at all.

9. The academic

Cindy got a job at City University after a short career at a university in the midlands. She started her working life in a firm of accountants. Academia was her second career. Born in 1972 she had gained a master's degree and PhD. She lived in a one-bedroomed flat in Chelsea. Chelsea, she said, felt 'very safe and comfortable. I like the area... Chelsea is safe, green, lots of things to do, a sense of community. The area I live in has a kind of village centre with a supermarket, doctor, newsagent, hairdressers, butcher, baker... it is quiet. I talk to people at bus stops and in shops... it is quite a relaxed, friendly area'. Living in Chelsea was not always a bed of roses, however: 'Chelsea can sometimes be a little pretentious... that's why I like the bit I am in because it is away from the parading and posturing... not necessarily Chelsea residents, but visitors to Chelsea... it can be flashy. Sometimes I wish it could be a little bit more down to earth. I'd feel more comfortable in a more down-to-earth area'. Asked how the parading and posturing manifested themselves Cindy said: 'Chelsea tractors. Sometimes going out to a bar and feeling surrounded by very arrogant young things.... There are lots of very exclusive places around... lots of private members' clubs. You see the culture of exclusivity all the time in Chelsea. These days you do not just go to the night club you have to be on the guest list. It is all about where you go and where you are seen...'. Asked where she would most like to live Cindy said: 'I have recently been looking at the route between Battersea and Wandsworth. If you travel from Clapham Junction in the direction of Tooting along Northcote Road and you get to Wandsworth Common there is a lovely area, much more suburban, I think. I love that area. But having said that where I live at the moment is very well connected to the centre. It is very easy to get back to at night... so at the moment I am fairly happy where I am'.

Cindy, who lectured in social science, thought her university was well run: 'Yes it's well run. We have devolved budgets and management. We have good strategic managers at school and department level, transparency, openness. I feel there is a lot of experience and competence here that is reassuring. As a junior member of staff I don't feel I have to get heavily involved in how things are working because they work well and I am comfortable with how they work. I don't feel I have to jump in and say "we should not do it like that but do it like this"... that is quite relaxing for me... I trust people to do things in an appropriate way so I can be a junior person and get on with the things I need to do, and advance my career...'. Cindy thought her colleagues were the best aspect of the job: 'I really like and respect them and enjoy their company'. She got on well with her boss. 'I think he is excellent, very kind, fair and encouraging' she said. She went on: 'I think from the encouragement and support I have had from him I think he thinks just as positively about me as I do about him. For example he has agreed to fund trips to Australia. I see that as a reward, I suppose, for doing a good job. If I was not seen to be doing a good job then I would not have got that funding...'. Cindy felt that promotion was a definite possibility 'to Senior Lecturer then Professor. I have been told that promotion is conditional upon an additional book publication at each stage'. Her working week was 'fairly nine-to-five, Monday to Friday. Sometimes I'll leave early one day and work late another... generally I do a forty-hour week'. Asked to summarise her experiences at City University Cindy said 'very nice organisation and people... there's teamwork... I'm close to professional networks... I have a good social life at work... there's lots of encouragement and perks and rewards... I feel that there are promotion prospects'.

Cindy had quite a busy social life: 'At the moment things are a bit hectic. I go out four or five nights a week'. Social venues included house parties or bars. Her hobbies were keeping fit and collecting: 'I run quite a bit. I have just taken up roller-blading. I am a sporadic and not particularly good skier and scuba diver. I am very keen on antiques and twentieth-century design and I collect furniture and lighting... I like wine and good food...'.

Cindy was pleased with the government's record on funding university research but felt it could do more for workers with families: 'There should be better paternity leave arrangements and more crèches. Because there is an imbalance between what a man and woman can expect, there is much more burden on a woman. It pigeonholes men and women to the detriment of both genders. There should be much better provision for men and women to have children. I would feel more comfortable about the future knowing that there was that complete flexibility...'. Cindy had strong views on the trades unions: 'I have a very mixed opinion of them. The unions I like the least are the rail and tube unions. They really push the boundaries and they get away with murder. We [Londoners] do not see them delivering the standard of work that justifies all of the benefits they are able to achieve through aggressive strikes and action over the slightest thing... so I think they give the unions a terrible name. I would like to see a huge clamp-down on them... I would like to see them quite crushed. I would not say I am a die-hard unionist... I have taken part in industrial action and within this union [the university lecturers' union] it has been very measured. I have seen how painful it has been for people to take the action because they have felt that students would suffer as a result. As it happens when I have been involved in action ultimately a settlement has been achieved before it has caused a major problem. That has been a huge relief. So I suppose I am a member of the union for insurance purposes... it is something to fall back upon were any problems ever to arise. I think our union is pretty moderate and reasonable and most people have very honourable intentions... I like the balanced approach we have. I am very anti the very militant unions.... I think some unions know they can hold their employers to ransom, and they do. Unions can be very valuable in helping to set standards in a profession and in that respect they can be a very good thing. The transport unions are successful because they have such a high proportion of employees signed up and they are in a position to really challenge the employer over everything. They have got a disgraceful attitude'. Asked to define her term 'aggressive strike' Cindy said: 'For example when large numbers went on strike over the way the organisation was dealing with one specific case – the man who was on sick leave and was caught playing squash – the fact that they would disrupt travel for the whole of London for one specific case, and a very dubious case at that, reflects how they will go on strike at the drop of a hat. It is going back to the Seventies...'. Regarding the wider political process Cindy believed that voting did have an impact on policy and the tone of government: 'I believe very strongly that people should exercise their vote... and I would not be averse to people being pushed much more strongly to vote with penalties for not voting. We have no licence to complain if we do not vote. I guess I do vote because I like to think it makes a difference'.

Turning to city politics Cindy was broadly happy with Ken Livingstone's record: 'Over the years he has been in power he has done a good job.... He is there as a champion for London. He has had lots of big events and initiatives celebrating London tied up with his office... and I feel he has helped to instil a sense of pride about London. He is pushing multicultural events as well as events celebrating London as a whole. I think, however, he may be getting to the stage where he is starting to lose his touch. He may be starting to get too distant from his public. There is strong feeling around the extension of the congestion zone. Some feel he did not really listen to people in the affected areas. Some feel he has become quite arrogant'. Asked to explain the negative aspects of extending the Congestion Charge Cindy said: 'In my area most businesses seem to have been against it. I suspect it would not have affected traffic levels that much... it has pushed more traffic into the centre of London... it means that people in my area can now drive around London at a very low rate [low cost] which they could not do before. It has moved into residential areas now. I'm still on the fence about it.... There has been a lot of hostility about the whole approach. There is a feeling that he has not been listening to people and is starting to impose things more'.

Asked what three things she would do if she were mayor of London (and money was no object) Cindy said: 'I would do more to curb traffic... more pedestrian areas. I'd try to find ways of discouraging people from driving. In the centre I'd like to see most vehicles being buses and taxis... in the rush hour a lot of the cars on the roads are occupied by one person... they tend to be the more powerful cars, sports cars, large saloons, four-by-fours. There are certain areas I don't like because I feel they are in a real state of disrepair and disorder... if you are out in Camden on a Saturday night you will be offered drugs blatantly in the street. That is an area that is very dirty and grimy. There is a real difference in the quality of your surroundings depending upon where you live – which borough you live in. I would like to see some of those areas cleaned up.... And I think policing needs to be improved.... The police in London are very badly run.... I don't know whether it is because they are overstretched... you just do not get any service from them when you need it. You see drug dealing on the streets in certain areas and nothing is happening... and I can't believe in a place like this that you would see that, but you do. Police in London don't give you any kind of service unless you are in the City of London'. Asked whether drugs were more an issue for the law than for the NHS Cindy said: 'They have to be completely joined up... I don't necessarily want to see people who are caught with drugs having the book thrown at them... I would rather see them given some sort of help. But drug dealers on the street are a threatening sight'. Asked whether she found the act of being offered recreational drugs intimidating Cindy said: 'Yes... and I would turn around and have a go at them but I don't want to run the risk of getting stabbed. I know what these people are like'.

London may have had its distasteful aspects but it was still a special place: 'I think it is very special. It could well be the most multicultural city in the world... any public transport you are on you hear languages from all over the world... you meet incredibly interesting, diverse people all the time and so although it is fast paced and sometimes seemingly unfriendly I actually find it very friendly. Once you start meeting people and get introduced to people they are very friendly. You can build up a social network through informal contacts. People tend to stay in touch with each other.... It is easy to have a good social life in London... there are lots of things to do. Life in the suburbs is completely different to life in the West End. In the centre there is such an incredible range of places to go...'.

Cindy was enthusiastic about the 2012 Olympic Games: 'It will be a fantastic thing. Certain parts of London that people would not normally go to are now going to have fantastic facilities. The marketing of London that will be achieved through the Olympics will bring lots more investment and interest in London so those of us who have properties in London will benefit financially. If you are a Londoner there are plenty of benefits and very few costs... we are obviously paying for it but I think the amount will be completely overriden by the benefits...'. Asked to comment on the view that the money being spent on the Olympics would have a greater impact if spent directly on housing and infrastructure Cindy said: 'Well I think they are spending money to make money. After the same event in other cities it has been said that the investment those cities have seen has been enormous.... I think our government is spending a significant amount of money expecting to get a huge return on that investment...'. Cindy's one-word adjective for London was 'vibrant'.

I interviewed Cindy in what appeared to be a new building sited very near the City of London proper. The building was light and airy. Cindy's office was small but clean, with a large window. The building had the mandatory porter and barrier-controlled entry. There was an atrium cafe, *de rigueur* these days in academia. This, I mused, was a pleasant place to work, and Chelsea was a pleasant place to live. All in all a pleasant lifestyle. I made my way to the ground and removed the necessary padlock from my bicycle. Cycling within the Congestion Charge area was an enjoyable experience. There was less traffic. There was less chance of being terminated. I headed north to the testing environs of Hackney, Tottenham and Edmonton.

Verstehen

My London blooding occurred in the early 1980s when a friend offered me temporary accommodation prior to my taking up a post in social services research. Until that point I had only experienced London on day trips. This, I sensed, would be altogether different. And so it proved. My friend met me at Blackfriars station. We caught a bus to Herne Hill, Brixton. We walked from the bus stop until we got to a corner shop in a three-storey Victorian terrace. The shop's side wall bulged outwards such that it overhung the pavement. 'No. It can't be this' I thought. It was. This was where my chum and several of his university friends lived… or, more exactly, existed. We entered via the side door and climbed the bent and creaking stairs. I got the visitor's tour. The toilet and bathroom were accessed through the kitchen. The bath had a grey lining that no amount of scrubbing could shift. It was simply too *old*. There were four bedrooms and a rather impressive dining room whose large windows rattled when the wind blew. There was a two-inch gap under the dining room door through which the wind escaped. There were mice (they left their footprints in the fat that coated the top of the gas cooker). I once found a long-drowned mouse floating in the toilet. Mice can be flushed. The fixtures and fittings were old. The carpets soiled and threadbare. Everyone was broke. But they always seemed to have enough money for beer and a take-away meal of chips and saveloy (they celebrated unhealthy eating, as did I). We used to drink in a pub around the corner. It was a dive but it was our second home. It felt comfortable. One night a fight broke out between two regulars. One of the regulars picked up a bar stool and brought it down on his friend's head. Crack. We gawped. It seemed to happen in slow-motion. I can still recall the arc of the stool as it was lifted then dumped down with enormous force. Fearing a Western-style bar-room brawl we told the female members of our party to 'Go to the ladies', which they did. We prepared to defend our corner, territorial males to the last.

10. The educational administrator

Evelyn was born in 1951 in Dominica. Married with four children and one grandson she lived with her husband in a semi-detached house in Tottenham. Evelyn's husband taught leisure and tourism. Evelyn herself worked as an administrator for the Workers' Educational Association. She had worked there for twenty-eight years. Her worst experience was 'doing temping work. I didn't know where I was going most times. I got to the venue quite late. The places you went to you either needed to get there quite early or leave home quite early and that was after I took my first child to her minder... it was kind of erratic'. Her best work experience was working for the WEA: 'I have a lot of freedom to work as I please, but within reason... I'm not monitored for everything I do'. When she first arrived in Britain, Evelyn lived in a hostel. She took a secretarial course at the Lucy Clayton Secretarial College in Kensington then landed a job at the Jamaican High Commission. After that she worked for Grey-Green Travel, then for the WEA.

Evelyn enjoyed her work: 'I like interacting with the staff and prospective students and the public. I get quite chatty with them. My colleagues have made comments like "Do you know who these people are that you are talking to, you know, you are talking very friendly with them". I think that's quite nice because some of them don't know what they want, and you can always help them to make up their minds. Sometimes I recognise accents, especially if they are from the West Indies'. Evelyn had a good relationship with her manager: 'She is a very nice person. She is fairly new to the WEA. Just over a year. She is getting quite used to the way the Association works. She is trying to build us up quite a lot now... things had got so bad... we had a very low staff morale.... She has tried to help us be more proactive and build the London region up to what it used to be about five, ten years ago'. Asked whether she had ever thought of leaving the WEA when things got tough Evelyn replied: 'I was made redundant. All the admin staff were made redundant because the WEA were making a hub outside London, and I didn't go for it because another post came up. It wasn't quite what I wanted but I felt it was the right thing to do at the time.... The PA post came up so I went for that. I was the only one who went for it. It was done internally. I got it because the others didn't want it. They wanted to move out'.

Evelyn felt the WEA had turned a corner: 'I think the Association is well run. The general secretary and the other trustees are doing a fantastic job. Things had got pretty bad at one time. I think we are on the right track now...'. Asked why she thought the WEA had got itself into a mess Evelyn said: 'I think there was an element of bad management at the time. Also the WEA wasn't advertising a lot. Many people had no idea about us at all even though we had been around for just over one hundred years. We are trying to rectify that now but it seems to be taking a long time'. Despite being stuck on her grade Evelyn thought she was paid a fair rate for the work she did: 'I think I'm paid a fair rate for the job. We have just had a restructuring of the salary and grading process and unfortunately I'm one of those on a "mark time" basis... they think I have been paid too much'.

The best feature of her semi-detached was its separate kitchen: 'At the time we bought it I liked it because the kitchen was separate from the dining room. That was something I grew up with... I like separate kitchens'. Its worst feature was 'its messy garden'. Evelyn liked where she lived: 'I live in a very good area. We have got several large parks that you can take children to. Just a few minutes down the road from me there is the New River Sports Centre... the area is quite conducive for schools and for travel because we have got Wood Green tube station. It is also very good for shopping. I am always at Wood Green Shopping City. It is very good for catching buses to and from work or anywhere you want. It is fairly central for my kind of life'. Tottenham had its down side, however: 'At the moment we seem to have a lot of young people's crime... some of it may be racist... we also have a lot of drugs. We also have lots of, I don't want to say foreigners, but that's the best way I could put it at the moment. It's not really the right word, but, a lot of foreigners who are bringing in a lot of nasty things. I don't think the police can deal with it at the moment'. Evelyn's ideal locale would be Kensington in the west of the capital: 'I quite enjoyed living in Kensington, a posh area. It was very quiet at the time. That was then, I don't know about now. When I visit that area it almost seems like Tottenham. It is not as posh as it used to be when I first came here'. Evelyn planned to leave London when the right time came: 'I have every intention of returning to Dominica from Britain when I retire. But I would visit London often because my kids would not want to return. They are British. They'd come over for holidays. Of course I'd visit them quite often'. Evelyn's church activities were a big part of her social life: 'I used to have a lot of hobbies. Now I don't do very much. I like reading, I like watching documentaries on TV, I like dancing but I don't do very much of that. I do lots of things with my church... that's part of my hobby. I like going to church and meeting my friends there'.

Evelyn thought the government had helped working parents: 'The best thing they've done is provide nurseries for working parents and also child care vouchers. My daughter uses that and it's helping her quite a lot'. Evelyn was a committed trade unionist: 'I am with Amicus. They've just joined with the T&G and the new union is called Unite. We are quite active here. I think the unions do quite well. They do try to help their members a lot. I just have to say "Thank You" to Amicus as I have just got my twenty-year badge'. Evelyn was less sanguine about the electoral system, however: 'I have voted all my life in Britain. There hasn't been much change that I've noticed. It should help but it doesn't'. Evelyn's verdict on Ken Livingstone was 'could do better': 'I think he's doing a good job but I think he could do better. Sometimes it seems that he can be too radical. I don't mind a radical person, but sometimes it seems like he's over-the-top and he does need to cool down a bit. Maybe he should not take on so many American advisors. We are British and we should stick with our British policies. Not everything from America is good. A lot of the politicians think all of America is good, and it's not'. Asked to reflect on the fact that the underground had benefited from American know-how Evelyn said: 'The tube seems to be doing OK. Actually I like the cool seats in summer. I stopped travelling on the tube regularly... and started travelling by bus'. Evelyn caught two buses to get to work in the City. The journey from Tottenham to the City took 'just about one hour'. Evelyn said she would pedestrianise more of London, do more for parents and scrap the Congestion Charge if she were mayor of London: 'I'd close the streets to make big shopping areas. I would cut out the Congestion Charge... I am glad it has not gone up further than eight pounds... and I'd do more for parents, open up child care nurseries at a much cheaper rate'.

Evelyn, who had lived in London for over three decades, thought it a special place: 'It's a special city. It's the capital of England and of the Commonwealth. When I was growing up in Dominica everything was London. You must go to London to study. London has got golden streets, golden roads, golden everything.... It can be special... there are lots of things to have a look at, although time and money do not help people to take advantage of that. A lot of things are quite expensive for visitors, even home visitors'. Evelyn's verdict on the Olympics was positive: 'I think it's a good thing for London. It will bring in lots of visitors, lots of money. The Olympics will make London and Britain proud again. It will help younger sports people, or prospective sports people, the children, to think of the future'. Her one-word description of London, her home for thirty-two years, was 'Beautiful'.

What I found most memorable about the WEA office was its friendliness. Everyone wanted to help, none more so than Evelyn whose enthusiasm was almost overwhelming. The interview concluded, I headed back up the High Road to Haringey. Almost straight (the High Road follows the line of an old Roman road) the road is an experience for anyone with an interest in urban transport. It is invariably choked with cars, vans, lorries and buses. Ambulances, fire tenders and police cars have a devil of a job making way in the dense traffic. The road is sooty and grimy. It is dangerous for both cyclists and pedestrians. The argument for more investment in London's road transport infrastructure seems overwhelming, especially when those roads are experienced on a bicycle.

11. The surveyor

Except for a four-year spell in Canada, William, born in 1954, had lived in London all his life. He lived in Wandsworth with his long-term partner. His answer to the question 'single or married?' was 'Both. I've always been single, but coupled'. His education was 'A piss-poor one. I left comprehensive school because they more or less told me to. I had not been to school for a few months. So they wrote to me and said "We take it you've left because we haven't seen you for a few months".[12] So I left. I hated school. I couldn't stand the authoritarianism of it. I did not like the environment. I hated it completely. I used to dread going. I loved lessons and learning. But I hated the environment. Then I went to a College of Further Education for a year or so. Then I got a few jobs. Then at 24 years I went back into full-time education, to polytechnic. I did an OND and a degree'. Asked whether his peers were also going to university he replied: 'No, not really. Of the kids I grew up with hardly any went to university'.

William could recall eight jobs: 'I've been a wallpaper salesman. I worked at Steakaway [a fast-food outlet] as a general manager. Surveying at the GLC. Then surveying at a private firm. Then Poly. Then two local authorities. Surveying at a housing association. Then self-employed surveyor'. One of the hardest working days of his life was '"The Paving Slab Day". I was working as a labourer for a building company in Fulham. The chap had about ten jobs on the go that all needed paving slabs. So he ordered a lorry-load and decided to distribute them around the sites that day. So I lifted a huge amount. I was on my back for two days. It was hard work in those days. There wasn't any health and safety. Bags of cement used to weigh a hundredweight. If you couldn't lift a hundredweight, bad luck. It comes in smaller bags these days. I remember one time we were demolishing the back of a house that had a horrible bulge in it and the scaffold was tied to the building. We were up on the scaffold and the bricklayer announced that he was going to hit the wall with the bulge in it, and he wasn't sure what was going to happen. As the scaffold was tied to the building he thought it might collapse. So his suggestion was that we should all work out a route off the scaffold, so if it started to collapse we would all jump. That's what we did. He hit the wall. Obviously it didn't collapse because I'm still here. But that's how things were run in construction in the 1970s'. Asked whether he was ever injured William replied: 'No. I probably inflicted some damage, though. I remember I was so knackered when lifting the paving slabs I dropped one on someone's foot. He was a big Irishman. He didn't seem to notice'.

Looking back over his extensive working career William mused: 'I've had some shit jobs but the only thing to do in those circumstances is to get on with them. The worst day's work I've ever done was in a factory on an Easter Monday. The production line was not running so they put me in the box department making cardboard boxes. They come flat. You fold them then staple the bottom. The only way I could sustain myself for eight hours was to see how many I could do in an hour. I was working alongside an Asian woman who obviously did it for a living. She had a different idea. She got through it by seeing how little she could do. The only way I could stay sane was to say "I did thirty in the last hour, now let's see if I can beat that". That was probably the worst day of my life in terms of work'. Asked if he thought the Asian woman saw him as a 'rate-buster' he said: 'No. I don't think she saw anything, really. She just had a rhythm. I suppose if you are doing it for the rest of your life you maybe get a rhythm. She was making ten boxes an hour. But if I had to do the same thing the next week I may well have joined her on ten an hour. Or shot myself'.[13] William's best job was 'Working as a surveyor for the London Borough of Croydon. It was the most fun. It was very varied. I ended up refurbishing a swimming pool and windmill'.

At the time of the interview William ran his own surveying practice in the London Borough of Wandsworth: 'We're in our fifteenth year. It started off with me working out of my mother's front room. My mother could be a problem. When I was out she'd answer the telephone. We had a very posh client. When I saw the client a couple of weeks later she said "Oh, I telephoned you the other day at your office. Your mother told me you hadn't been home that night and that you would probably be home in the morning because you hadn't got enough shirts with you". That's really what you need when you are struggling in your first year. They were interesting times. Then I moved into a house that was fairly derelict. I had an office there. I took on my first member of staff when I was there. He was very understanding because the WC consisted of a toilet and a bucket of water to flush it with. I'm amazed I got away with it. After a year we took on another member of staff. I ended up with the front room of the house being turned into an office. That lasted for about five years. It was grim. You couldn't have a day off. You'd take a day off and staff were coming in to your house and working. You couldn't have a lie-in because it wasn't good to have the staff around when you were in bed. Then fate intervened. I met someone who had an office for sale so I bought it. That was eight years ago. We've taken on some more staff. I'd like to take on yet more, but they're just not there at the moment. It's really frustrating. We're turning away work. I hate doing that. It goes against my instincts. But it's better to turn work down than end up the richest surveyor in the graveyard. There's a shortage of people attracted into the building industry'.

Asked what had kept him going through the lean times he replied: 'Enthusiasm. My father buggered off in 1960... consequently I've taken charge of my destiny.... Once you've worked for yourself you can't imagine going back to work in a job again. Also I enjoy what I do. There are always new things coming in, so that keeps me going.... I enjoy making all the decisions'. Asked what he thought the government could do to help small businesses he said: 'I'm going to sound like a grumpy old man but graduates these days are so poor. I've brought three up to RICS standard, but it's such hard work, and it gets worse every time. After twelve months I had to tell the last graduate he had to find another career. He graduated in building surveying from Reading'. William worked on average 'seventy to eighty hours per week... although weekends are fairly free of work.[14] Personally, I like to get things done for people. I like to do them properly, and if it takes a bit longer then I don't begrudge that. Money isn't what drives it. It's really a wish to prosecute some work to someone's satisfaction. If that means staying late then you do it. I don't think my health suffers. But perhaps my private life does a bit. So I'm trying to address that'. William thought his staff considered him to be 'A curmudgeonly bastard and a grumpy old man.... If people are nice to me I try to be nice to them'. Asked if he took pleasure in creating employment he said: 'I feel we're a sort of team... I don't feel they are employees so much as colleagues'.

William thought the best aspect of the job was its creativity: 'I like the doors that open and reputation we build. It's important that we build a quality service and maintain it. We develop new client bases and it's done by word of mouth. We have never had to advertise. I do feel wretched if we ever let ourselves down in that respect. If we ever do something substandard or miss a trick I am mortified by it'. The worst aspect was 'Keeping all the balls in the air. There's a bit of pressure involved. I suppose I've learned to deal with it, though. I don't let it get to me any more. A few years ago I would go on holiday and still be doing my work on the aircraft. I've got over that now. Now I think if something is not done it's only going to be a week. I explain to people and they usually understand. You have to get over that stage or you end up dead. The thing you learn is that you are a resource and that if you burn yourself out you are no good to anyone. I learned the hard way by coming close to burning myself out. So the pressure is what I like the least about this job. I'm better at it now'. As an employer William felt he had an obligation to pay a fair wage for the job: 'I'm very conscious about the staff. I try to pay them as much as I can. I don't worry too much about money. One of the things about building a team is recognising people's effort. I never wanted to run a sweat-shop. I review salaries every six months and try to keep the staff happy in terms of their remuneration. My share is what's left. As I point out to them they get the money and I get the change'.

Like many William had bought a house for renovation. Unlike most, however, he had lived in it as it was being renovated: 'It will be a five-bedroomed terraced Victorian villa. It was run-down to the point of being derelict. Over a period of fifteen years I've made it almost habitable. I added two bedrooms but then took one away to put a bathroom in'. William had done most of the renovation himself: 'I take some satisfaction in turning a tap on and seeing water come out, because I actually made that happen. I have renewed virtually all the plumbing, electrics, walls and ceilings. I love doing it and I still get a kick out of the fact that it still works... or some of it, anyway. The thing I like most about it is the grandeur of it. I've re-established the cornicing in the reception rooms. It is rather nice to sit down and admire the marble fire place, and the tiling, and the workmanship that was put in originally'. Did he think of himself as a frustrated artisan? 'Well if it hadn't been for Harold Wilson's commitment to higher education I'd be an electrician or something like that, or a plumber'. Did he think he would have been happier as a plumber? 'No'. Did he think of himself as an aesthete? 'Yes'.[15] Asked what he liked least about his current accommodation he replied: 'That I haven't finished it yet. To be honest I never intend to finish it. It's a hobby, really'.

William liked Wandsworth because it made him feel at ease: 'It's relaxed, I suppose. It feels comfortable. There are no areas that I wouldn't go in to. I was talking to a guy from New York once. We were talking in the pub about what New York was like, because it's one of the places I want to go. I was talking to him about Brooklyn. And he said he doesn't go there because it's dangerous. I couldn't live in a city where there's an area I wouldn't go into because it's dangerous. Maybe I'm being naive. But I feel there's nowhere in London that I wouldn't go. There are places I wouldn't relish going to, like Peckham and certain areas in the East End... you don't walk around with gold watches and chains and stuff. Tooting is relaxed. It's always been mixed-race. There have always been West Indians. They're some of the friendliest people in the town. The Asians took over the corner shops, and for the first ten years a bit of London life disappeared because the newsagent used to be the locus of gossip.

When they became Asian that stopped. It was all very commercial. But the second generation has moved on and the shops are back to where they were. You can now get a pint of milk at eleven at night, which is a huge bonus, and they talk to you as well'.

Although community relations were harmonious the pressures were changing: 'Yes relations are good. But the community is under different pressures now. In the last year there's been a huge influx from central Europe. That has affected the building industry. I'm meeting them every day on building sites. I think that's causing a bit of tension. They are not a different colour so you can't tell who they are. That makes people worried in a different way. They are not worried that they're a different colour or culture. They're worried because they don't know how many there are and where they are and what they're doing. So that's created a different sort of fear. What worries me is that they may well displace the West Indian community from the job market. That I feel is a fear for the future. The Muslim thing has caused a few tensions. You do pick up anti-Muslim feelings around here. There's a mosque in Balham which they tend to congregate at. I think people tend to worry about the sheer volume. There are very wealthy and very poor people living here and they manage to co-exist reasonably well. There don't appear to be ghettos where a couple of streets are posh and a couple are shit. They seem to be mixed up, somehow. In my road there are about ten West Indian families who came over here in the 1950s. At that time they did not pay a lot for their houses. Now the area is more wealthy but the West Indians are not going anywhere because they live here. Some of my friendliest neighbours are West Indian. Incomers take three or four years to say "hello". The West Indians will come up and say hello from day one'. Asked whether prosperous white incomers were less community spirited he said: 'They used to live in Islington and Clapham, but they moved out of those areas. There is a breed of people that is more interested in money and where they're going for the weekend than the local area'. Asked if he found that sort of behaviour disappointing he said: 'Yes, but I'm a hypocrite. One of the things I love about living in London is the anonymity. I frequent five or six pubs. The ones I go to a lot are the places where you get to know people. You can go in and have a chat. There are other places where I want to go and have a beer and sit on my own. It's nice that you can do that. So on the one hand I love being anonymous, and on the other hand it would be nice if it was friendlier'.

William thought one of the worst aspects of living in Wandsworth was 'Parking. The fact that the local authority uses it to raise money rather than control problems. But that's just a moan. I don't think there are any serious things that piss me off. The brewery closing. When I was a lad I believed in two things. One was the Labour Party. The other was Young's Brewery. Both shafted me. Blair turned the Labour Party into the Tory party, so I took solace in Young's bitter. Then for £65 million they sell up. They sell 200-years-worth of history and 400-years-worth of brewing on that site... and bugger off. That's not what Young's is supposed to be about. It's the jobs and the tradition of it. It was up the road and it was something we used to be proud of. We had an independent family brewery. It's not just the brewery that I miss. It's a way of life. I used to go to a pub near Wandsworth prison. I used to know a chap in there. He was always there. He sat at the corner of the bar. He was quite an intelligent chap, but he was unfortunately a piss-head. He was a painter by day. He used to sketch by night. He was nice to talk to. Very erudite. He used to quietly get pissed and then he'd go home. He never caused any problems. He didn't get violent. Everyone knew him. When Young's refurbished the pub he went in there and he was given £10 by the landlord to fuck off and not come back. I thought that was outrageous'. Asked if he wanted to move out of London he replied: 'Yes and no. My partner is very keen to move out, and I don't know if I can. So it's going to be interesting'.

William thought the government had done one or two good things: 'They've extended the licensing hours and have helped families with tax credits and the like…. If you need the minimum wage it's such a terrible indictment of the government isn't it? It's set at such a low level. If there were people being paid less than that then the minimum wage has been brilliant. It's hard to believe that there are people being paid less than the minimum wage. Who would pay anyone the minimum wage? Our cleaner gets more than the minimum wage'. William thought the trades unions had been diminished: 'They seem to have disappeared up their own orifice. I used to be a very active trade unionist. I was a NALGO shop steward in a local authority. I got a lot out of it. As a shop steward I used to get very frustrated at getting people off the hook for misdemeanours they should have been caned for. Because the local authority managers were so bloody awful they never made any of the charges stick. Mrs Thatcher managed to castrate the unions. I think they struggle to be relevant now. At the time I didn't think the unions deserved the treatment they got. But looking back, possibly the unions were a little too negative. Perhaps there were some abuses'. William said he did vote. Asked if he thought voting changed anything he said: 'No. If it did they wouldn't let you do it, would they?'

William was a tad disappointed in Ken Livingstone: 'He's a bit like everyone else involved in local politics these days… a bit of a disappointment, I suppose. One expected more. I think it's a shame he didn't stay as an independent. I think it's a shame he has not been more outspoken or stroppy about things. He's capitulated to the government. He hasn't taken them on. Maybe he is being adult, but who wants to be adult about these things? Politics is about passion. I would have preferred him to be a bit more passionate. The tube, for example. If he was convinced that privatisation was wrong and public ownership was best why didn't he fight for it? He had London behind him. He had an electorate and a mandate. But all he did was go quiet and ask if he could be let back into the Labour Party. I never understood that'. Asked if Livingstone had sold out to the establishment William replied: 'It does appear that way. Possibly he's being political. But it's not my sort of politics… and I didn't think they were his. There used to be passion'.

Asked what three things he would do if he were mayor of London and money was no object William said: 'I would introduce a serious system of cycle ways to make cycling a realistic alternative to cars. Painting a line down the road is not anything like what is required. It's a licence to kill yourself, really. I've just come back from a cycling trip to Belgium where they have an incredible network of cycleways. If you go into the towns you find that bicycles rule. So many people join gyms and drive to work. Why do that when you can cycle to work? It's cheap, noiseless, pollution free. My bank is half an hour's walk. So I thought I'd cycle to the bank. I came back from the cycling holiday and thought "this is the answer. I'll cycle to the bank". So I cycle down the High Road two days running. On one day someone opened their car door into me and on another a coach passed by me so close that the rivets took the skin off my elbow. That's the sort of tolerances you are dealing with here in London. You could be dead. People do die. It's not worth it, really. The tube system is outrageously expensive. It should be subsidised. We need another of Ken's "Fares Fair" policies. If Paris lets you travel anywhere on the Metro for fifty pence, why is it five pounds here? I don't know. Unless it's a device to stop you travelling on it because it's so decrepit. Thirdly I'd have more beer and circuses. The arts establishment like the Royal Opera House should get out more. Go to the suburbs and put on a show. There should be a festival of beer and circuses on every common in London'. Although London had its irritations it was still a special place, thought William: 'Some of the things you see in other cities which make you think "Why don't we do that at home?" have actually happened here. Why didn't we have the Oyster Card twenty years ago? I don't know. London is the best place in the world. It's vibrant, energetic, wonderful, familiar, historical but modern. I think it's very comfortable with itself, most of the time'. One development failed to inspire William, however – the Olympics: 'I sort of dread it, really. I was hoping they'd go to Paris so we could hop over on the Chunnel and congest their city. All the trades will be sucked into building the Olympic site. That will create labour shortages in my industry'. William's preferred adjective for London was 'optimistic'.

I had interviewed William in his Wandsworth office. Located in a Victorian terrace of small shops it was imaginatively converted, clean and bright. The staff were well provided for. There were large windows and good facilities. The enterprise persuaded you that change was possible: that London would be a much better place to live if more citizens cared about the place and did something for their neighbourhood *at the grass roots*. Bottom-up change endures. Small is beautiful. Grandiose, politically motivated schemes (the Millennium Dome, for example) are doomed. Brutal in scale, they are generally unwanted and unloved interventions. No-one owns them in an emotional sense. So no-one cares. And it shows.

12. The off-licensee

Graham ran an off-licence cum general store cum Internet cafe in Camden. It reminded me of a Victorian emporium, but contemporised. There was something for everyone; tinned food, cigarettes, sweets, alcohol, lively conversation and on-line access. I had the warmest of welcomes in one of the most unique shops I have ever encountered. I did the interview in the shop's small kitchen which doubled as an office. From time to time Graham's friends would enter the kitchen to make toast or grab a coffee. Through the kitchen window one could hear bird song – and nothing else. That is one of the curious things about London. You can live or work on a busy arterial road (Camden is overrun with traffic) and still find peace and quiet in a back garden.

Graham was born in London in 1954. Although a father he was single at the time of the interview. His school career produced one O-level. 'I left school with an O-level in art. I studied for nine and got one' he said. At the time of the interview he was studying for an Open University foundation degree. Graham had travelled widely. He had lived in the United States, the Bahamas, Germany, Austria, Ireland and elsewhere. He liked to travel and experience other cultures. Graham had tried several occupations before settling on shop ownership: 'I was a police officer in the Met Police. I was an auditor with Thomson Holidays. I worked in the City for a firm of stockbrokers. I worked for Rank Xerox. I worked in Playboy casinos. They were the most important jobs. I got the travelling bug after I left Thomson Holidays'. Graham found the Metropolitan Police a somewhat frustrating employer: 'Police work was illuminating. When you leave school you have an idea of what work will be like. The reality is often very different. You encounter the complications of people in organisations, and how they interact with each other. I don't think we are really prepared for that'. Graham was ambitious but found little outlet for his ambitions within the police service. Too young to 'get on' he left out of frustration.

Graham's least interesting job was 'Stuffing envelopes. We did it every three months at Thomson Holidays. The entire staff would go into the post room and send out the brochures for the next holiday period. We'd spend an entire week stuffing envelopes to send to people who had booked holidays. I left Thomson's after a year and a half. They replaced me with a computer'. Until he became a shopkeeper Graham's best job had been 'working for the Playboy organisation as a croupier. It provided an insight into a society that I did not have access to. The rich. The powerful. The famous. Decadence. I worked as a croupier, first in London, then the Bahamas, then the USA. If you are relatively naive then you have certain expectations of people who are in privileged positions. These preconceptions tend to disappoint. People don't necessarily use their wealth and influence and power in the way that you might. In fact it is often a means to pervert people who are less fortunate. In some ways they get pleasure out of seeing what it costs to buy somebody. How to manipulate and degrade them. I think that was true of a lot of people connected with the Playboy Club. There is just no sense of human worth or values. Money takes a completely different meaning. If you are standing at a table earning £140 per week and a gentleman the same age as you comes along with a briefcase containing £250,000 and he loses that money to the casino in forty minutes, his perception of the value and meaning of money is very different to your own. He'll click his fingers and he's got another £250,000 because his father earns one million dollars a day. These people have an entirely different perspective on life'.

Graham enjoyed running his emporium: 'I'm the manager of a shop. I was a house-husband for a number of years. As a consequence of divorce it was necessary for me to find my way back into a working environment. My partner was a purser for an airline. I enjoy the interaction with customers. They are a very broad representation of the entire area [Camden]. There are some very interesting people. It's nice to sit down and have a cup of tea and listen to people's experiences. We have loads of people who come here who are very knowledgeable about computers. They give and take. Young people are very keen to make positive contributions and help others. Everybody benefits. I learn a lot'. Running a shop in Camden was not without its annoyances, however: 'People using my kitchen. That can be frustrating. There are aspects about living in Camden that I find frustrating. We have a well-established "Care in the Community" scheme. We have a community but we are not quite sure where all the care is. We have a lot of people with problems. People being rehabilitated out of prisons and mental health institutions. We are not really pre-warned or prepared for these people. Their presence in the area creates problems for neighbours. Their problems tend to be discussed in the shop and we try to find out what the solutions are. But the information isn't available. I think there is a tension between protecting the individual and providing society with information. At the moment, on balance, I think it goes too far in terms of protecting the individual. I've frequently had to ask people to leave the shop. As an off-licensee you have to ask people to leave if they are under the influence of alcohol. If someone has a psychological disorder you shouldn't serve them alcohol. The social workers don't come in and say "We're moving a chap in next door, don't serve him alcohol". Most recently children were too frightened to walk down the road because a chap who was released would be ranting in the street. Everybody wants to know what sort of potential danger is posed by this individual. They want to know what we are going to do about it? To some extent the police are powerless. The social workers say "We are in control here". It seems to me we have built up layers of bureaucrats who are supposed to be part of the solution, but they seem to me to be part of the problem. The Human Rights Act has given people lots of protection and I don't think it is being used fairly'.

Graham worked hard as a shop owner: 'I work all hours... seven days a week from nine-thirty in the morning to ten-thirty in the evening'.[16] A set lunchtime was an alien concept: 'When you are working for yourself things like scheduled lunches don't have any meaning'. Graham drove to work from Paddington. The drive took twenty minutes. Although he liked living in Paddington (because of the pubs) he hankered after something more convenient for running: 'I'd like to live opposite Regents Park in a penthouse. I could put my jogging kit on and have a morning jog each day without any parking problems or risk having my bicycle stolen'. Graham shared the Paddington flat with his brother. Asked if he'd like to buy a house or flat of his own he said 'Accommodation for me is just a place to stay. It's a roof over my head. I don't regard it as a home. It's just a place to protect me from the elements. I like to feel that if the opportunity to travel arises I'm not going to be tethered by mortgages or commitments. Travel is a very fulfilling experience. And the world changes all the time. Just because you've been to a place once does not mean it's not worth revisiting. I think if you settle down in one place the process of switching off has started. I'd rather die on my feet than on a couch somewhere'. Graham had a real issue with the way Britain's housing market worked: 'I find the whole concept of housing and ownership so opposite to my views that I choose not to think about it too much. I don't want to think about a Labour government that has presided over a huge boom in house prices and made housing almost unaffordable for young people. I don't think that banks should control the property market.... You have a nation enslaved to the bankers. We are all mortgage slaves'.

Graham displayed a good deal of cynicism about local and national politics. He was no fan of the Blair–Brown axis: 'I don't think this has been a government of the worker. The problem with the minimum wage is that it is artificial. We are told that inflation is two-and-a-half per cent [2007]. That's rubbish. Salaries are to some extent determined by that level, so living standards have been eroded. People have gone into debt just to survive. Very little has been unaffected by inflation. Prices have risen dramatically. Many, many people who would like to go to work can't afford to go to work. I know these people personally. They would lose their housing benefit and other benefits. If you were offered twenty-one or twenty-two thousand a year that would not justify coming off the dole. We have a production studio nearby. They have runners, young people. One of the runners, a lady, was paying fifty pounds a week in travel costs. The cost of travelling one stop on the underground is extortionate. The cost of getting on a bus is extortionate. And under a Labour government! None of this affects rich people. Heating. Insurance. Every aspect of modern life has drained the resources people have. I can't think of one good thing the Labour Party has done for working people. The government has got to provide affordable housing. That is everything... if housing is affordable. If a man, a postman shall we say, can go out to work and earn a wage such that his wife can stay at home to look after the children then many of the social evils that we have got will stop. When you put the housing market in the hands of bankers, these are not benign people. They are there to make as much money as they possibly can. We now have a situation comparable to that which existed in Japan fifteen years ago where the government authorised multi-generational mortgages. You would buy a house with the intent of paying the mortgage off via your son and your grandson. Now we are talking about people getting mortgages to the tune of ten times one's annual salary. Nurses cannot afford a proper place to live'. Graham's final judgement was: 'The rich have never been richer and the poor have never been more disadvantaged. It is at the cost of anybody who is in work. We have all become mortgage slaves. I would be better off if I went and signed on'.

Graham was as disaffected with the trades unions as he was with the New Labour project: 'I've never been a supporter of trades unions. I think they ruined this country in the 1960s and 1970s. They are politically dangerous. The government is there to look after the people. If we need unions then the government is not doing its job properly'. Asked whether voting in elections changed anything Graham replied 'Nothing'. Graham did not vote 'because it implies there is a choice and there isn't one. I think democracy is essentially an illusion. It is a numbers game. It is flawed to start from the assumption that the majority knows best. If we projected Britain thirty years hence and the Muslim component of the population had increased their number to perhaps thirty per cent they may well vote for an Islamic state. Just because there is more of them I don't necessarily think that would be a right or a good thing. To base the evolution of society on those who can reproduce most is dangerous. We should put the most talented people into the most important positions. Unfortunately we don't get anywhere near that in this country. You need to build a strong society. That means that the strongest and most able are given the best resources. The benefits of those efforts are distributed to those who are less advantaged. To place people who do not have the necessary skills into certain positions is a burden on society'.

Graham had little time for the then mayor of London, Ken Livingstone: 'In terms of building up a huge bureaucracy he has done well. In terms of covering the city with cameras and charges he has done brilliantly. It is of no benefit to me. The Congestion Charge is a disaster for small businesses'. Graham did not see any environmental benefits arising from the Charge: 'The truth is the biggest polluters out there are the diesel buses and taxis. They are the worst polluters on the planet. He has filled positions with his buddies. No-one really knows what they do except that many are paid over £100,000 a year'. Asked what three things he would change if he were made mayor of London Graham replied: 'We need higher-profile policing. The police have disappeared. We are told that crime has declined. That's rubbish. The reason for the decline in crime figures is because you can't telephone the police and report the crime now. They never answer the telephone. People have just given up. We try and there's no-one there. Crime is now out of control. People feeding drug habits. People just trying to survive. We need to deal with the drug problem and deal with housing and deal with policing. That would make London more comfortable – more liveable – for people. The problem with drugs is that the authorities don't know how to deal with them. We didn't stop people taking heroin or smoking marijuana by putting people in prison. In fact the opposite is true. The use of illegal drugs has gone through the roof. The only way to solve the problem of drugs is to make them legal. Get them dispensed over the counter. Get the crime out of drugs. And get people into detox and rehabilitation if they want it. That is the way to deal with drugs. Accept they are going to be there, because you are not going to get rid of them'.

London's Olympic project left Graham cold: 'I would like it to be something that would be really good, but I suspect it's going to be something that's a negative. A lot of money will be spent down in the East End, which will be good as it's regeneration. But as with any city that takes it on it's a great deal of work and responsibility and mostly they make a loss at the end of it. We can't even agree on what sort of logo to use. The logo says nothing to me.[17] I think they should stop taking the drugs. I think the Olympics would be a lot more interesting if they allowed all the people who come over to admit they use drugs. The Olympics now is a farce. Most people can't be bothered to watch it because they know that the biggest and the fastest achieved their records through drug use. I won't go. It's a nonsense. People don't want to see someone jumping twenty-three feet without drugs. They want to see someone jump twenty-nine feet with drugs. They'll have to address the issues of drugs and amateur status before it'll have any significance for me'.

Graham celebrated London – despite its many social and economic problems and the 'farce' of the 2012 Olympics: 'London is a very special place because of its history. Because of its location, its creativity. It is an extraordinary place that contains extraordinary people. You find them in the most unlikely places. Coldplay used to live in next door's basement. It attracts people who want to do something'. Graham's last word on his birthplace was 'Vibrant'.

13. The journalist

Neil was born in the South Wales town of Neath in 1947. Married with three children he had enjoyed a long and illustrious career in journalism. He had worked on the *Sunday Telegraph*, *Times* and *Independent*. His degree in behavioural science had probably helped him in his work. He had lived in or around London for about forty years. He came to Fleet Street by a circuitous route: 'I worked as a painter and decorator. Then taught in a secondary school. Then I did a post-grad course in journalism at Cardiff. I worked at the *Kent Messenger*, Maidstone, for four to five years. Then I worked on the *Sunday Telegraph* as chief City sub-editor for about seven years. Then I became deputy features editor for *Times Business News*. Then a City reporter, then labour reporter, writing about trades unions. Because I refused to cross the picket line during the Wapping dispute I was fired. I went to the *Independent* for 20 years. Now I'm freelance and have been for three months'.

Neil's worst job had been 'probably chief City sub-editor for the *Sunday Telegraph* because I was working for a right-wing newspaper and I'm not particularly right-wing myself. And I was working for a difficult man'. Asked how he had reconciled his personal politics with those of the *Sunday Telegraph* he replied: 'Personal ambition, on the one hand, and I wasn't writing about politics, so that certainly helped'. Neil's best job had been 'labour editor of the *Independent* because I had a kind of free hand to report facts as I saw them. But then the newspaper changed slightly. It used to be a kind of general newspaper that accommodated all kinds of specialisms. These days it is concentrating on certain areas and as a consequence certain other areas are not covered to any significant extent. During my last two or three years I enjoyed it decreasingly. I was pleased to leave in the end. It is a left-of-centre newspaper but it's a rather middle-class left-of-centre. So it's interested in the environment and it's interested in civil liberties and so on. But it's not desperately left-wing when it comes to the workplace. It is not interested in trades unions any more. I think the editor regards trades unions as boring, basically, and in a strange kind of way antiquated. When the *Mirror* bought a portion of the *Independent* a few years ago one of the first things they did was to derecognise the union. We had to wait for a Labour government to be re-elected to pass legislation which meant that if we held a vote we could lawfully set up a union which had to be recognised. We got ourselves re-recognised'. Taken in the round Neil enjoyed his long career at the *Independent*: 'I liked my colleagues. I thought they were talented people and I got on with them. Most of them were interested in doing a good job. I got on with them very well.... At the *Independent* I did as I pleased, although that sounds a bit sparse. Because I was quite experienced I sorted my work out myself. It was a bit like being self-employed but employed at the same time. It was a question of bringing home the bacon to the paper. If one brought home the bacon they didn't really mind. I was slightly semi-detached, I suppose, because I had been around for quite a long time and I had developed my own way of working. Regimes changed at the *Independent*, but overall they were quite relaxed about that'. Asked whether he liked working in the Westminster Village Neil commented: 'I enjoyed it. It could be a bit claustrophobic. But villages tend to be. You are continually meeting the same people. I enjoyed reporting on politics. Some of the journalists can be a bit arrogant. But once you get to know them and puncture their egos a few times they turn out not to be so bad after all'. One of the down sides of doing freelance work was losing one's work colleagues: 'I don't see my colleagues in work so often which is a bit of a down side because I'm a reasonably social animal. That was a part of the job that I liked'.

At the time of the interview Neil was living in a pleasant, detached house in Gravesend, a village that had become a dormitory for London's workers: 'We've just paid the mortgage off with the help of "redundo". It's reasonably desirable. It has quite a lot of original Victorian features in it that we have exposed bit by bit. It is reasonably spacious. When we had our three sons there it was good because we had a bit of space'. Neil enjoyed Gravesend's social variety: 'It's multicultural. There is a big Asian population. There are lots of Indian restaurants. I'm mad keen on curry, and it's a fairly lively area. Housing is quite cheap. It's pretty harmonious. It's mainly Muslim and Sikh. People seem to rub along quite reasonably'. Like many London satellite towns Gravesend had its social problems: 'There is a fairly large population of quite low-paid young people with nothing much to do, sometimes. They can cause a bit of trouble. But it doesn't deter me from living in the area'. Asked if he considered fear of crime to be a more serious problem than crime itself Neil said: 'In some areas of London you have lots of poorly paid people with drug problems. There are certain areas where you would not walk around on your own. But I think you are OK in most parts of London'. Asked where in London he would most like to live Neil said: 'Covent Garden or Soho because there is so much going on'.

Neil was in little doubt as to the government's best decision: 'It was introducing the national minimum wage. That was largely the result of pressure put on the government by trades unions'. Without union pressure Blair would have balked at a national minimum wage, said Neil: 'Blair's instincts are free market. If the trades unions didn't have an input into the Labour Party I doubt very much whether we would have had a national minimum wage. Or if we had it would have been a lot weaker than it is'.

'You could still strengthen employment laws' thought Neil. 'For instance you have to work somewhere for a year before you get protected by the law. It seems to me you should be protected from things like unfair dismissal from day one. I think they should support manufacturing industry to a greater extent. I don't think the country can survive on the service sector alone. I think there should be some kind of manufacturing base. I think people should be encouraged to become more highly skilled. It seems to me that whenever we have a large construction project there simply aren't enough brickies, scaffolders and joiners to go around. We have to import them. I don't think that's necessarily a good idea in economic terms. And I don't think it's a very good idea in social terms either because you get people who are disenfranchised, who are unskilled and who see no future for themselves'. Neil did not relish the prospect of Britain depending solely on the service sector for its wealth: 'I think any sensible stewardship of the economy should involve manufacturing. It should be a mixed economy. I do not think it is sensible to concentrate on the service sector because services ebb and flow. We need a solid base in terms of energy production and the basics of manufacturing. I think our manufacturing should be high value-added, so people are skilled. I don't think we can compete with the Asia-Pacific region in terms of costs, but I think we should be able to compete with anywhere in the world when it comes to sophisticated manufacturing... aviation, electronics. I think there should also be a motor-manufacturing industry and general engineering industry'.

Not unsurprisingly, given his having been sacked for refusing to cross picket lines during the Wapping dispute, Neil supported the trades unions: 'I think they are struggling because people are less trade-union minded. Where there are trades unions people have a better deal than where there is no trade union. But I think there is a crisis of confidence. We see that in the constant merging of different unions in order to make themselves more powerful and enjoy economies of scale. In political terms it has been better under Labour but it could be even better'. Asked if he thought the unions would get a better hearing under Brown than Blair he said: 'Yes, but only marginally so. I think Brown is more a creature of the Labour Party than Blair ever was. I don't think there is much between them politically but I think the unions have a slightly better chance under Brown than they had under Blair'.

Neil was a committed democrat who used his vote: 'When I look at other countries where there is no voting culture I think people should use their vote. I think broadly speaking, with major exceptions like the Iraq War, the government reflects the consensus. They might not agree with the consensus but I think broadly they reflect it. There are notable exceptions. I think the Iraq War was always unpopular, but generally speaking I think broadly in terms of policies it reflects what the electorate wants it to reflect'. Asked if he thought he was offered a real policy choice at elections Neil said: 'I think the Tories have tried to move into the centre ground. The leader of the Tories has a problem because the rump, well not quite the rump, the grass-roots of the Tory party is still quite right-wing. So in terms of choice I think all the parties are in the centre of politics these days, or near the centre, so there is less of a choice than there was. There was always a choice between Labour and Thatcher. Thatcher was very right-wing. There is less of a choice now because the Tories are trying to steal some of Labour's clothes'.

Neil was a fan of Ken Livingstone: 'I think he's doing an excellent job. I think the Congestion Charge was a very good idea, although it is not progressive in the sense that the more you earn or the bigger your car the more you pay when you travel into the centre of London. In terms of transport he's presided over a huge increase in bus use, for instance, which is a very good idea. He's very good for London in terms of transport'. Asked whether the mayor should be given more power Neil said: 'I think he has quite a bit of power already. He has had to bow to the government so perhaps he should have more power over transport'. Asked what he would change if he were mayor of London Neil focused on transport and youth services: 'Public transport is the life-blood of the city and I would like to see Transport for London having slightly more power than it has to run London Underground, for instance, as it sees fit rather than have a public–private partnership forced on it. I'd like to see more people employed on public transport to ensure that travellers aren't harassed by people who are hopelessly drunk. London is more aggressive than other parts of Britain. I'd like to see them engage young people in deprived areas more. Money isn't necessarily the answer but I'd like to see more effort put into engaging young people from poor areas to become more educated'.

Asked if he thought the 2012 Olympic Games would be a good thing for the capital Neil said: 'Yes, a good thing. It will enable more people to see what kind of city it is and that multiculturalism can and does work and that tolerance of other people and other people's ideas can and does work. Drawing people in to experience that for themselves will be a good thing. It's a very good idea to engage young people in sport. Sport is a very important element in people's lives. It can only be a force for good, from that point of view'. Asked if he thought it would be better to spend the money directly on social amenities he said: 'I would tend to agree with that, but we are where we are. It is like somebody saying, well, should the Americans have gone to the moon. Well, they went there. Generally speaking humans like big occasions. They like big expeditions. They like something new, something different. I understand why people would want the Olympics. The money could probably be better spent but I don't think that's realistic. I don't think that the money that would have been spent on the Olympics would necessarily be spent on housing and so on. It would just dissipate in other ways'.

London, said Neil, was notable for its social variety and tolerance: 'It's special because it is, broadly speaking, quite a tolerant city. I think it has more diversity than a lot of other cities, in terms of ethnic groups, and so on. I think it is special because it is multicultural and multiracial, and long may it live'. Asked if he thought London had more in common with other capital cities than with England and Britain he said: 'It's a capital city so it soaks up people from different parts of Britain and the world. Although places like Manchester and Birmingham are similar to that extent it is not quite as marked as it is in London. It is more of everything. It is more of an international city. It is more varied and therefore possibly has more in common with other big cities abroad. It is more multicultural than most'. 'Multicultural' was the adjective Neil used to summarise his London experience.

We had talked in a Strand wine bar frequented by journalists and politicians. We sat outside in the summer sun, chatting, drinking and, between exchanges, listening to the tuneful band practising in the adjacent pleasure garden. When I got my first full-time job in London I took a bed-sitter in Ealing, west London. I tried to describe Ealing to my girlfriend (later to become my wife, then ex-wife). Ealing was, I wrote, 'a comfort, like an old monochrome film'. I got the same comforting feeling sitting outside the old Strand wine bar. This was a comforting, familiar, warming London. A *pleasure*.

Verstehen

London can be both a pleasure and a pain. In my years there I have experienced both. If the capital magnifies personal pleasures it also magnifies personal pains. When my wife told me she was upping sticks and leaving I felt pretty desolate. It was a Sunday. I went to see a film in a Leicester Square picture house. The film was Mike Leigh's *High Hopes*. This was not the best entertainment choice, as it turned out. Like much of Leigh's work, *High Hopes* is a bleak commentary on life. He has a knack of stripping away the noise we create. That shrill noise that blanks the pointlessness, tedium and banality of our lives. We all like to think we're important and that we do important things. But we aren't and don't (this is especially true of academics, including the author of this tome). Please don't misunderstand me. Leigh's film is a carefully crafted indictment of yuppie greed and immorality, a window on the sharp social, economic and political fissures of London life. Just don't go and see it when your life falls apart. You might be found floating face-down in the river.

14. The bookie

Vince was born in Shaftesbury in 1957. After getting a good degree from King's College London he got a job with a large firm of bookmakers. Apart from a brief interregnum with a firm of tax accountants Vince had worked for the same bookmaking firm for three decades. The worst job Vince had ever had was, unfortunately, his current one 'which is not good news. The role of district operations manager means I'm doing tasks I don't particularly enjoy... but they have to be done. Currently I'm not a particularly happy bunny. My least favourite task is the structured visit to the betting shop where you are committing yourself to visit all twenty shops within a monthly time period, which can be done, but as Mr Macmillan used to say "events, dear boy, events"... other things happen which means you are trying to multi-task and it's difficult keeping all the balls in the air. I currently feel a bit stressed. There are many times when I'd like to cancel my commitment to go to a certain shop at a certain time, but you have to go. At the same time as doing the visits you are responsible for recruiting, training, disciplining, doing their wages, visiting shops, doing checks. They have a programme designed to improve customer care, which is worthwhile, but it's very structured and it's very time-consuming and it does feel as if you're a little bit trapped, I think'. Vince's best time at work was when he managed his own betting shop: 'I think managing my own shop in north London from 1990 to 1998 was the best time I've had at work. I worked hard. It went rather quickly, looking back. The good thing was that you were managing your own shop. You had responsibilities to your line manager but on the whole they let you get on with things. I had a good team with a good team spirit. We achieved our objectives. The customers were happy. In retrospect, now, when I see other managers I realise that I was a good manager. At the time I possibly wasn't aware of that'.

As a district operations manager Vince had major responsibilities for service quality, profitability and staff: 'I'm the line manager for twenty managers and also their staff, deputy managers, cashiers – who are now called customer service assistants – and the cleaners. My current payroll has got about one hundred and forty people on it. It's my job to make sure the shops are open and maximising their profit, that they are staffed and that the staff are trained. I've also got to train a manager to cover me. You are a bit of a social worker because you are listening to people's problems. At the same time you are trying to develop them to work in teams, to give better customer service, so the customers come back more often to lose more money and increase profits for the company'.

Despite the stresses of the job, Vince drew strength from and enjoyed the company of his workmates: 'What are my peers like? They're a good bunch. There is not much jealousy amongst us five. We help each other out. I've got no gripes with any of them. We've got a lot on our plates and we try to help each other if we can'. Asked what he thought his fellow managers thought of him he said: 'They think I'm dependable and reliable. They know if I can help them I will. I don't step on their toes. They probably think I'm a reliable soul who is not ambitious and therefore not to be worried about'. Vince had a female line manager whose support he valued: 'She's very good, very fair. You can always talk to her. She's aware of the problems. The stresses. If she can help she will. If I had a problem I'd go to her so, yes, I am quite lucky with my boss'. As to what he thought she thought of him he said: 'She thinks I'm dependable; that I should have more confidence; probably that I worry too much'. Despite its challenges and stresses there were certain aspects of the job of district operations manager that Vince enjoyed: 'I'm quite good at recruiting, training and developing. I still enjoy identifying people with talent and then ensuring they go on to do the relevant courses. I enjoy trying to develop them to become deputies and managers'. The worst aspect of the job was 'multi, multi, multi tasking'. 'There does seem to be a little bit too much of that' said Vince.

Like many of those who work with the general public (like Graham in Camden) Vince had crossed swords with punters: 'I have had arguments with customers which in hindsight could have been handled better... but at the time the rules were such that you had to stick to a decision. Ten, fifteen, twenty years ago rows in bookies were common. They were heated and they got irrational. In the last ten years I think we've got away from that. Ten, twenty years ago all the bets were over the counter, so the bets were settled by the managers and if there were disputes over race times or prices it was down to the manager to explain the situation and deal with it as best he could. You had good days and bad days. It was down to you and your staff to handle the situation. In the last few years they have decided to give the customer more advantage, in my opinion, so you have fewer rows now. Instead of arguing with the customer you pay him his £50, even if he's not entitled to it. The reasoning behind this is simple – in the long run he will lose that £50, so why argue with him? That's the way they look at things. However, in the last eight years machines have been introduced into the betting shops. These machines are called "fixed odds terminals". They've attracted a younger crowd, in London often of eastern European origin. These are machines where they lose money and it's not down to the manager to assuage them when they lose. If they lose they take their aggression out on the machine. So most of the violence in the shops is from guys breaking machines, smashing the glass. So the violence is there but it's not directed at the staff. The people who use the machines are not old-fashioned gamblers. We have attracted a new crowd. If we didn't have the machines we wouldn't have the arguments in the shops, on the whole'.

Vince lived in what he described as a 'Three-bedroomed semi-detached ex-council house in Edmonton'. Edmonton is not a glamorous suburb. Home to 'white van man' and London's cab drivers Vince offered this description of Edmonton's social heart, Edmonton Green Shopping Centre: 'It's full of white trash. Middle-aged women with lots of kids, and their daughters who look exactly the same as them, with kids already'. Despite Edmonton's distance from the bright lights of London Vince made an effort to travel in: 'I have two nights out in a week, I'd say. Saturday I go out with friends and have a few drinks. Sometimes I go clubbing it, sometimes I don't. Sunday, having hopefully slept, I do the same thing. I go back and go drinking and clubbing it. I come back on Monday morning at about 8 a.m.. I can't do it every weekend but most weekends I can. I'm doing the things in my forties I should have done twenty years ago, so I've got catching up to do. I have a good time'. Reflecting on Edmonton's remoteness Vince said: 'I can see the convenience of living closer to the centre and possibly south of the river. Maybe somewhere like Pimlico or Vauxhall but I probably have not got the ambition at my time of life to move there'.

Verstehen

I know Edmonton. I lived there for a short while. Edmonton is symptomatic of a shameful period when urban sprawl seemed natural and inevitable. Vast tracts of good-quality farmland were bought up, often by local councils, for development. Huge council estates sprayed across London's green environs, replacing green lung with alienated youth, corrosive low-level crime, regressive social attitudes, concentrated poverty, ugliness, banality and hopelessness. Edmonton is one of the centres of London's pernicious shell-suit culture. I defy anyone not to be depressed by London's reservations for the poor. How can intelligent people (councillors and university-educated planners) do such violence to a city? It's not as if they built one estate, learned a lesson, then stopped. They kept on building. Didn't they talk to colleagues in other boroughs? Didn't they think of visiting other boroughs' failing developments to understand the pitfalls? Edmonton is flat. The council estates seem to stretch to the horizon. All the houses are the same. The estates are rotting from the inside... and at the same rate. Someone is going to have one hell of a mess to clean up in 50 years time. Meanwhile, on the estates, hopeless families reproduce hopelessness. Girls continue to start families at sixteen. They and their offspring smoke, glue-sniff, binge-drink, dabble in drugs, shun education, exist on a diet of take-away food, believe what the tabloids say, do as the tabloids say, watch garbage television – 'bubblegum for the mind', as someone once said. Talent, unable to flourish in a social and cultural desert, dies on the indifferent streets. What an achievement. Well done central government. Well done London's boroughs. Well done the universities. Take a bow.

Asked to name the best thing the government had done for working people Vince said: 'They give too much time to maternity women. It certainly is a woman's world. It doesn't do anything for me. As a single bloke I don't think the government does much for me'. Although he believed that voting could change things Vince saw a convergence in national politics: 'Yes I think the parties have converged, but I would still guess that they possibly represent about eighty per cent of voters. I'd say there's possibly ten per cent on the right and ten per cent on the left who probably do feel that they've been swindled. But for the vast majority of people who are centre, centre-right, centre-left, I would have thought that the two main parties, and the Liberal Democrats, do actually cover most of their ambitions'.

Regarding London's administration Vince thought Ken Livingstone as mayor had been doing a reasonable job for Londoners: 'I would say he's been good for London. Even though I didn't vote for him he's been successful in giving the impression that he does care about London. Whether its spin or not he gives the impression he does things for London and works efficiently for London. Even though I don't agree with most of his politics I do feel that he's actually a voice in doing something for London'. Asked what three things he would change if he were mayor Vince mentioned transport, crime and accommodation: 'I'd run the tubes during the night. You would have to do something about the gangs in London and the culture of knives and guns that go with it. I'm not saying I've got the answers and I'm not saying that Ken doesn't care about it, but it is a problem. Even though law and order sounds like a right-wing thing something has to be done to stop the blacks killing and gunning each other. But what the answer is, I don't know. Something needs to be done about the teenagers and the gang culture. I'd build more affordable homes. I'm not so sure it's sensible to build homes in the Thames Gateway. From what I can see it's prone to flooding. Obviously you have got problems like more houses need more water and all the stuff that goes with it. And I'd make sure all new homes had solar panels in their roofs for solar energy'.

Vince, an athletics fan all his life, thought well of the Olympics: 'They'll be a good thing for London. I've got no time for people who moan – those "everything is half empty" people – the last Olympics held here were in 1948. I'll be honest. I never thought there'd be any in this country in my lifetime. I know it's the fashion now to give them to Third World countries. OK, it's going to cost money, but think how much money is spent in this country anyway. Hopefully at the end of it there will be good facilities for people. It might not tick all the boxes but London should go into it and make the most of it and enjoy it... and stop whinging about it... I'll attend on one or two days just to say "I was there"'. London was a special place, thought Vince: 'My instinct is that it is special because it is the centre for the press and television and tourists. With the Olympics coming I think you'd have to say there is something special about London'. As to whether London had more in common with other capital cities than with the rest of the United Kingdom Vince said: 'I suppose there is some element of truth in that. But that's not to say that multiculturalism doesn't exist in Birmingham and Manchester and Glasgow or Edinburgh or Cardiff'. His one-word summation of London was 'busy'.

I had interviewed Vince in the front room of his ex-council property. The house was well kept with a bit of garden front and rear. I walked to the bus stop on the Great Cambridge Road. I passed street after street of almost identical properties. Purchased houses had been tinkered with. Owners had added stone cladding (something that should be outlawed) or black-painted wood to achieve a mock-Tudor effect. Sometimes a plastic porch – freezing in winter, boiling in summer – had been glued to the front entrance. When I lived in Edmonton I noticed how salesmen would blitz an area in order to shift as many porches, car ports and other types of plasticated carbuncle as possible. Cars and vans were parked everywhere – in driveways, on pavements, on the engine-oil-sodden, litter-strewn grass verges. Many cars seemed better tended than their owners' houses. Thanks to Ken I didn't have to wait too long for a bus to Turnpike Lane underground. My big red bus sped through an ocean of urban sprawl, everything the same, characterless, boring, anaesthetic for the eye. 'There's no hope', I thought. 'We're all doomed, and we deserve to be'. The most daunting thing about London is the sheer scale of its badlands.

15. The web designer

Robert was born in 1977 in Leamington Spa. Single, he had lived in London for two years. At the age of fourteen he moved to Canada where he trained as a chef. Later he moved to New York to work. 'My education is slightly unorthodox' he said. 'I went to school in Canada but I never got my high school diploma. However I eventually got a higher national diploma and a degree in the UK'. As to why he left catering he said: 'Catering was exploitative in the UK and I was in that frame of mind to do a degree. I think I was twenty-five when I decided to re-educate myself. It was incredibly challenging and rewarding work. That was partly down to my motivation. I really wanted to change what I was doing'.

Robert's worst-ever job had been in catering: 'When I came back from New York I was very de-motivated as a chef. I went to get a job as a waiter in a very small establishment. They thought of themselves as very elitist. I was the only waiter there. It was a dreadful place to work in terms of attitudes towards the clients and the staff. I found the owner of the restaurant an abominable person. It was awful working with him so in the end I jacked it in'. His best job was his current one: 'This job is the best one I've had because it's mentally very challenging. They push me to my intellectual limits. They are investing in me. I'm getting trained. It is very, very rewarding work'.

Robert lived in Whitechapel, an area he liked for its liveliness and convenience for central London: 'I share a two-bedroomed apartment with my twin brother. It's in a gated community that has a twenty-four-hour porter. It's a converted schoolhouse with double-height ceilings and a mezzanine level. It's a pleasant place to live with a nice Zen feeling. I like the space the apartment offers and the location. It's easy to see my friends in Shoreditch. I really like hanging out in Brick Lane. There's a lot more character there and ethnic diversity. The best feature of Whitechapel is its proximity to Brick Lane and the museums in the city like the Tate Modern gallery. It's easy to get anywhere you like because it's right on the cusp of zone one'. Whitechapel had its negative aspects, though, including poverty, crime, litter and the many social problems found in Tower Hamlets (as described earlier in this book). Asked if he had ever been a victim of crime Robert said: 'I've never been a victim of crime, but it's fear of victimisation, more than anything else'.

Robert's ideal London location would be 'Somewhere closer to the City, possibly somewhere next to London Bridge'. Robert could see himself moving out of London at some point: 'I'm definitely not here for good. I think I'd want to get away from the rat-race more than anything else... I might want a slower pace. Those are the reasons why I could see myself moving outside London'. He went out three or four nights each week. 'Sometimes you can take things for granted and not go out' he said. He played sport and designed his own T-shirts, which he gave to friends and family.

Robert did his web-development work for a leading cancer charity: 'I'm involved in getting information about our scientific research out onto the web. The charity has a big fundraising department that runs campaigns... I'm instrumental in helping to develop those campaigns on-line. I also do a lot of the intranet development. So I'm primarily a technical resource for anybody who wants anything done on the Internet or intranet'. Robert secured the job through an agency. At the time he was fortunate in having a choice of two jobs: 'The charity's salary and benefits package was very attractive. I must admit, however, that it wasn't my first choice. At the time I wanted to go into a more creative agency. I was worried about stifling my creativity by going into a business such as this. The charity's primary need is informational, more than anything else. I had a choice between two jobs, between this place and an advertising agency in Hoxton Square... I really wrestled with this decision. I ended up choosing the cancer charity because of its training. It was better for my career, more than anything else. Plus the benefits package was very good'.

Asked how many hours he worked in a week Robert said: 'It depends how busy we are, really. Recently I have been getting to work at nine and finishing at five... that's nowhere near what I could do in catering. In the UK catering industry there is an over-reliance on split-shifts. That requires you to come in very early in the morning to work the lunch shift, then go home for a couple of hours, then come back and work the evening shift. Sometimes a restaurant will stay open late, so you'll come back at six and work until closing. Fridays, Saturdays and Christmas are mental. You are very busy from Thursday to Sunday. The only quiet months are January and February'. Asked which was the harder job – catering or web design – Robert said: 'Catering was a very manual job. Web design is very analytical. I seem to find that I'm as exhausted at the end of each day as I was in catering. After I finished my shift in catering it took me a couple of hours to wind down. That pattern tends to be quite destructive. If it's eleven at night and you need a couple of hours to wind down what happens is you go for a few drinks here, and a few drinks there, so it can be quite destructive, potentially. With cerebral work it's very difficult to switch off. It's difficult not to think about the problems you are dealing with, particularly coding problems, which you tend to mull over. You are desperate for a solution. Sometimes you wake up in the middle of the night. It keeps on turning. But with the manual stuff, it's over. But I really enjoy what I do'.

Asked what he thought of his colleagues Robert said: 'I make an effort to get along with people... it's my nature to get along. And also I think it's part of my job as well. Being a web analyst/developer means I have to be approachable. People who have problems with the web will get intimidated because of its technical nature. If I'm not approachable to staff I am making myself redundant... I'm not doing my job very well'. Asked if he found working with academic researchers a strain Robert said: 'No. Fortunately by the time they've decided what they want, they want it yesterday'. Asked if he thought he received a fair wage for the web-design job he said: 'I think I'm due for an increase in salary... but the benefits package is very good... there's a final salary pension scheme. There are not many people out there who can say they have a final salary pension scheme supported by their employer. Then there's the holidays. Twenty-five days plus Christmas plus the bank holidays. We get loans... bike loans, transport loans, and that sort of thing'. Robert caught a tube to work which took forty minutes (on a good day).

Asked to name the best thing the Labour government had done for working people Robert said: 'The minimum wage. I was working as a chef at the time and there was a massive discrepancy in minimum wages. The poor waiters were getting nothing, so they had to live off their tips. Considering Britain is such a terrible place for tipping the legal minimum wage did bolster their income a lot. That's about it, really. I don't think I've seen a massive number of improvements'. Asked if he thought the legal minimum wage harmed the restaurant industry (as some had predicted it would) Robert said: 'No, because the mark-up on food is astronomical. There is a healthy enough profit-margin there to increase waiters' wages. Your food cost in general is 35 per cent. That's the cost of food. Then you've got overheads which always stay at about 15 per cent to 20 per cent. Then you've got 50 per cent pure profit'. As to what else the government could do for working people Robert said: 'They could make transport more efficient. Because the tube failed today I had to take four tubes to get here. A decent transport system would be great'. Asked what he thought of the trades unions Robert said: 'The catering unions were pretty ineffectual. When I worked in the US as a chef I worked on some movie sets and their teamsters' union was very, very powerful. I got a very good salary from that'.

Asked if he thought that voting in elections changed anything Robert said: 'If you don't vote, why bother? Why complain about it? It's probably because problems are so complex that you don't see a difference. Only if you have a personal problem and they solve that problem for you do you see a difference. Only if you have a particular gripe and it is addressed do you see a difference'. Despite his left-of-centre politics Robert disagreed with Tony Blair's policy on Iraq: 'I think it was totally inexcusable to get involved in a war in Iraq and align ourselves with such a fascist in the United States. This guy Bush is pure evil. I am utterly opposed to what Blair did. Tony Blair was a hidden politician.... I like the fact that Gordon Brown has distanced himself from Bush'. Asked what sort of job Ken Livingstone was doing as mayor of London Robert said: 'I think he's doing a good job. I like the Congestion Charge, although there are rumblings about that. You walk around Chelsea and you see these four-million-pound houses and apartments and the owners are moaning that they have to pay a bit more in Congestion Charge when they can afford these absolutely stunning houses that nobody else can afford. You have to be absolutely stinking rich to live around here'. Asked if he might be peddling the politics of envy with such views Robert said: 'No. I choose not to drive. Why do you need to drive in London? There's not much point driving around London. It's too congested'.

Asked if he thought of London as a special place Robert said: 'London is unique. It has higgledy-piggledy streets. It's a very different entity from New York. It still has those big city attitudes, though, like rudeness. You don't make eye-contact on the tube. As to differences between London and New York there's a bit more social responsibility, I think. There's a certain type of flamboyance within London... you tend to see it in major metropolitan areas. We have the Shoreditch Twat – a guy dressed up like Nathan Barley – really, really cool. He's wearing his pants down to his knees, that sort of thing. Skinny jeans. Über, über trendy. You see that sort of creative look here where people follow their own trends and styles. There are more restrictions in small communities'. Asked what he would change if he were mayor of London and money were no object Robert said: 'I'd improve transport. I'd provide a greater amount of affordable accommodation for first-time buyers. But I'd want that housing to be innovative, not just a block of council houses. So it'd have to be dynamic and funky and trendy. I would also clean the city up'. The Olympics, said Robert, would be 'a good and a bad thing' for London: 'In terms of transport it will be a plus. In terms of the cost of living and housing in particular it will be a minus. House prices will go through the roof. I'll definitely go, though, but I hope they don't blow the budget too much'. 'Exciting' was Robert's London-in-a-word.

Robert's comfortable, modern office was located in a salubrious west London neighbourhood. There were quiet streets of stuccoed three- and four-storey Edwardian residences. The white-painted houses looked comfortable and rich. There were Range Rover Vogues and Porsche Cayennes for the mummies and daddies and Toyota buzz-boxes and Minis for the driving-age children. The gardeners and nannies and deliverers of organically grown fresh garden produce and painters and decorators went about their business. There were plenty of tourists, too, mostly American and Japanese. This was the London they expected to see, I thought, the London of the biscuit-tin illustration and Conan Doyle novel. I considered engaging a party in conversation and suggesting they took a train to Green Lanes or bus to Bermondsey or Brixton. Then I thought 'No. They've paid good money for this white-washed Metropolitan pantomime. Don't be nasty. Let them be'.

16. The poet

Geoff was born in Walthamstow, north-east London in 1959. He and his wife, who worked as a teaching assistant at a special school, had two children. Geoff's education included an HNC in Business Studies and various professional qualifications in public relations, marketing and advertising. Since getting his HNC Geoff had held four main jobs: 'I worked at the London Borough of Waltham Forest. I worked in the Leisure Department. I was there from 1981 to 1989, doing the marketing and public relations for the leisure services in the borough. Then I moved on to work in a corporate communications and PR position with Westminster City Council from 1989 to 2002. Then I moved to customer service management within Westminster Council in 2002 and worked there until 2005 when I went part-time, four days a week. I spent one day a week building up my new business which is my own company. I use poetry as a way of increasing people's communications skills, self-esteem, confidence and literacy skills. It's for adults and children. That's quite an unusual job'. The Waltham Forest job was the worst: 'I've liked all my jobs, but looking back the first job I did was the worst because it was two-dimensional. But at the time it seemed very exciting'. Running his own communications company was the best job: 'The best job is what I'm doing now by a long, long way. It's the first job I feel I was built to do'. Geoff elaborated: 'I think I'm fortunate in that I can actually combine something I think I'm actually good at, and have a talent for, which is writing poetry and performing, with a lot of the transferable skills I learned in other jobs. Most of them relate to communications, whether it's mentoring, dealing with difficult people, dealing with people in special target groups, people who don't speak English very well, elderly people, ex-offenders, people with mental health problems. The variation in what I do is fantastic. I work all over London'.

Like many, Geoff seemed to stumble upon his ideal job: 'In my previous jobs I used to say "This is not what I want to do when I grow up". I didn't really feel I was built for the jobs, even though I enjoyed them and did them all well, they were just jobs. But I have got high expectations of myself and life generally. I was always striving for something that was, perhaps, rather special. At forty-five years I didn't really think I was going to find it. Then, one day, when I was working in customer service management at Westminster Council a colleague at another council asked me if I'd like to come along and do some poetry at their Adult Learners Day. Then I said "Why don't I use writing and performing poetry to teach presentation and communications skills?" So I ran two workshops in one day. Based on the feedback I got from people they went absolutely brilliantly. My colleague said "When are you going to give up what you are doing and do this full-time". I asked Westminster if I could work for them for just four days each week instead of five. I spent one day a week building up my business... then in January 2006, six months after I went part-time, I gave my Westminster job up and, hopefully, I haven't looked back since... touch wood'. Asked if he ever came close to losing his nerve and staying in local government Geoff said: 'I think I did but it wasn't a question of losing my nerve. The reason why I stayed in local government is because there were no options outside. I never really saw that I could develop the kind of transferable skills that I had to move into what I am now doing. It was only a set of circumstances that tested me... that made me realise I could do it. The reason why I stayed in local government before that... wasn't because I was dull and boring, didn't want to move, not a risk-taker.

The reason was simply that I enjoyed the jobs. I thought that's what work was. I didn't realise – or perhaps I did realise – that you could enjoy work more. But I didn't think there would be an opportunity to do that. Then everything kind of fell into place and I took the opportunity and grabbed it with both hands. Probably if I had thought about it more I wouldn't have made the jump at all. The other factor is that work has never really ruled my life. I've always enjoyed work. I do it for the money. I do it for a reasonable wage, not a fantastic wage. I work to have a reasonable amount of leisure time so I can spend the money. I can't understand people who work every hour of the day, push themselves to the top of the organisation, probably end up with a divorce, lots of ulcers, got lots of money, but can't spend it. That's not really me'. Asked if he would have made the jump without his wife's support Geoff said: 'No. Because my family is always more important than anything to me. If my family wasn't happy with it there is no way I would have taken it. And I'm not just saying that because my wife might be reading the book'.

During his long working career Geoff had had one or two run-ins with colleagues: 'I've had a few arguments and confrontations, which I never shy away from. They have probably all revolved around one thing which is normally someone trying to exert their power over me or other people. I don't like injustice. I don't like people abusing their power. I don't like people taking advantage of their position. I think working in local government, which is a political environment with both a large and small 'p', was often quite political. There were a lot of egos bouncing around. A lot of stress and tension. People can get quite excited, quite forceful, and often for the wrong reasons. I think in this country a lot of people work their way up to the top because they have good technical skills but their person-skills are rubbish.... There are a lot of people in powerful management positions in leading organisations who are just rubbish at dealing with people'. Asked how he thought we might address that issue Geoff said: 'First you need to take risks. For example, when I was at Westminster Council there were people who were appointed as chief officers of departments who had no experience of the technical side of that department. Secondly, we need to get away from the mind set created by the current education system where we are into ticking boxes and looking at qualifications rather than looking at people's ability to do the job. Thirdly, perhaps we need to stop appointing people in our own image... we tend to think two-dimensionally when we interview people. We tend to appoint people who are similar to us, despite everything we say and do about equal opportunities and monitoring the way people are employed. I don't think we've really cracked that as a country yet'.

Asked to give a precise definition of his work Geoff said: 'On my business card it says poet/trainer. That's what I put on my tax form as well. The reason I say poet/trainer is because many who say they are poets just write poetry. I think if I market myself as just a poet the expectation from the people I'm trying to sell myself to is I'm just a poet. There are many people doing that. Because of my background in communications I like to stress the training side as well. I take commissions in corporate settings as well as in schools, libraries, etc. In those sorts of settings they are looking at getting a corporate trainer in or somebody a bit like myself who is a bit more whacky, a bit more off-the-wall in his approach, but nevertheless someone who is a trainer all the same. So I think poet/trainer just about sums it up'. Geoff, who could work up to forty hours in a week, loved his job. 'It's my passion' he said. Geoff used public transport to get to work: 'I get to my clients any way but driving. I'm not a driver. I cycle. I walk. I take a bus. I use the tube. I travel by rail. Sometimes a mixture of all. I haven't tried river bus yet, or tram or plane. I don't like flying.... My longest journey to work in London is two-and-a-half hours'.

Geoff was less than enthusiastic about New Labour's record: 'I don't really see a lot of positives coming from this government despite the fact that I voted for them. The only thing I would say is they have created a sound economy and the economy has been extremely robust. Under the Tories it was rather shaky during the latter stages of the Major administration. Whether or not that is down to the government or whether or not it is just the economic cycle of ups and downs I'm not quite sure. There are probably more negatives really that the government has created'. Asked what New Labour's reasonable economic record [prior to the economic woes of 2008, that is] had done for his one-man business Geoff said: 'I am often very frustrated because people have not got the money to employ me. Everybody wants to work with a poet, get a poet in for the day, whether it's a school, or a youth offending team or a library. So I could argue that it's the government's fault because the money isn't there. There isn't enough spent on public services. Not enough spent on the arts which one could argue is a social service. But perhaps there would be even less if we were still under a Tory administration. I'd like to see more money spent on the arts. More money spent in education. More money spent on the NHS, which is terribly, terribly poor when it comes to the kind of work that I do. Occupational therapists are keen to get people doing creative writing and poetry. But nobody has ever got any money. I find that very sad'.

Asked if he thought politicians routinely lie Geoff said: 'I don't think there is a straight answer to that. I think politicians are very economical with the truth, in the sense that they are always very keen to get their own agenda across, rather than answer a question directly. Most statistics can be manipulated in any way you want... to say anything you want. What politicians do is to always present a story that shows them in a favourable light. I would say politicians are manipulative, rather than lying. I don't think that most politicians do lie. I don't trust many of the politicians that I have worked for. But I wouldn't say that they would out-and-out lie because they are too worried about getting caught out, especially in today's accountable government. There is normally some kind of audit trail of papers, figures, whatever, that you can track back to find out if somebody is lying. What they are is very, very manipulative and economical with the truth'. Asked if he thought the media did a good job of holding politicians to account Geoff said: 'On the whole, no, because I think a large part of the populist media don't make them account for themselves. And the quality papers aren't read by most people. The vast majority of the media that the vast majority of the people read don't hold politicians to account. It's the eighty–twenty rule. About eighty per cent of the media is in the hands of twenty per cent of the people. People like Rupert Murdoch, etc. So we have a very stilted view of things, like asylum seekers. Trying to find a positive case for asylum seekers is very difficult because ninety-nine per cent of the media will be against them, including many of the quality papers. But thank God there are some serious journalists out there who do project the right image for the media and are able to dig up stories. But there's not enough of it'.

As to what else New Labour could do to help working people Geoff said: 'There are things the present government could do without any doubt. But I think a lot of them go beyond the power of the present government. We need to perhaps look at the way the whole of society is structured. There are all sorts of things I am not happy with in society. I don't think the government can just wave a magic wand and solve them all. But there are things they could do. I'd like to see tax more even'. Asked if he thought there was anything more the government could do to help the small businessman Geoff said: 'Mine's a very straightforward business. It's just me. I've got an accountant. I'd love to say "No, the government should help me do this, that and the other" but I don't think it would make a great deal of difference or impact on the kind of business I run'.

Unlike New Labour fundamentalists Geoff was right behind the trades unions: 'I agree with unions. I think there was perhaps a time in the 1970s when they were too powerful and needed to be tamed. But I think it has got to the stage now where it's completely the opposite. People are in a situation now where they are just exploited consistently at work. For example my wife was appointed on a certain grade. She's now working at a higher grade. She was told by her manager that there wasn't enough money to pay her on the higher grade. She was told if you want to get on, basically, just be sensible and do the extra duties. If that was twenty years ago there would have been a mass walk-out. But there is just no power in people's hands nowadays. I could not believe it when the Labour Party dropped Clause Four. I think it's sad that we are now in a position similar to America where there is no difference between the two main parties... so I think it's a bit sad that unions are so much weaker than they used to be. I wouldn't like to see them any stronger than they were in the Seventies, though. I think there was a lot of mismanagement by government in the 1970s as well. I don't think the situation in the 1970s was just down to the unions by any means'.

Geoff believed that voting in elections could have an impact: 'I think it changes some things because if you have a different government it's going to run the country differently. But I don't think it changes enough. I don't think governments really listen to people. It's a democracy by definition. In practice I don't think it's a democracy, however, because the government doesn't listen to the people. It never really has done, to be frank. If it did it wouldn't have walked into Iraq. Clearly most people did not want that to happen'. Geoff chose not to vote in Tony Blair's final general election (which saw New Labour's parliamentary majority reduce): 'In the last general election, for the first time ever I'm sorry to say, I didn't vote. I could not believe I didn't vote. I'm a socialist at heart. I looked for a socialist party but couldn't find one. I would have voted Socialist Alliance or Green Party, but there wasn't a candidate who represented those parties in Chingford, unfortunately. I felt terribly guilty not voting. But I did read quite a lot of articles before the last general election and there were many people – a lot of quite learned people – people like John Pilger and Alexei Sayle, who said they were not voting because they felt the act of not voting in itself said more to a government than the act of voting. I strongly believe that. I think if nobody voted we might get to a stage where the government does become more accountable and starts to listen to people. All you are doing when you vote a government in is you are giving them the licence to do what they want'.

Geoff applauded Ken Livingstone's efforts to improve London's transport infrastructure: 'I think in terms of transport he's making a fantastic difference. For somebody who uses public transport all the time I can't believe how frequent the buses are. OK the prices have rocketed up. But I don't mind paying more to get a good service. I'd say the same about the tubes as well. I think Ken Livingstone is quite a clever character. As he showed in the past when he used to run the Greater London Council he knows which strings to pull to make it seem like he's doing a lot more than he actually is. I see Ken Livingstone as quite an opportunist. I think if you look for the other things that he has done which have made a difference I'm not really sure what impact he has made.... But I'd still vote for Ken every time, because I think he's far and away the best. I think his heart is in the right place, and I also think as a politician he's one of the few who says what he believes and does what he believes, but does actually listen to people as well... most of the time. So he's as honest a politician as you will get. But a man of contradictions as well'. Geoff singled out crime, poverty and transport for more attention: 'Crime must be addressed. It's important that crime is tackled. While I know the fear of crime is more than the actual level of crime itself, and crime is going down, although violent crime is going up, I'd like to see that tackled with more police men and women on the street, and more clever policing. There's a vast amount of inequality. I've been in Southwark this morning. The poverty in some parts of Southwark compared with other parts is quite stunning. In the south of the borough you've got Dulwich which is a very, very rich middle-class area. In the north of the borough around the Elephant and Castle you have poverty and urban decay, inner-city crime, kids hanging around. The third thing I'd improve is probably transport. Despite the fact that Livingstone has done a good job I'd like to see more of a strategic approach because to get from one side of

London to the other can take two-and-a-half hours. That's how much time it takes me to get from Chingford to Hampstead. I asked my friend who does drive and he said it would take him three hours if he was driving in the rush hour. That can't be right. I think an outer circle tube line would be a good thing. As soon as the M25 was opened we all knew it didn't have enough lanes. It's not been extended. I'd link that to the number of cars on the road, as well'.

Geoff was looking forward to the London Olympics: 'I think it's absolutely fantastic. It's an opportunity. It doesn't mean we are going to take it, but hopefully we will. I certainly hope whatever benefits we get from it we manage to sustain. There's no point in it being a flash in the pan. I hope it creates jobs. I hope it puts London on the map. I hope it creates a great sense of civic pride for people'. Asked what he thought of the 2012 logo he said: 'Well my daughter drew one in school the other day that was better. I think that says it all. But I'm a marketing person as well who used to make a living out of designing logos or commissioning the design of logos, and I think it's very, very weak. I saw many on the BBC web site that are far stronger. But I've seen many a rubbish logo in my time from many a company'. Geoff's one word description of his birthplace was 'buzzing': 'This could be a poem. "Buzzing" is how I'd describe it. I went across Southwark Bridge this morning on a bus and I just felt my heart go up. I was elated as I went over the Thames. I looked to the right and I looked to the left and I thought "I've just got to get up here very soon, bring my wife up here because we've not been here for a little while". I love the vibrancy of it. It's fantastic'.

Geoff's 'It's fantastic' marked the end of the interview and the end of my journey through contemporary London society. We had chatted in a local authority conference facility. The building was old but elegant, probably one of the numerous great houses built by London's wealthy entrepreneurs in the eighteenth or nineteenth century. Of course when it was built it would have stood in tens or hundreds of acres of rolling farmland, with uninterrupted views of the City. By 2007 it was bounded to the south by the raucous North Circular road and shambolic North Middlesex Hospital, and to the north by a desert of council estates, dark and dowdy corner shops and vile-smelling, greasy-floored kebab and fried chicken take-aways. The house was an allegory for London's topography: elegance and grandeur diminished by automotive violence, planning error and tastelessness. Why do civil servants commit such crimes? Why don't politicians act? How can sentient human beings tolerate such visual vandalism? Don't they find it offensive? Or have they simply surrendered, given up, rolled over and turned off? The answer doesn't bear thinking about.

Endnotes

1   Galbraith (1992) p. 33

2   Because of these and other limitations (age range, gender, country of origin, etc.) one
     should be wary of generalising from the sample.

3   This observation, that there is a 'dangerous other', a 'dark pit of despair and destitution'
     awaiting those of us who do not knuckle down is resonant of the way in which social
     control was achieved in Victorian society. In Victorian times the spectres of alcoholism,
     family breakdown, sexually transmitted diseases, diseases of dirt and filth, prostitution
     and drug addiction (cocaine and the heroin pipe) were deployed to keep the masses
     in line. The popular press reproduced images of 'fallen women', street urchins,
     alcohol-fuelled brawls, the poor house and the insane asylum *ad nauseam*. Ironically,
     prostitutes were as popular with middle- and upper-class males as they were with any
     other social stratum. Victorian society was as hypocritical and inconsistent as our own.
     Inevitable, perhaps, as human nature does not change.

4   Epsom is an exurb of London, prosperous and manicured.

5   Cassandra had a contract to make leaded lights for a period London Underground
     station. The station was being restored.

6   Both Cassandra and her partner drove.

7   Lance's partner had just given birth.

8   Geoff described three sub-cultures within London Underground.

9   The National Union of Mineworkers (NUM), led by Arthur Scargill, struck over the
     government's pit-closure programme. After an acrimonious and sometimes violent
     dispute that saw Metropolitan Police officers bussed around the country to support
     overstretched county forces, the strike was defeated. The programme went ahead. Mines
     and their supporting communities were eviscerated. Pockets of high unemployment
     emerged. Hard drugs moved in. Crime soared. Community cohesion melted away. The
     term 'underclass' was coined to describe the social consequences of engineered de-
     industrialisation. Britain's social complexion was irrevocably changed.

10   The Public–Private Partnership funding arrangement. New labour has been a big fan
     of PPP as it provides for risk-sharing between government and the private sector on big
     construction projects (like the long-overdue comprehensive refurbishment of London's
     underground system).

11   Samantha did not clarify the exact object of his affection (his children or his dogs).

12   This anecdote reminded me of a scene from the TV show *Men Behaving Badly* in which
     the landlord of the local pub was selling such small quantities of beer he received a
     memo from the brewery. The memo asked whether the pub was still open.

13   In *Human Safety and Risk Management* Glendon, Clarke and McKenna observe:
     'Features of repetitive work are switching off and letting your mind go blank
     – strategies used, for example, by many assembly workers for coping with repetitive and
     monotonous tasks. A source of dissatisfaction and stress could be lack of control over
     the task... with workers enjoying little autonomy or responsibility'. See Glendon, Clarke
     and McKenna (2006) p. 236.

14   It is worth pointing out the obvious. In an eighty-hour, five-day week William works an
      average sixteen hours each day, leaving eight hours a day for sleep and recreation.
15   I had to define the word 'aesthete'.
16   This is a seventy-seven-hour working week.
17   London's 2012 Olympic logo caused something of a stir when first revealed. It was
      considered too obtuse, too abstract. The press had a field day. The Olympic team was put
      on the defensive. The soaring cost of London's Olympic project put the organisers under
      more pressure. (The financial crisis of 2008 provided supporters of the Olympic project
      with a different frame of reference: the Stratford development could be seen as a vehicle
      for pumping much needed investment into London's economy. The Olympics 2012 could
      be framed as a Keynesian financial instrument.)

· CHAPTER FOUR ·

Eternal city

L IKE Paris or Rome, London endures. Greater than the sum of her parts[1] Britain's capital is a phenomenon of interdependencies and social collisions. London is simultaneously constituted, experienced and served by her denizens. Much more than a geographical feature, London is a distinct experience, a land in her own right. Whatever one's social class, ethnicity or religion, to be a Londoner is to be special. To be a Londoner is also to be a part of history. The workers interviewed for this book are the labour descendants of those interviewed for the WEA's original studies. They form part of a labour *continuum*. The nature of the work done by today's Londoners may be somewhat different, but the experience of working in the Great Wen is broadly similar.

As evidenced by interviewees' statements, working in a twenty-first-century London can be as tiring, frustrating and demoralising *or* inspiring and rewarding as working in a twentieth-century London. Consider, for example, demolition worker John Welch's testimony from the first volume of *Working Lives*:

> My introduction to really hard work was at [one of the] big department stores in Oxford Street on nights. Gawd, was it hard! I was one of a gang of four men loading the skips and occasionally it became necessary to use a 14lb. hammer to reduce large lumps of brick to liftable proportions.... I was trembling at midnight when we knocked off for sandwiches and cups of tea... [2]

Now consider modern Londoner William's recollection of The Paving Slab Day: 'I was working as a labourer for a building company in Fulham. The chap had about ten jobs on the go that all needed paving slabs. So he ordered a lorry-load and decided to distribute them around the sites that day. So I lifted a huge amount. I was on my back for two days. It was hard work in those days. There wasn't any health and safety. Bags of cement used to weigh a hundredweight. If you couldn't lift a hundredweight, bad luck.... I remember I was so knackered when lifting the paving slabs I dropped one on someone's foot. He was a big Irishman. He didn't seem to notice'. John Welch started work in the London of 1919. William did his labouring in the 1970s.

There were similarities between John Welch's experience of health and safety in the 1920s and 1930s and the experiences of some of those interviewed for this book. Asked to describe his work as a demolition labourer Welch said:

It was dangerous work. You were always hearing of casualties from the other men on the jobs.... Bootnose [a demolition man] was killed at Cannon Street, when a cast iron girder fell on him. At Peter Robinson's one bloke fell off the front wall... he never walked again. They put him into a wheelchair... and he got £250 compensation. It ruined his life and that is all he got.[3]

Health and Safety could be as lax in the 1970s as it had been in the 1920s. As chartered surveyor William recalled: 'I remember one time we were demolishing the back of a house that had a horrible bulge in it and the scaffold was tied to the building. We were up on the scaffold and the bricklayer announced that he was going to hit the wall with the bulge in it, and he wasn't sure what was going to happen. As the scaffold was tied to the building he thought it might collapse. So his suggestion was that we should all work out a route off the scaffold, so if it started to collapse we would all jump. That's what we did. He hit the wall. Obviously it didn't collapse because I'm still here. But that's how things were run in construction in the 1970s'. Like John Welch and William social entrepreneur Steve knew the risks of demolition work:

[D]emolition was a horrible, horrible job, and invariably you are working with people who are not protected. Certainly at the time when I was doing it, masks, helmets, health and safety just did not exist... we are talking not that long ago... beginning of the Eighties. Quite a lot of work was carried out in an ad-hoc fashion. If you know you are just doing a job for a short while, passing through, you can observe people doing it and you can say 'this is a dreadful job'. One demolition job involved carrying breeze blocks up stairs and rubble down for two days... there were no chutes... just physically draining and mind-killing... but we were doing it at a sort of run with student heads thinking it was a bit of a challenge. The old boys who had been doing it for years thought we were mad... which we were.

Despite its deprivations both John (in the 1920s and 1930s) and Steve (in the 1980s) got something out of labouring. John put it this way: 'Housebreaking was a rough job, hard work [but] I liked it because you always had different ways to work and different jobs to do'. Steve put it like this: 'I worked with an Italian bricklayer... about fifty years old, still lived with his mum... quite an odd sort of cove... he just happened to be a fantastic bricklayer. Working with someone who on the surface was not very bright but as a craftsman was just incredible was enjoyable. So all of that was very interesting, quite enjoyed it'.

Clearly there are continuities of labour and outlook across London's generations. There are, as noted above, also continuities of conditions. For John Welch housebreaking was uncomfortable and dirty work. Brick-cleaning was physically demanding: 'It was a back-breaking job at first, as there is a certain posture to be held while you work: you stand close to the pile of bricks with the trowel handle gripped in the right hand. You bend forward and pick up a brick and strike at the joint where the mortar sticks to the brick.... Housebreaking in the 20s was done without many tools.... Men stood on a wall and knocked it down piece-meal...'.[4] Some six decades later soon-to-be-redundant bank employee Derek found himself working underground, stock-taking bank records:

> We were working in those cellars you see under the pavements. You know the sort, with glass plates in the pavement... we could see vague shadows passing overhead. I could not stretch to full height under there. We were stooping trying to get these boxes out. They were filthy. There had been damp in there. Cobwebs. Dirt. Dust. At the end of a stint if you blew your nose you would have like black gunge coming out. I went down there in rough clothes every morning, and when I got there changed into even rougher clothes.... That final job for Barclays was really awful, filthy work.

Cabbing has changed little since Ron Barnes was interviewed in *Working Lives. Volume Two*. True, modern black cabs may have better heaters, sound-proofing and seats, but the basic elements – the driving, waiting on rank, tipping, lifting of suitcases and shopping, crawling in heavy traffic, soot, grime, fumes, spilled tea and bolted snacks – remain the same. Barnes's description is worthy of reprise:

> When you first get your licence you feel that you are really someone. But the noise, smell and heat of your cab in the summer, and the force nine gale all around you in the winter, and the humiliation of being tipped soon alters that. A well-spoken woman from Kensington... asked me to wait while she popped into Harrods. I agreed. On her return she told me that she didn't need her services any longer, and with that she paid me off. She then gave me twenty pence over the usual and said 'That's for being so good'. As well intentioned as she may have been, the words she used were those I would have spoken to a child of five on giving him or her a little something for not wetting themselves.[5]

Like Ron Barnes, Michael could work long hours. He could be out driving for up to nine hours each day – and actually earn very little if trade was sparse.[6] Other interviewees worked hard, too. Ali the bus driver was at work for 'fifty-five to seventy hours' each week. Cassandra the stained-glass artisan usually worked nine-to-ten hours each day (in her dank basement). Lance the advertising executive could work up to sixty hours each week. Samantha the City worker typically worked a ten-hour day: 'My contractual hours are nine to five, but the hours I actually work are eight to six. Depending on how busy we are it can often be a lot longer than that'. William the surveyor worked up to eighty hours each week. Graham, owner of the Camden emporium, worked extremely long hours: 'I work all hours... seven days a week from nine-thirty in the morning to ten-thirty in the evening'. As mentioned above there are continuities between the workers interviewed for this book and those interviewed by Centerprise in the 1970s. Like Graham, Mike Christou, the Fish and Chip Man of *Working Lives. Volume Two*, worked long hours. And like Graham he sometimes had to deal with antisocial behaviour at work:

I worked six days a week for many years but after that I worked five days. I closed one day. Now I have two and a half days off. On Thursdays I go to the market very early. I leave my house at 5:30 a.m. and then I finish at 4:00 p.m. I call it a half-day because I've got the night free with my family.... The only thing wrong in our shop is that you get a few rough people. Someone comes into your shop and says, 'You blooming foreigner!' I was up at six in the morning to go to market and this person is coming in at 11:30 in the evening, swearing and all that business.[7]

Derek the London Underground manager talked about his experiences of shift work. He disliked shift work, especially when he was rostered to work a staggered shift pattern by inexperienced staff:

We had a guy a couple of years ago. He didn't have his eye on the ball. He had me working on three consecutive days. He had me doing an early shift. Then I went the following day onto a late shift. Then he wanted me to do a night shift as a favour. When you have to get up at 05:00 to do an early turn, the following day your sleep pattern is all over the place. You tend to get up early. When you are on 'earlies' you tend to get up at the same time every morning. For example, I woke up at five this morning. I have been on earlies. I tried to go back to sleep until six, but I couldn't sleep any more. And to go from one shift pattern to another like that, bang, bang, bang, I felt absolutely drained at the end of it, and I swore I would never do it again. I get this kind of grinding noise in my ears. It is like when you are under the water... I don't know if you have ever heard that sound of the sand sliding around. Sometimes I get that in my ears. It's lack of sleep and stress. Sometimes you are sitting in a chair at work and your eyes close, and you'll hear a noise and you'll wake up with a start. You have just dropped off to sleep. It just happens like that. All of a sudden you will hear the phone... so you have to shuffle out and deal with something. Shift working is really difficult. We jump from one shift pattern to another – you do a week of earlies, then lates, then nights. They say it takes years off your life, doing shift work, and I can believe it. It is very stressful and tiring. So when I got my annual leave I just flaked out. I tried to recharge my batteries.

Derek's experience of shift-working confirms the Health and Safety Executive's (HSE's) analysis of the short- and long-term social and health impacts of night work:

Shift workers, particularly those who work at night, may be at risk of ill health because shift work can disrupt our body clock (by interfering with the production of hormones by the body), disturb sleep and cause fatigue.... Individual and social factors may also contribute to the risk of ill health effects.... As well as chronic fatigue, there is some evidence associating long-term exposure to shift work and the following ill health effects: gastrointestinal problems such as indigestion, abdominal pain, constipation, chronic gastritis and peptic ulcers; cardiovascular problems such as hypertension, coronary heart disease; increased susceptibility to minor illnesses such as colds, flu and gastroenteritis.[8]

Most of those interviewed for this book worked long hours. Working long hours and being away from home for extended periods can put relationships under strain. Psychologists Cary Cooper, Philip Dewe and Michael O'Driscoll say this of the work/non-work conflict:

[The] inter-role conflict has consistently been linked with psychological strain... and is especially prevalent among women, employed parents and dual-career couples.... One prominent form of conflict arises because people have finite resources in terms of time and energy [note Derek's comment (above) regarding his annual leave, which he used to recover from his shift work], and demands from different roles will tax those resources.... [T]he more time and energy required to perform specific roles successfully, the greater the extent of inter-role conflict.... [I]ndividuals may have to engage in a process of accommodation, where they limit or modify their involvement in one sphere to accommodate the demands of the other. For instance, intensive demands from the job may require them to significantly reduce their input into family life.[9]

Regarding the length of the working week in the UK, the Office for National Statistics notes: 'The length of the working week varies by occupation... 40 per cent of managers and senior officials worked over 45 hours a week – the occupational group most likely to work these long hours.... Government policy over recent years has stressed the importance of maintaining a healthy work–life balance'.[10] The general secretary of the Trades Union Congress (TUC) has drawn attention to the wider social impacts of long working hours:

Increasingly people are balancing the demands of caring not only for children but also dependent adults, and these workers need support and protection. But long hours working is the biggest demon facing UK workers. Many fathers find themselves spending extra hours at work when they would really rather be at home, which in turn forces their partners to reduce their hours and pay to run the home and look after children. A better work–life balance where men and women could spend more time with their families and be less stressed at work would be in everyone's interest.[11]

Post-industrial Londinium?

It is often said that Britain has become a post-industrial, service-sector-dominated society. Britain's economy may, indeed, be dominated by the service sector but if one looks at the *nature* of work, much of it is still unskilled, manual, dirty, unpleasant and poorly paid. Derek hit a personal low-point in Barclays' grimy vaults. In Britain today east European, Chinese and African economic migrants work long hours for low pay in menial jobs. There are no clean breaks between epochs. Epochs (here defined by specific modes of production) interpenetrate and overlap. Such overlaps can be seen across the length and breadth of London. As mentioned in Chapter Two, Docklands – perhaps the brightest and shiniest of Britain's business centres – has a vibrant manufacturing sector. The data is worthy of reprise:

> A 1997 survey of Docklands employees showed that while 56% held white-collar jobs (in the financial services sector, real estate, local government, etc.), 43% had blue-collar jobs. Surprisingly, perhaps, 19% of Docklands employees worked in manufacturing (plus 9% in transport and communication and 8% in wholesale, retail and repair). By 1997 there were more manufacturing jobs in Docklands than in 1981.

Docklands lies roughly at the junction of the Lea (or Lee) Valley and the Thames basin. The Lea Valley is home to a tremendous variety of industry, from waste recycling and waste-to-electricity plants, to vast warehousing facilities, to bakeries and bottling plants, to coach repair and engineering shops, to transport depots, to clothing manufacturers and purveyors of pretentious, over-priced, Swedish-designed flat-pack furniture. It also has an elaborate canal and reservoir system and hundreds of acres-worth of parks and recreation grounds. Some vistas are idyllic. Some disastrously ugly. The point is not how it looks, however. The point is that it exists close to the heart of one of the most go-getting capitals in the world. The Lea Valley is simultaneously Victorian (the scrap dealerships, dress-manufacturing and car repair shops are a sight to behold) and contemporary (the valley is peppered with 'shopping sheds' – corrugated, flat-roofed, air-conditioned, artificially lit, security-guard patrolled, CCTV-surveyed temples of consumption).[12] There are Lea Valleys all over London. True, some may be no more than small pockets of industry – residues, as it were. The important point, though, is that they *persist*. And they persist because they are *necessary*.

History is messy. Society is messy. Londonland is *simultaneously* an industrial and post-industrial locale. Londonland's luminous and ever-so-clean glass and brushed-aluminium business hubs are underwritten by industrial neighbourhoods (sometimes small, sometimes large) and the labours of an underclass of native and migrant workers. Atomised, these workers are vulnerable to exploitation. To paraphrase Bauman, such workers (indeed, all workers, educated and non-educated, rich and poor) exist 'in a situation without obvious levers of control'.[13]

Change and continuity

The Britain of today, of Thatcher, Blair and Brown, is a Britain of multiple realities, of change and continuity. If the changes are interesting (the accelerating rise of the service sector, for example) so too are the continuities. Like all great cities London nurtures non-conformity – a kind of Metropolitan Bohemianism. One of the characters featured in *Working Lives. Volume One 1905–45* was Phil Anderson.

Born in 1911 Phil lived in south Hackney all his life. He had a succession of jobs interspersed with periods of unemployment. Eventually he found his equilibrium, an unconventional lifestyle of acting and asceticism: 'In his later years [Phil] took control of his own life. He enjoyed and made money from acting and lived according to his own rhythms. These included daily early morning swims in Victoria Park, much cycling, reading, yoga and meditation. He also collected books, paintings, records and Chinese vases, mostly from East London markets, where he was a familiar figure'.[14] Phil Anderson would have felt at home in Graham's Camden emporium with its eclectic clientele or in the company of social entrepreneur Steve with his cycling business. He would also have had much in common with chartered surveyor William with his bottom-up approach to job and wealth creation and enthusiasm for traditional London industries (like brewing) and pastimes (socialising in the 'local'). Like Phil Anderson, William was also a collector – of anything from juke boxes, bought on eBay in the middle of the night when sensible people were abed, to elaborately painted pub mirrors.

If London is today a city of multinationals and manufactured business districts it is also a city of small-scale enterprise and community industry. Take William's surveying business, for example. William's story is very much that of a London lad – made good, of a restless soul (William detested school because of its authoritarianism and in later life fell out with his housing association boss) who eventually created a niche for himself. Like William, Steve blossomed as a social entrepreneur. Disenchanted with the state's efforts to satisfy local needs he decided to do it for himself by creating community-based micro businesses. Cassandra, too, seemed to revel in her work, despite having to labour long hours in a damp and sometimes flooded basement. Finally, after spending many years in local government Geoff found satisfaction combining his love of writing poetry with teaching communications. All these people could have played it safe. All could have remained employees of some large public or private enterprise – anonymous office-fodder. To their credit, however, they took a risk. They exploited whatever opportunities existed and struck out on their own. They self-actualised. They benefited themselves and others. They *took control*. As William put it: 'I've taken charge of my destiny.... Once you've worked for yourself you can't imagine going back to work in a job again.... I enjoy what I do. There are always new things coming in, so that keeps me going.... I enjoy making all the decisions'.

Successful businessman Lance also *took control*. Dissatisfied with the prospect of spending the rest of his life (lucratively) working for someone else he took a risk and, with his partner, set up a successful advertising agency. His standard of living suffered but at least he was running his own show. Finally we have Michael the cabbie and Samantha the City worker. After seemingly being thrown on the scrap heap Michael decided to give himself a leg-up. He became a cabbie. Samantha, erudite and intelligent, saw her City job as a means to a more personally satisfying end. She intended to start her own business when she had saved enough money. Londonland, then, is not just a haven for big corporations. It is a breeding ground for entrepreneurship. A place where people with energy and ideas and access to cash or credit can have a go. In this author's opinion London's economic resilience is as much a function of its native entrepreneurs as it is of its multinationals. More so, perhaps, because small businesses are more rooted than multinationals (the 'unanchored power' of Bauman's globalised world). Unlike peripatetic corporations, small businesses cannot indulge in 'space war'. They are where they are and have to make the best of whatever comes along.

How to build resilience

In 2008 the wheels began to come off Britain's extended economic boom. House price inflation began to slow as commodity prices began to rise. Oil prices soared. There was talk of 'stagflation' – the economic paradox of zero economic growth and inflation. Stagflation had not been seen since the 1970s, the decade of Britain's economic nadir when industrial action, under-investment, low productivity and mediocre management conspired to bring the country to its knees during the Three Day Week.[15] There was talk of another round of job shakeouts in the City. The barrow-boys in suits, Porsche dealers and Kensington estate agents held their breath. By the autumn the City had hit the buffers. In a swirl of bad debt (much of it originating in the United States' sub-prime mortgage market) banks stopped lending to one another. Investment banks, insurance companies and mortgage providers reaped the whirlwind. The failure of US investment bank Lehman Brothers threatened Lehman's 5,000 London employees.[16] The takeover of the Halifax and Bank of Scotland (HBOS) by clearing bank Lloyds TSB put at least 14,000 jobs at risk. (The most pessimistic prediction was that 40,000 jobs would be lost through the merger.) Lloyds TSB's chief executive said he expected to see £1bn-worth of cost cuts. Some feared that as many as 500 Lloyds TSB branches could close.[17] All Britain's towns and cities, including London,[18] would feel the chill.

Across the water commentators made dire predictions. 'This is a very severe economic and financial crisis where hundreds of banks are going to go bust' said a New York University professor of economics.[19] 'This is the worst financial-services crisis of our lifetime. You have major firms that have imploded or are at risk of imploding. It is a deconstruction – and a reconstruction to follow – of the financial-services industry as we know it' said a finance industry recruiter.[20] Surveying the US economy the *Economist* wrote:

> [A]round 159,000 Americans lost their jobs in September, the most since 2003. Some industries are hurting badly: car sales are at their lowest level in 16 years as would-be buyers are unable to get credit. General Motors has temporarily shut some of its factories in Europe.[21]

Across the water indigenous European manufacturers fared little better. '[O]ne of the more startling statistics in recent weeks [is] that Volvo's European truck sales in the third quarter fell from last year's 42,000 to just 115' noted the *Financial Times*'s Tony Jackson.[22] *Observer* journalist Richard Wachman characterised the events of September 2008 as 'the biggest economic crisis since the Great Depression'. Wachman continued: '[T]he world is a hugely changed place and... the legacy of the near meltdown of the global financial system will be with us for a long time to come'.[23] The *Economist* noted that 'whole countries have begun to get into trouble. The government of Iceland has had to nationalise two of its biggest banks and is frantically seeking a lifeline loan from Russia'.[24] Several of London's local authorities had money invested in Icelandic banks.

The crisis in the world's financial markets was a major theme of the autumn party conferences (and even distracted attention from Gordon Brown's electoral woes). According to some, the Conservative Party conference, held in the week when the world banking system looked especially shaky, was all but eclipsed by the crisis. This was Gordon Brown's moment. David Cameron, Conservative Party leader, was little more than an onlooker. As Brown put it: 'This is no time for novices'. At the end of October 2008 the *Economist* reviewed the political balance sheet: 'The past month has seen an emboldened prime minister, a diminished opposition, an improbable cabinet reshuffle [that saw one of Brown's least favourite politicians, Peter Mandelson, returned to government], and the rise and fall of a political truce between the government and the opposition'.[25]

By the end of October 2008, after much thrashing around, the G8 nations appeared to have a workable salvage plan in place – a plan designed not in the New World but in the old. As journalist Nelson Schwartz noted in the *International Herald Tribune*: 'After initially dithering, European leaders came up with a financial bailout plan that has now set the pace for Washington, not the other way around, as had been customary for decades'.[26] Where Washington was happy simply to buy up bad debt, European governments got to the heart of the matter: banks' lack of capital and fear of lending, even to each other. Schwartz again: 'While Congress and the White House were focused on simply buying up hundreds of billions in mortgage loans gone bad, leaders like [Gordon] Brown sought to fix a deeper, even more serious threat: a lack of faith in the banks themselves. That was why their tactic – becoming the investor of last resort and the guarantor of loans between banks – worked to staunch the panic...'.[27] Despite this concerted effort, however, the world economy continued to stutter.[28] Markets remained unstable. Trade dipped. Unemployment rose. The International Monetary Fund published a *World Economic Outlook* that made devastating reading. Tony Jackson summarised the IMF's prognosis in the 3 November edition of the *Financial Times*:

In a study covering 17 developed economies over three decades, the IMF came up with three findings of particular relevance. First, recessions preceded by a financial crisis tend to be deeper and longer than others. Second, they tend to be worse again if the crisis is in banking, rather than in securities markets or foreign exchange. And third, the countries hardest hit are those with so-called arm's length financial systems, such as the US or UK.... In practical terms, the IMF found that recessions linked to banking crises lasted twice as long on average as those not linked to any financial crisis, and the cumulative loss of output was about four times as great. *The present recession, plainly, ticks all the boxes....* [my emphasis][29]

In times like these London needs a vibrant indigenous business sector. It needs Londoners to take control of their own destiny. It needs people like William, Cassandra, Lance and Samantha. Building resilience also requires that London's talent is recognised and nurtured. This process begins at school. Or rather it *should* begin at school. Unfortunately Britain's one-size-fits-all education system runs the risk of alienating a significant portion of its charges. Not everyone is temperamentally suited to taking tests and exams in their early teens. Youngsters mature at different rates. Not everyone can take teachers' authoritarianism. William, for example, found it intolerable: 'I left comprehensive school because they more or less told me to. I had not been to school for a few months. So they wrote to me and said "We take it you've left because we haven't seen you for a few months". So I left. I hated school. I couldn't stand the authoritarianism of it. I did not like the environment. I hated it completely. I used to dread going. I loved lessons and learning. But I hated the environment'. In contrast to his school experience William enjoyed his time at a College of Further Education. He appreciated being treated like an adult. He appreciated being able to exercise *choice*. He felt more in control.

Verstehen

I was a moderately bright junior school pupil. At eleven years of age I was transplanted to a state-run grammar school. At first all went well. I usually came in the top three of one of the top classes in the school. At about fourteen, however, I began to lose interest in learning. I found the lessons, which consisted for the most part of taking dictation, boring. Today, of course, teachers would hand out photocopied notes, or even e-mail class notes to pupils' accounts. In the early Seventies, however, dictation was *de rigueur*. I began to bunk off school. I used to wander around Swansea, the nearest city. I would go to the art gallery, to the museum and to the city's main library with its beautiful reading room. The life I created for myself was infinitely more interesting than anything the dead-hand of state education could offer. Interestingly no-one ever worked out what I was up to. I suppose I had teachers' trust. Not unsurprisingly I did badly in my O-level examinations. I gained two b-grade and three c-grade O-levels. I compounded my unhappiness by progressing to A-levels. More dictation. Always dictation. And tests. Tests to check whether we had taken our dictation correctly. By the second year of sixth form I was bunking off again, this time with a group of friends. We would drive to the Gower Peninsular where we would play tennis, chat up women, go drinking, play darts and generally mess around. Looking back the Gower days were the best days of my life. After enduring a third year of sixth form I scraped into Sheffield City Polytechnic. A revelation. We were treated as adults. We weren't chased. We weren't humiliated. We were tested only when absolutely necessary. The important thing was to *learn*. The important thing was to *get it*. And I did get it. I got an upper second. Later in life I got a master's degree and a PhD. Why? Because I was more in control of my education. I helped set the agenda. Consequently I had no reason to kick against the system. Because it was *my* system. Ownership motivates people. They feel involved. They feel valued, empowered. They feel like every citizen should feel.

In my opinion forcing teenagers to stay on at school is a bad idea. Education should be flexible. Young people should have the opportunity to work and to return to education when they feel ready. An education system that fails to accommodate difference is a failed education system. Just ask William. Some, of course, might label such ideas dangerous or unworkable. But if William's career is anything to go by we have nothing to fear. Because he gave himself the space to develop at his own pace and *think* William eventually got a degree, a career in surveying and his own successful business. He is now a pillar of the community. He creates wealth. He employs local people. He beautifies the capital. He plays a part in local politics. No doubt William's comprehensive school labelled him a failure. How wrong can you be?[30]

Creating resilient, stable and prosperous communities means striking the right balance between top-down and bottom-up approaches to government. Resurrecting London's devastated Docklands was clearly beyond the capacities of its local inhabitants. It was beyond the capacities (both financial and creative) of its local authorities. It needed government intervention. It needed international capital. It needed the multinationals to take an interest. The results may not be pretty (in fact they are often pretty vile) but at least the area is economically viable again. And there are jobs for east London's working class. As noted above, in 1997 forty-three per cent of those employed in Docklands held blue-collar jobs. Nineteen per cent of Docklands employees worked in manufacturing, nine per cent in transport and communication and eight per cent in wholesale, retail and repair.

Not unsurprisingly the £10 billion-worth of private investment mainlined into Docklands has benefited the entire East End. In September 2004 Jane Padgham, economics correspondent for the *Evening Standard*, described the 'trickle-down effect' of Docklands' structural investment: '[T]he Jubilee Line extension, the Channel Tunnel Rail Link and the office developments of Canary Wharf have fostered conditions that have encouraged budding entrepreneurs'.[31] A spokesman for the London Chamber of Commerce concurred: 'These enormous [investments] have transformed the East End into a commercially vibrant area which is tailor-made for entrepreneurs and small businesses. When small companies start, they look for local suppliers. So, as more and more firms locate in this part of London, a beneficial circle [i.e. virtuous circle] is generated which will alter the economic geography of the capital'.

When I worked as a temporary employee for a firm of architects in east London I saw at first hand how small amounts of private capital levered by imagination, energy and a determination to win out over bureaucracy can transform neighbourhoods long abandoned by local and central government, and indeed the multinationals. Sure the small-time entrepreneurs who invest their own money are looking for a return. That's business. But it is worth asking what would have happened to the East End without these new-wave investors. The trick for government, of course, is to channel seedcorn investment such that it creates viable, living 'mixed-use' communities (as opposed to sterile business districts whose patrons evacuate at sun-down).

There will always be the potential for conflict between local/central government and local enterprise. All bureaucracies are potentially self-serving. There is always a risk that a bureaucracy will devote more money to sustaining itself than the community it was set up to serve. Bureaucracies can, in short, be self-referential. This was Steve's experience in Stamford Hill. Steve realised that his cycling scheme would work best if it used local residents as tutors and if the locus of control remained in the community. For Steve 'top-down' meant no-hope: 'We are still put in a position where the local authority – even though it has no knowledge of cycle training – feels it should dictate what cycle training takes place. This comes from people who are not grass-roots in the community; people who are not seeing what is happening on the ground; people who are not seeing the benefits of training local people to be skilled, and keeping that skill in the community. They are looking at what they think is important: "Is this profitable?"; "Surely we should buy in the skills because it is cheaper?" The fact that it takes money away from the community does not seem to hit home'. Steve's experience was that economic localism (small-scale, community-owned, managed and staffed enterprises) worked.

As mentioned earlier in this book I hail from an industrial, working class Welsh town called Neath. Neath has always been a Labour stronghold. I used to think this was a good thing. Not any more. Monopolistic power breeds complacency and stifles creativity. The healthiest, most resilient communities are those that embrace a variety of world-views and ways-of-doing. Healthy communities are built on local initiative. Instead of imposing itself local government should facilitate. It should play an enabling role. It should encourage participation by providing economic support and advice – tutelage, if you like. At Neath Boys' Grammar School I had the benefit of being taught history by a chap we nicknamed Twitch (because he had a nervous twitch that was probably caused by having to teach us unruly teenagers). He wasn't the brightest of teachers but he did make one observation that has stuck with me. 'If the Neath Labour Party put a sheep up as a candidate it would get voted in' he said one day. This observation was both funny and tragic. Funny because any mention of sheep in Wales always gets a chuckle. Tragic because it might well have been true. There was a view that Neath had been Labour for so long its electorate had lost the ability to think outside the box... that the electors of Neath had become dependent on a political apparatus that had run out of ideas. The same criticism has been levelled at London's councils. Specifically that as Docklands crumbled all they could offer was superannuated rhetoric based on a misreading of how the global economic system was evolving. In a globalised world capital is highly mobile. Businesses locate in those countries with the lowest production costs and best government inducements. Business mobility is supported by emerging technologies (the Internet, for example) and novel financial arrangements (electronic dealing floors and money-market products supportive of global capital). The organising principle of business mobility is laissez faire capitalism which, in the words of economist John Kenneth Galbraith, 'is an attitude, the belief that it is in the nature of things, and especially of economic life, that all works out for the best in the end. Nothing that happens in the short run is in conflict with longer-run well-being. The intervention of the state, with its controlling or sustaining hand, is not necessary, and except as a bank or a corporation needs to be rescued[32] or the common defence furthered, it is never benign'.[33]

Room for local initiative?

I have kept a flat in the London Borough of Haringey for many years. Haringey is not a bad place to live. But it is always bumping along the bottom. Always grubby. Always crumbling. The local authority does its best. Communicates its plans to residents. Applies for this and that grant. Makes representations. Celebrates the borough's cultural diversity. But self-evidently it is not enough. Self-evidently a different approach is needed. *Self-evidently* the energy that is bottled up inside the community needs to be set free. *Self-evidently* the nature of governance must change. If this means relaxing bureaucratic controls, so be it. A way has to be found of bringing about a sea change in how London's boroughs are governed. Londoners are not short of energy and ideas. That much we can see from the life stories documented in the previous chapter. But they must be given the skills, support and opportunity to put those ideas into practice. Perhaps we as a nation have travelled too far down the path of control. Control for control's sake is an oppressive paradigm.

To its credit the Blair–Brown Labour government has tried to encourage local initiative. Its City Growth Strategies (CGS) programme, for example, encourages local businesses to engage with the community to generate synergies and local economic growth. The CGS programme is derived from a US initiative pioneered by Professor Michael Porter of Harvard Business School. Professor Porter summarised the US experience of CGS thus: 'Our experience has shown that sustainable economic development will only happen in urban deprived areas as it has elsewhere by building competitive businesses and a business environment that supports these companies and attracts investment based on competitive advantages. This is the only way to move economically isolated communities into the mainstream economy, thus greatly expanding opportunities'.[34] In the summer of 2002 the London Development Agency (LDA) launched four CGS pilot schemes, one of which was centred on the London Borough of Haringey. In a 2004 *Daily Mail* article Chancellor Gordon Brown said he wanted 'a renaissance of British entrepreneurship'. He wrote: 'During the Industrial Revolution, Britain led the world in innovation, science and enterprise. It is time to rediscover that spirit and genius in the world of the Internet and digitalisation.... We know how much stronger our economy and our society will be if all the dynamism, creativity and potential of everyone is released – if people can see that enterprise is not for an elite but potentially for them as well'. He went on to list some of the government's entrepreneurship initiatives, including the National Council for Graduate Entrepreneurs, the Enterprise Capital Fund and CGS. What the chancellor failed to mention, however, was the fact that the Industrial Revolution and subsequent Machine Age was a more-or-less spontaneous event facilitated by the *absence* of government intervention. It was the Victorians' penchant for laissez-faire capitalism that greased the wheels of industry. Certainly laissez-faire capitalism had its problems – poverty, ignorance, exploitation, disease, misery and fear – but it created an environment in which ambitious people felt inclined to have a go. What is interesting about the self-actualisers described above (people like Lance, William, Cassandra, Geoff and Michael) is that none of them either sought or benefited from any kind of top-down support. They did not avail themselves of any bureaucratic munificence. They simply decided to create a career and life *for themselves*. In the parlance of the old Tory party they 'got on their bikes'. Perhaps what Londoners need most is encouragement and advice. They need role models. They need people like Lance, William, Cassandra, Geoff and Michael to tell them they too can do it. They need 'face-time' with success stories.

To its credit the government acknowledges the need for successful entrepreneurs to evangelise. As Gordon Brown wrote in the *Daily Mail*: '[T]o inspire teenagers to be enterprising I want local businessmen and women to go into our classrooms to help every young person learn about and experience the world of business before they leave school and make business leaders role models for the young again'. So, Prime Minister, let's have much less testing in schools[35] and much more contact with successful people (both those who run their own businesses and people like Michael who turned their life around, who *found a way*). Schools should be less self-referential and more porous.[36] They should be clearing houses for ideas. Schools (and colleges) should be the ideational bedrock of every community.

Up the workers

While interviewees' political views were varied some themes did emerge. Trades unions, for example, received a mixed reception. Views ranged from unconditional support to barely concealed hostility. As university lecturer Cindy remarked: 'I have a very mixed opinion of them. The unions I like the least are the rail and tube unions. They really push the boundaries and they get away with murder. We [Londoners] do not see them delivering the standard of work that justifies all of the benefits they are able to achieve through aggressive strikes and action over the slightest thing... so I think they give the unions a terrible name. I would like to see a huge clamp-down on them... I would like to see them quite crushed'. Even William, who had been a trade union representative at a local authority, had misgivings: 'Thatcher managed to castrate the unions. I think they struggle to be relevant now. At the time I didn't think the unions deserved the treatment they got. But looking back, possibly the unions were a little too negative. Perhaps there were some abuses'.

Surprisingly, given his 2008 defeat at the hands of the Conservative mayoral candidate Boris Johnson, there was broad support for Ken Livingstone. Most interviewees thought he had done a reasonable job for London, and were especially supportive of his transport initiatives. William, however, felt he could have been a tad more radical: 'He's a bit like everyone else involved in local politics these days... a bit of a disappointment.... One expected more.... I think it's a shame he has not been more outspoken or stroppy about things. He's capitulated to the government. He hasn't taken them on. Maybe he is being adult, but who wants to be adult about these things? Politics is about passion'. It remains to be seen whether the new mayor of London will have an impact on the capital. With a budget of over £11 billion he should be able to do some good. Whether he'll be able to do much about crime – one of the interviewees' most serious concerns – remains to be seen, however. Between January and June 2008 fourteen London youths met with violent deaths. Many were knifed to death by peers. The Metropolitan Police Service set about targeting youth offending. As the *Times* reported: 'Sir Ian [Blair], the most senior policeman in Britain, said yesterday that his force was "bending every sinew" and using every available resource to stem the youth violence crisis. Recent figures from the Met show that young people are committing an increasing proportion of serious crime in London and that, in the past 18 months, murders of and by youths have shown a significant increase on previous years'.[37] Interestingly the 2004 British Crime Survey found 'a distinct lack of confidence in the juvenile justice system with only 25% saying that they are effective in dealing with young people accused of crime'.[38]

Both Ali the bus driver and Michael the cabbie talked about youths' attitudes towards civil society. Ali said: 'Now kids have free pass, free travel, and they are taking the piss. They are vandalising the buses. They are disrespecting the old people. It's really bad'. Michael said:

> We get threatened over here... we get cut up on the road... people pull knives out... and they say 'no, no, our figures don't show this'. Well I'd like them to come out at midnight and go on the top of one of the double-decker buses around Tottenham and places like that and see how much they like it or send their wife out and get harassed by the hoodies that's in and around the area, but they won't do that will they? Their figures don't show that. Makes you a bit bitter, doesn't it?

Crime, of course, is an age-old curse of city workers. *Working Lives. Volume Two* included an interview with Ron Barnes, like Michael a black cab driver. Ron, interviewed in 1977, reflected on the risks of his profession:

> There have been numerous incidents that never hit the headlines of cabbies being violently assaulted and their night's takings stolen. I never take doubtful characters into cul-de-sacs.... A passenger could complain to the Carriage Office if I refused to drop him at the end of a cul-de-sac, but if I feel a bit dodgy about the geezer [male passenger] I have to take that chance. To chance being reported [to the Carriage Office] is the lesser of the two evils, the other being the loss of an eye, your cash or perhaps even your life. That has been known.[39]

University lecturer Cindy resented being offered drugs on the street in bustling entertainment centres like Camden Town in north London. The fact is, of course, that recreational drug use is now commonplace in British society. Some hold that the best the authorities can do is to manage the fallout. This policy does nothing to address the intimidatory aspects of drug dealing, however. As Cindy put it people should be free to go about their business without the public insult of being offered drugs. In this author's opinion round-the-clock street-level policing would help reclaim the streets for law-abiding citizens. Visible policing costs money, however. It means substantial long-term investment in community-based law enforcement. Closed-circuit television is no substitute for pavement work. City worker Samantha had her bag snatched while returning home one night. She put up a fight. She got injured. She might have been beaten senseless or knifed. Like too many victims of crime she blamed herself: 'But I think it was partly my own carelessness being out late at night alone'. Clearly the blame lies with the perpetrators and, to some degree, with a society that fails to invest sufficient resources in proven crime prevention strategies (like beat officers who are on the streets through the night).

Crime *per se* is just one aspect of the problem, of course. Other aspects include fear of crime, the sheer cost of crime (higher premiums and deterred tourists, for example) and the physical manifestations of crime, both direct (graffiti, broken windows, vandalised street furniture and burned out cars, for example) and indirect (razor wire on garden walls, pointless burglar alarms on houses, death-trap bars on windows, etc.).

Most interviewees believed London to be a reasonably tolerant society – a melting pot of different races. A couple of interviewees voiced their concern about immigration. Ali the bus driver said: '[T]he worse thing is immigration… they immigrate a lot of people from other places and they are unuseful [*sic*]'. Ironically Ali was himself an immigrant. Then there was Michael the cabbie: '[They need to] stop us – white middle England – becoming the minority, the put-upon people. They could do that, but they won't…. The racial political correctness is what we need to change…. I feel there are lots of people, white, middle-England, working-class people that are prisoners in their own country at the moment through this political correctness rubbish'. Others felt they could sense a certain unease about London's Muslim community following events in New York and Washington and the later terrorist attacks on London's transport system. But the consensus view was that Londoners generally rubbed along together quite well. As to why this was so one interviewee noted: 'Being a large city with a large population you are quite anonymous. That can work both ways. It is not a tight-knit community where you would have to get along with everyone very well. Perhaps it is just that people do not have to have so much to do with each other'. In other words London's size facilitates integration by taking some of the pressure off its residents. You don't have to mix if you don't want to.

One of the most interesting (or tragic) aspects of London's social geography is the spatial separation of its classes. Consider, for example, university lecturer Cindy's home turf, Chelsea. Chelsea is, for the most part, the preserve of the upper-middle and upper classes. Neighbouring Fulham is being gentrified. Wealth colonises pleasant, convenient-for-the-City neighbourhoods. Hammersmith, on the other hand, is still being contested. Because London, as a city, is a *contiguous* assemblage of residential and commercial properties it is quite possible to turn a corner and find yourself in a different world. This was my experience when I did my doctoral research in the Fulham neighbourhood of Sands End. Sands End, a prime riverside location, was being colonised by developers and gentrifiers. This process had created a kind of social parallelism with the well-to-do rubbing up against London's traditional working class. I did my research in the early 1990s. I have no doubt that by 2030 or thereabouts Sands End will be as solidly middle-class as, say, Putney or Richmond or Blackheath. Today, though, Sands End is still a neighbourhood of disjunctures and surprises, like the contrast between new-build Chelsea Harbour (described to me as a 'jerry-built pile' by one ex-councillor) and Sands End's Victorian terraces. There are also grass-roots political disjunctures. To get my PhD I investigated residents' attitudes towards the demolition of Sands End Power Station in the early 1980s.[40] The power station contained large amounts of blue and brown asbestos (a suspected carcinogen). My research led me to the local community association. Unsurprisingly, perhaps, the association did not draw heavily on Sands End's indigenous population for its members. It is possible that Sands End's working class residents were less concerned about asbestos than about getting rid of an eyesore as quickly as possible[41] and creating new jobs in the area.[42]

A meritocratic, Olympic future?

Is Britain a meritocracy? Partly. As William said, many people of his generation (including me) benefited from student grants provided by the local authority. Nineteen-Sixties socialism (even in its non-threatening British form) gave us both a leg-up. Does this mean we now reside in the bosom of the Establishment? No. We do not. We went to the wrong schools and universities. We speak in the wrong accents (Welsh Valley and south London). We never seem to be able to satisfy the dress code. We still feel awkward around toffs. We are still bemused by too much cutlery. Tony Blair set out to create a harmonious meritocracy. Journalist Giles Hattersley says he failed. A visit to Royal Ascot 2008 provoked this diatribe from Hattersley: 'If you are in any doubt as to why the class divide still haunts Britain, I suggest you pop down to Royal Ascot.... Forget your dreams of Britain as a classless meritocracy. These days Ascot is where the haves meet the chavs [monied lower orders] head-on. In fact, it's a turf war. In the royal enclosure the cream of Britain – i.e. rich and very thick – wear top hats and tails, talk form and sip their champagne. Outside – in the numerous Pimm's bars and beer gardens – first-generation lower-middle-class types get wrecked [drunk] in the sunshine. Boobs out, legs akimbo.... As you might imagine, tensions are rife...'.[43]

When asked about the 2012 Olympics most interviewees were generally supportive. Some emphasised the importance of maintaining the site and facilities after the event. Such views have been echoed in the press. As journalist Nick Ross observed in the *Evening Standard* in April 2008: '[T]he more important task is to secure London's legacy. The lessons of previous Games is that host cities often get saddled with inappropriate infrastructure and huge debts – and London (together with the Lottery) will have to make good any overruns'.[44] On 25 August 2008, Team GB (Britain's Olympic team) returned home from Beijing. The team's performance attracted significant political and media interest. 'Britain's Olympic stars returned home yesterday to a heroes' welcome.... They were greeted by a beaming Gordon Brown.... The athletes... won 19 golds, 13 silvers and 15 bronzes in China' wrote Jo Steele in *Metro*.[45] Team GB's medal haul was the best in 100 years – a welcome fillip for Prime Minister Gordon Brown whose popularity rating had plummeted during 2008.[46] The media was in gushing mood. *Metro*'s Steele talked of 'the pride of Britain' and 'our heroes'.[47] The *Guardian*'s Sunder Katwala judged that 'Team GB's Beijing gold rush has lifted the national mood'.[48] Clearly sporting success *per se* has many positive outcomes. It can brighten mundane lives and inspire even the most slothful to take up exercise – no bad thing in a country where obesity is now a major health issue. But sporting success does not come cheap. And, as some interviewees pointed out, Olympic investment must produce a healthy, long-term return. 'I hope facilities will have a life beyond the Olympics. I find the major overspend and under-budgeting that has taken place quite alarming' said one interviewee. 'I think people will learn out of it for those three or four weeks, but after that we'll have empty stadiums' said another. 'I think it will be a good thing in the sense that hopefully some areas in the East End will be regenerated... I think jobs will be very welcome if that does happen. But I wonder what will happen after the Olympics is over, actually, and what will happen to those people and all the buildings?' said a third. As mentioned earlier in this book the regeneration of London's Docklands took a great deal of money. The project sometimes went off track. Economic downturns slowed renewal. Developers went bankrupt. Local residents voiced concerns over employment opportunities. Environmentalists opposed the new airport (a vital adjunct to London's newest business centre). In time, however, the new Docklands assumed an economic momentum of its own, creating both white- and blue-collar jobs (see above). Perhaps it would be wise not to expect too much too quickly from the Stratford project. There will be ups and downs. There will be successes and failures. The Stratford project is best seen as one element of London's general renewal.[49] And its success or failure must be judged in the context of the wider economic picture (which, in 2008, looked bleak).

The need to modernise London's infrastructure was mentioned by most interviewees. London may be one of the most energetic cities in the world but its citizens labour long and hard in the midst of decay and damage. The old bits need to be replaced. And the new bits need to be maintained properly (which means sorting out the revenue side of the London account). What is the point of engaging the best architects and engineers to build impressive infrastructure if it is allowed to rot? Governments and councils and development agencies should eschew short-term thinking in favour of strategic planning. Chasing political Brownie points is all well and good but it's a betrayal of London's heritage and potential.[50] Who wants to live with filth and ugliness?

Publicly at least the mayor of London supports long-term, sustainable investment in London's infrastructure (although, perversely, he opposes expansion at Heathrow, one of the capital's biggest employers and an engine of economic development for southern England). At the height of the 'credit crunch' he wrote this in the *Evening Standard*: 'These are difficult times. We have been in extended talks with a range of business groups, small companies, finance houses and leading multinationals to develop an Economic Recovery Action Plan for London.... We may not all be Keynesians now but we must not shelve the major infrastructure projects such as Crossrail that not only safeguard jobs in the short and medium term but ensure London's competitiveness in the long term. I have lobbied the government hard on this.... Moreover I am looking at whether it is possible for any other projects currently in the pipeline to be brought forward'.[51] Conscious of the need to show leadership in a time of despondency Mayor Johnson issued a call-to-arms: '[A]mid all the capital gloom, we mustn't forget that London retains the strengths that propelled it to becoming the world's leading city. We speak English, the modern *lingua franca*. Our time zone hasn't changed, and 90 per cent of the world still shares some of its working day with us.... Our workers are still among the most productive on the planet, our highly skilled and flexible workforce is still second to none. We are world leaders not just in financial services but in the media, fashion and high technology, with world-class universities pumping out ideas and talent. We are still the best city in the world to live in'. The mayor concluded with typical Johnsonian flourish: 'To those who say Zurich is a more attractive place to do business, the joke goes: have you ever spent an evening there?'

The last word

This book complements the two volumes that inspired its writing. Like *Working Lives. Volume One 1905–45* and *Working Lives. Volume Two 1945–77* its intention has been to foreground a few of the ordinary people who make London work.[52] London isn't just Leicester Square film premiers or Buckingham Palace ceremony or Saturday football derbies or marathons. London is an economic force that stands on the shoulders of its workers. Its heroes aren't its gormless 'supermodels' or even more gormless footballers. Its heroes are its computer programmers, bus drivers, cabbies, tube drivers, brickies, corner shop owners, office workers and cleaners. London's heroes are the uncelebrated, quiet millions who struggle to the office or factory or shop each day to make it work. Their story is the only one that matters.

Endnotes

1   This term is borrowed from *gestalt* psychology.

2   Centerprise Trust (1976) p. 32. Welch started work at sixteen.

3   Centerprise Trust (1976) p. 36

4   Centerprise Trust (1976) p. 33

5   Centerprise Trust (1977) p. 142

6   There is a four-month-long slack period in the cab trade that runs from about January to April. Black cab drivers know it as the Kipper Season.

7   Christou cited in Centerprise (1977) pp. 161–2

8   Health and Safety Executive (2006) p. 6

9   Cooper, Dewe and O'Driscoll (2001) p. 50

10 Office for National Statistics (2005) p. 54

11 Barber cited in Osborne (2005)

12 Retail park managements actually call their buildings 'sheds'.

13 Bauman (1998) p. 57

14 Centerprise Trust (1976) p. 75

15 I remember studying by candlelight. And this in the country that had saved Europe from Nazism. In the country that had won the World Cup. In the country that possessed the Mother of Parliaments. My teenage experience of borderline anarchy – of a kind of societal insanity – haunts me still. It shapes my politics. It confirms the wisdom of Churchill's dictum that jaw-jaw is better than (economic) war-war.

16 Mathiason (2008)

17 Mathiason and Connon (2008)

18 There were even fears for London's extravagant party season. According to *Evening Standard* journalist Benedict Moore-Bridger, in 2007 'a record £120 million was spent on London's office Christmas parties in two nights'. Christmas 2008 would be very different. 'City companies being hit by the collapse of world markets are cutting costs by cancelling office Christmas parties... the global economy's downturn has left institutions struggling to justify the expense' said Moore-Bridger (2008).

19 Roubini cited in McGeehan (2008)

20 Sloan cited in McGeehan (2008)

21 *Economist* (2008a)

22 Jackson (2008)

23 Wachman (2008)

24 *Economist* (2008a)

25 *Economist* (2008c)

26 Schwartz (2008)

27 For many years Brown had presided over a system of 'light touch' regulation. This had given the City of London certain advantages over other financial centres (like New York). See Hall and Eaglesham (2008).

28 Given the speed at which our modern world can change the reader should note that this summary was written in the late autumn of 2008.

29 Despite having no support from Republicans in February 2009, President Obama secured a multi-billion dollar aid package for the US economy. Like Brown, Obama

believed that doing nothing was not an option. In early 2009 the US economy was deteriorating at an alarming rate. According to the new president the recession had cost the US economy some 3.6 million jobs. Despite the protectionist origins of the Great Depression there were calls for indigenous industries to be firewalled from international competition. In Britain wildcat strikes were called in support of a 'British jobs for British workers' agenda (an agenda hijacked in some locales by the racist British National Party).

30 Clearly it would be wrong to decide policy on the basis of such limited data and my personal opinion. It would be right, however, to undertake research into youngsters' experience of modern schooling. The *only* people who really know what goes on inside the school gates are the people we send there. So let's ask them what they think. What have we got to lose? For those who doubt the utility of 'back-to-the-floor' management see Bennett (2008).

31 Padgham (2004)

32 The British government has intervened to save a number of businesses, including Rolls Royce Aero Engines (Edward Heath) and the Northern Rock Bank (Gordon Brown). In September 2008 the Brown government waived competition rules to facilitate Lloyds TSB's takeover of struggling HBOS.

33 Galbraith (1992) p. 51

34 London Development Agency (2003)

35 The current testing epidemic is, in my opinion, a political stunt. It's the government trying to persuade us it's on top of things. When patently it isn't. Instead of dissipating teachers' finite energies with SATs why not task them with re-creating a culture of self-discipline and mutual respect amongst London's schoolchildren? (Interestingly, in the autumn of 2008 the government abandoned some SATs testing, although it allowed schools to continue testing if they wished.)

36 During my time at Neath Boys' Grammar School we had three external visits. One from the Army. One from Bangor University desperate to persuade us to spend three years on the edge of civilisation. And one from a troupe of travelling players who pranced around a lot (it seemed to us they were mourning the death of hippiedom). It was the first (and only) time I saw simulated sex on stage.

37 Ford and Fresco (2008) p. 7

38 Travis (2004)

39 Barnes cited in Centerprise Trust (1977) p. 146

40 A copy of the dissertation is kept at Brunel University, Middlesex.

41 The safe removal of asbestos from a building adds significantly to demolition costs and timescales.

42 I used the Sands End study to critique Ulrich Beck's theory of the Risk Society. In his book of the same name Beck (1992) claimed that western social and political discourse had become fixated on risk management. My research suggested that one's attitude towards environmental risk is, in some degree, influenced by one's economic status and life chances.

43 Hattersley (2008)

44 Ross (2008)

45   Steele (2008) p. 1

46   Miles (2008) p. 17

47   Steele (2008) pp. 1–4

48   Katwala (2008)

49   In 2008 London had several major infrastructure projects in hand, like Crossrail, the £16 billion railway line between Heathrow and Shenfield.

50   The chase becomes especially frantic in election years. Monies are miraculously found. Fortuitous underspends come to light.

51   Johnson (2008)

52   I am conscious that my survey has been, perforce, limited in scope. More ethnographic research is required if London's varied workforce is to be comprehensively surveyed. Every type of worker deserves a voice. Every nationality deserves a voice. Migrant as well as indigenous labour must be surveyed. We need a new Mass Observation.

Bibliography

Al Naib, SK (2001) *London Docklands: Past, present and future*. Romford: Research Books.

Anselmo, JC (2008) 'Small Problems', *Aviation Week & Space Technology*, Monday 19 May 2008.

Atkinson, R (2006) 'Going Strong', *Guardian Weekend*, Saturday 25 November 2006.

Balakrishnan, A (2008) 'New data fuels house price fears', *Guardian*, Saturday 1 March 2008.

Bale, J (2007) 'I miss London, but life is much better (and cheaper) in Perth', *The Times*, Friday 20 April 2007.

Bates, D (2007) 'Houses rise by £8,000 a month', *Metro*, Monday 16 April 2007.

Batty, D (2002) 'Q&A: poverty', *Guardian*, Thursday 12 December 2002.

Bauman, Z (1998) *Globalisation. The Human Consequences*. Cambridge: Polity Press.

BBC News (9 March 2004) 'UK "divided by regional poverty"', *BBC News*, <http://news.bbc.co.uk/> accessed 29 January 2007.

BBC News (20 February 2006) 'Commission to fight child poverty', *BBC News*, <http://newsvote.bbc.co.uk/mpapps/pagetools/print/news.bbc.co.uk/> accessed 29 January 2007.

BBC News (30 October 2006) 'Soaring City bonuses "hit £8.8bn"', *BBC News*, <http://news.bbc.co.uk/go/pr/fr/-/hi/business/6098162.stm/> accessed 27 January 2007.

BBC News (2007a) 'Breadline Britain', *BBC News*, <http://news.bbc.co.uk/1/shared/spl/hi/business/05/breadlinebritain/> accessed 29 January 2007.

BBC News (2007b) 'Migrants "deceived and exploited"', *BBC News*, <http://news.bbc.co.uk/> accessed 30 April 2007.

Beck, U (1992) *Risk Society: Towards a New Modernity*. London: Sage.

Bennett, R (2007) 'Charity attacks "disgrace of child poverty con trick"', *The Times*, Wednesday 28 March 2007.

Bennett, SA (2006) *A Sociology of Commercial Flight Crew*. Aldershot: Ashgate.

Bennett, SA (2008) 'Crew Resource Management Über Alles?', *The Log*, October/November.

Beynon, H (1973) *Working for Ford*. London: Penguin.

Brown, G (2004) 'Britain Needs More Start-Ups', *Daily Mail*, Wednesday 2 June 2004.

Campbell, B (1984) *Wigan Pier Revisited. Poverty and Politics in the 80s*. London: Virago.

Campbell, B (1993) *Goliath. Britain's Dangerous Places*. London: Methuen.

Carter, H, Pai, H-H and Butt, R (2006) '"Tell the family to pray for me... I am dying".

Desperate calls on a treacherous night as 23 lives were lost in Morecambe Bay', *Guardian*, Saturday 25 March 2006.

Carvel, J (22 March 2005) 'More cash, more flab in UK, but inequality gap grows', *Guardian*, <http://guardian.co.uk/> accessed 16 February 2007.

Centerprise Trust (1976) *Working Lives. Volume One 1905–45*. London: Centerprise Trust Ltd. in association with Hackney W.E.A.

Centerprise Trust (1977) *Working Lives. Volume Two 1945–77*. London: Centerprise Trust Ltd. in association with Hackney W.E.A.

Cheal, T (22 April 2004) 'London: Child poverty', *BBC News*, <http://newsvote.bbc.co.uk/mpapps/pagetools/print/news.bbc.co.uk/> accessed 29 January 2007.

Citizens Advice London (11 July 2003) 'Tackling poverty in London', <http://www.citizensadvice.org.uk/print/index/campaigns/social_policy/> accessed 29 January 2007.

Cooper, CL, Dewe, PJ and O'Driscoll, MP (2001) *Organisational Stress. A Review and Critique of Theory, Research, and Applications*. Thousand Oaks: Sage.

Cox, J (1994) *London's East End Life and Traditions*. London: Weidenfeld & Nicholson.

Daily Mail (2006) 'City bonuses feed the politics of envy', *Daily Mail*, Thursday 14 December 2006.

Daily Mail (11 February 2007) 'Hain wants £1m City bonuses shared with the poor', *Daily Mail*, <http://www.dailymail.co.uk/pages/live/articles/news/ > accessed 16 February 2007.

Datta, K, McIlwaine, C, Wills, J, Evans, Y, Herbert, J and May, J (2006) *Challenging remittances as the new development mantra: perspectives from low-paid migrant workers in London*. London: Queen Mary, University of London.

Davies, N (2005) 'Life on the breadline', *Guardian*, Wednesday 2 November 2005.

Davis, B (2008) 'IMF asks nations to plan strategies if crisis deepens', *Wall Street Journal*, Thursday 13 March 2008.

Denzin, NK and Lincoln, YS (2003) 'The Discipline and Practice of Qualitative Research'. In Denzin, NK and Lincoln, YS (eds) *Strategies of Qualitative Inquiry, Second Edition*. London: Sage.

Devine, F (1994) '"Affluent Workers" Revisited', *Sociology Review*, February, pp. 6–9.

Dovkants, K (1995) 'Grim reality behind the East End legend', *London Evening Standard*, Monday 9 January 1995.

Dubiniec, M (2006) 'Moving with the times', *Guardian Unlimited*, <http://www.guardian.co.uk> accessed 1 February 2007.

Economist (2000) 'Poverty in America: Out of sight, out of mind', *Economist*, Saturday 20 May, pp. 31–34.

Economist (2008a) 'Saving the system', *Economist*, Saturday 11 October, pp. 13–14.

Economist (2008b) 'Capitalism at bay', *Economist*, Saturday 18 October 2008, pp. 13–14.

Economist (2008c) 'End of the phoney peace', *Economist*, Saturday 25 October 2008, pp. 39–40.

Economist (2008d) 'Pain all round, please', *Economist*, Saturday 25 October 2008, p. 40.

Elliott, L (2004) 'Labour fails to stop widening of income gap', *Guardian*, Thursday 24 June 2004.

Elliott, L (2006) 'London employers forced to plug the skills gap with migrant workers', *Guardian*, Tuesday 12 December 2006.

Evans, Y, Herbert, J, Datta, K, May, J, McIlwaine, C and Wills, J (2005) *Making the City Work: Low Paid Employment in London*. London: Queen Mary, University of London.

Financial Times (1997) 'Variations persist', *Financial Times*, Thursday 16 October 1997.

Ford, R and Fresco, A (2008) '"Proper sentences" for knife crimes needed, police will tell magistrates', *The Times*, Wednesday 28 May 2008.

Fuller, T (2005) 'Europe's great migration', *International Herald Tribune*, Friday 21 October 2005.

Galbraith, JK (1992) *The Culture of Contentment*. London: Sinclair-Stevenson.

Gilbert, N (1993) *Researching Social Life*. Thousand Oaks: Sage.

Gillan, A (2007) 'Six hours away by ferry – a world apart for children', *Guardian*, Saturday 17 February 2007.

Glancey, J (22 September 2005) 'That sinking feeling on "estate from hell"', *Guardian*, <http://society.guardian.co.uk/print/> accessed 22 February 2007.

Glendon, IA, Clarke, SG and McKenna, EF (2006) *Human Safety and Risk Management*. London: Taylor & Francis.

Greater Manchester Low Pay Unit (1995) *Workers' Voices: Accounts of Working Life in Britain in the Nineties*. Manchester: GMLPU.

Guardian (2006) 'Should I chase the bonuses in the City?', *Guardian*, Friday 17 November 2006.

Guardian (13 January 2007) 'Behind these walls', *Guardian*, <http://books.guardian.co.uk/departments/politicsphilosophyandsociety/> accessed 10 February 2007.

Guardian (2007) 'London shootings: Diagnosis but no prescription', *Guardian*, Saturday 17 February 2007.

Guha, K (2008) 'Fed believes it can prevent a deep recession', *Financial Times*, Thursday 13 March 2008.

Hall, B and Eaglesham, J (2008) 'Sarkozy and Brown seek system shake-up', *Financial Times*, Monday 3 November 2008.

Hall, S and Jacques, M (1989) *New Times. The Changing Face of Politics in the 1990s*. London: Lawrence and Wishart.

Harrison, M (2005) 'End of the Road', *Independent*, Friday 8 April 2005.

Harrison, P (1983) *Inside the Inner City*. Harmondsworth: Penguin.

Hattersley, G (2008) 'Class division wins by a country mile at Royal Chavscot', *Sunday Times*, Sunday 22 June 2008.

Health and Safety Executive (2006) *Managing shift work*. Sudbury: HSE Books.

Hopkins, N and Hall, S (2000) 'David Copeland: a quiet introvert, obsessed with Hitler and bombs', *Guardian*, <http://www.guardian.co.uk/uk/2000/jun/30/uksecurity.sarahhall> accessed 29 May 2007.

Hudson, R and Williams, AM (1989) *Divided Britain*. London: Belhaven Press.

Humphrey, J and Schmitz, H (2007) *China: Its Impact on the Developing Asian Economies*. Brighton (University of Sussex): Institute of Development Studies.

Humphries, S and Taylor, J (1986) *The Making of Modern London 1945–1985*. London: Sidgwick & Jackson.

Hutton, W (1995) *The State We're In*. London: Jonathan Cape.

Independent (2007) 'Mind the wealth gap', *Independent*, Thursday 8 February 2007.

Institute of Development Studies (2008) 'Globalisation Research – Asian Drivers: China, India and Development', <http://www.ids.ac.uk/go/research-teams/globalisation-team/research-themes/asian-drivers> accessed 20 August 2008.

Jack, I (1997) *Before the Oil Ran Out: Britain in the Brutal Years*. London: Vintage.

Jackson, T (2008) 'IMF thesis gives no reason to think the worst is over', *Financial Times*, Monday 3 November 2008.

Johnson, B (2008) 'Times will be tough – but we can lead the fightback', *Evening Standard*, Monday 27 October 2008.

Johnston, P (2008) 'Migrant labour to "create new UK underclass"', *Daily Telegraph*, Friday 4 January 2008.

Kaletsky, A (2005) 'A vulnerable miracle', *The Economist: The World in 2006*. 20th Edition.

Kasperson, RE (1992) 'The Social Amplification of Risk: Progress in Developing an Integrative Framework'. In Krimsky, S and Golding, D (eds) *Social Theories of Risk*. London: Praeger.

Katwala, S (21 August 2008) 'The Olympics: non-transferable assets', *Guardian*, <http://www.guardian.co.uk/> accessed 26 August 2008.

Knight, J (2 August 2005) 'Voices from the poverty frontline', *BBC News*, <http://news.bbc.co.uk/go/pr/fr/-/1/hi/business/4103916.stm> accessed 29 January 2007.

Lawson, N (22 February 2007) 'New Labour has presided over a social recession', *Guardian*, <http://www.guardian.co.uk/> accessed 22 February 2007.

Lean, G and Ball, G (1996) 'UK most unequal country in the West', *Independent on Sunday*, Sunday 21 July 1996.

Little, A (25 April 2007) 'New evidence of "bonded labour"', *BBC News*, <http://news.bbc.co.uk/1/hi/uk/6593827.stm> accessed 1 may 2007.

London Development Agency (2003) *Press Release: Chancellor backs business-led growth for London's inner city areas*, Wednesday 8 October 2003.

London Docklands Development Corporation (March 1998) *Regeneration Statement*. <http://www.lddc-history.org.uk/regenstat/index.html> accessed 7 February 2007.

Mass-Observation Archive and the Centre for Continuing Education, The (1991) *The Mass-Observation Diaries. An Introduction*. Brighton: University of Sussex.

Mathiason, N (2008) 'Bid hope for Lehman's Canary Wharf staff', *Observer, Business and Media*, Sunday 21 September 2008.

Mathiason, N and Connon, H (2008) 'Silence over HBOS jobs alarms banking unions', *Observer, Business and Media*, Sunday 21 September 2008.

McGeehan, P (2008) 'In Finance, London Gains on New York', *New York Times*, Sunday 21 September 2008.

McRae, H (2007) 'The challenges of living in the super-rich playground', *Independent*, Thursday 8 February 2007.

Mecham, M (2007) 'Getting It Together', *Aviation Week & Space Technology*, Monday 21 May 2007.

Miles, A (2008) 'It's no U-turn: abandon the 2p fuel rise', *The Times*, Wednesday 28 May 2008.

Moore, J (2007) 'City corners global market in financial services sector', *Independent*, Thursday 8 February 2007.

Moore-Bridger, B (2008) 'Lavish Christmas parties over for City workers hit by credit crunch', *Evening Standard*, Tuesday 28 October 2008.

Morris, S (2008) 'Gangmasters face losing licences as crackdown reveals exploitation', *Guardian*, Wednesday 13 February 2008.

Morrison, B (6 January 2007) 'From hutch to home', *Guardian*, <http://books.guardian. co.uk/print/> accessed 22 February 2007.

Mortished, C (2008) 'Lack of wisdom laid bare, for what little it's worth', *The Times*, Saturday 15 March 2008.

New Internationalist (1996) 'Class: The Facts', *New Internationalist*, July, pp. 18–19.

Nicoll, R (2005) 'A tale of two cities', *Observer*, <http://observer.guardian.co.uk/comment/ story/> accessed 10 February 2007.

Office for National Statistics (2005) *Social Trends*. Basingstoke: Palgrave Macmillan.

Orwell, G (1974) *Down and out in Paris and London*. Harmondsworth: Penguin.

Osborne, H (2005) 'TUC attacks long working hours', *Guardian*, Thursday 9 June 2005.

Padgham, J (2004) 'East End is Hot Spot for Start-Ups', *Evening Standard*, Thursday 9 September 2004.

Pai, Hsiao-Hung (2004) 'Inside the grim world of the gangmasters', *Guardian*, Saturday 27 March 2004.

Pickard, T (1989) *We Make Ships*. London: Secker and Warburg.

Radnedge, A (2007) 'Britain is the worst country to be a child', *Metro*, Wednesday 14 February 2007.

Robins, D (13 December 2006) 'Inner-city blues', *Guardian*, <http://society.guardian.co.uk/ print/> accessed 10 February 2007.

Ross, N (2008) 'My Manifesto', *Evening Standard*, Friday 4 April 2008.

Schifferes, S (25 September 2003) 'US inequality gap widens', *BBC News*, <http://news.bbc. co.uk/go/pr/fr/> accessed 16 February 2007.

Schifferes, S (21 January 2007) 'Globalisation shakes the world', *BBC News*, <http://newsvote. bbc.co.uk/mpapps/pagetools/print/news.bbc.co.uk> accessed 20 August 2008.

Schwartz, ND (2008) 'Suddenly, Europe looks pretty smart', *International Herald Tribune*, Monday 20 October 2008.

Seabrook, J (1983) *Unemployment*. St Albans: Granada Publishing Ltd.

Seager, A (2006) 'City bonuses reach record £19bn', *Guardian*, Thursday 17 August 2006.

Steele, J (2008) 'A golden welcome for pride of Britain', *Metro*, Tuesday 26 August 2008.

Steven, S (1995) 'London Voice. Special Report: The Betrayed', *London Evening Standard*, Monday 9 January 1995.

Stewart, H (2007) 'Immigrants put UK in pole position', *Observer*, Sunday 7 January 2007.

Tagg, D and Pickard, M (1995) 'Smiling face of the East End', *London Evening Standard*, Monday 30 January 1995.

Taylor, D (1995) 'One in 3 households live on £4,500 a year', *London Evening Standard*, Thursday 12 January 1995.

Teather, D (2006) 'The bonus bonanza', *Guardian*, Saturday 4 November 2006.

Theobald, R (1994) *Understanding Industrial Society. A Sociological Guide*. New York: St Martin's Press.

Tighe, C (1997) 'Clear impact on the landscape', *Financial Times*, Thursday 16 October 1997.

Travis, A (22 October 2004) 'Large gap between public fear and the actual rate of crime', *Guardian*, <http://www.guardian.co.uk/> accessed 26 August 2008.

Treneman, A (1999) 'Hell is other people', *Independent: Wednesday Review*, Wednesday 31 March 1999.

Wachman, R (2007) 'City bonuses: after the long feast, time for some famine', *Observer*, Sunday 2 December 2007.

Wachman, R (2008) 'This transforms the financial system. Forever', *Observer*, Sunday 21 September 2008.

Ward, T (1997) 'A three-way split? The 30-30-40 thesis', *Sociology Review*, February, pp. 7–8.

Waters, M (1995) *Globalisation*. London: Routledge.

Weaver, M (20 February 2007) 'Report backs end to secure council tenancies', *Guardian*, <http://www.guardian.co.uk/> accessed 22 February 2007.

White, J (2001) *London in the Twentieth Century. A City and Its People*. London: Penguin Books.

Willis, P (30 May 2007) 'London drives house price growth', *Guardian*, <http://www.guardian.co.uk/> accessed 8 June 2007.

Woodward, W and Muir, H (2007) 'Father appeals for help to "catch my boy's killers"', *Guardian*, Saturday 17 February 2007.

Young, M and Willmott, P (1966) *Family and Kinship in East London*. Harmondsworth: Pelican Books.

Appendix

Questions

1	**History**
1.1	Male/female?
1.2	Year of birth?
1.3	Country of birth?
1.4	Born in city/town/village?
1.5	Single/married?
1.6	What does your partner do?
1.7	How many children do you have?
1.8	In how many countries have you lived for > 6 months?
1.9	What were those countries?
1.10	What education do you have?
1.11	How long have you lived in London?
1.12	Approx. how many jobs have you had in London?
1.13	What were those jobs?
1.14	What was the worst job?
1.15	Why was it the worst job?
1.16	What was the best job?
1.17	Why was it the best job?

2	**Social**
2.1	In London how many rented rooms/flats/houses have you lived in?
2.2	In London how many flats/houses have you owned?
2.3	What does your current accommodation consist of?
2.4	Where is it?
2.5	Does anyone share it with you?
2.6	What do you like most about your current accommodation?
2.7	What do you like least about your current accommodation?
2.8	What is the best feature of the area you live in?
2.9	What is the worst aspect of the area you live in?
2.10	Where in London would you most like to live?
2.11	Why would you like to live there?
2.12	Do you want to move out of London?
2.13	On average how many nights out do you have each week?
2.14	What do you do on a night out?
2.15	What are your hobbies?

3	**Current work**
3.1	What is your present job?
3.2	How did you find the job?
3.3	Are you full-time or part-time?
3.4	Are you on a permanent or temporary contract?
3.5	What are your hours?
3.6	How long do you get for lunch?
3.7	What do you do at lunch time?
3.8	Do you have any other breaks during the day?
3.9	Do you get paid holiday?
3.10	Is there any chance of promotion?
3.11	What do you think of your workmates?
3.12	What do you think they think of you?
3.13	What is the worst argument you have had at work?
3.14	What do you like most about the job?
3.15	What do you like least about the job?
3.16	What do you think about your boss?
3.17	What do you think s/he thinks of you?
3.18	Do you think the business is well run?
3.19	Do you think you are paid a fair rate for the job?
3.20	How do you get to work?
3.21	How long does your journey to work take?

4   **General**

4.1   What is the best thing the current government has done for workers?

4.2   Is there anything else they could do to help workers?

4.3   Are you in a trades union or staff association?

4.4   What do you think of the unions?

4.5   Do you think that voting in elections changes anything?

4.6   Do you vote?

4.7   If you don't, why not?

4.8   What sort of job do you think Ken Livingstone is doing as Mayor of London?

4.9   Is London just another city or is there something special about it?

4.10   If you were Mayor and money was no object what three things would you do to improve London?

4.11   Will the Olympics be a good or bad thing for London?

4.12   Can you sum London up in one word?